A Life for A Love

By

L. T. Meade

A LIFE FOR A LOVE

CHAPTER I

The time was July, and the roses were out in great profusion in the rectory garden. The garden was large, somewhat untidily kept, but it abounded in all sweet old-fashioned flowers; there was the invariable tennis-court, empty just now, and a sweet sound of children laughing and playing together, in a hay-field nearby. The roses were showering their petals all over the grass, and two girls, sisters evidently, were pacing up the broad walk in the centre of the garden arm-in-arm. They were dark-eyed girls, with chestnut, curling hair, rosy lips full of curves and smiles, and round, good-humored faces. They were talking eagerly and excitedly one to the other, not taking the smallest notice of the scene around them—not even replying when some children in the hay-field shouted their names, but coming at last to a full stand-still before the open window of the old-fashioned rectory study. Two men were standing under the deep-mullioned window; one tall, slightly bent, with silvery-white hair, aquiline features, and dark brown eyes like the girls. He was the Rector of Jewsbury-on-the-Wold, and the man he was addressing was his only son, and the brother of the eager bright-looking girls.

"I can't understand it, Gerald," he was saying. "No, don't come in at present, my dears;" he waved his white, delicate hand to his daughters. "We'll join you in the tennis-court presently. Yes, Gerald, as I was saying, it seems the most incomprehensible and unheard-of arrangement."

The girls smiled gently, first into their brother's face, then at one another. They moved away, going through a little shrubbery, and passing out into a large kitchen garden, where Betty, the old cook, was now standing, picking raspberries and currants into a pie-dish.

"Betty," said Lilias, the eldest girl, "has Martha dusted our trunks and taken them upstairs yet? And has Susan sent up the laces and the frilled things? We want to set to work packing, as soon as ever the children are in bed."

"Bless your hearts, then," said old Betty, laying her pie-dish on the ground, and dropping huge ripe raspberries into it with a slow deliberate movement, "if you think that children will go to bed on the finest day of the year any time within reason, you're fine and mistook, that's all. Why, Miss Joey, she was round in the garden but now, and they're all a-going to have tea in the hay-field, and no end of butter they'll eat, and a whole batch of my fresh cakes. Oh, weary, weary me, but children's mouths are never full—chattering, restless, untoward things are children. Don't you never go to get married, Miss Marjory."

"I'll follow your example, Betty," laughed back Marjory Wyndham. "I knew that would fetch the old thing," she continued, turning to her sister. "She does hate to be reminded that she's an old maid, but she brings it on herself by abusing matrimony in that ridiculous fashion."

"It's all because of Gerald," answered Lilias"she is perfectly wild to think of Gerald's going away from us, and taking up his abode in London with those rich Pagets. I call it odious, tooI almost feel to-night as if I hated Valentine. If Gerald had not fallen in love with her, things would have been different. He'd have taken Holy Orders, and he'd have been ordained for the curacy of Jewsbury-on-the-Wold, and then he need never have gone away. Oh. I hateI detest to think of the rectory without Gerald."

"Oh, Lilias," replied Marjory, "you really areyou reallyyou really are"

"What, miss? Speak out, or I'll shake you, or pinch you, or do something malicious. I warn you that I am quite in the mood."

"Then I'll stand here," said Marjory, springing to the other side of a great glowing bed of many-colored sweet-williams. "Here your arm can't reach across these. I will say of you, Lilias Wyndham, that you are without exception the most contradictory and inconsistent person of my acquaintance. Here were you, a year ago, crying and sobbing on your knees because Gerald couldn't marry Valentine, and now, when it's all arranged, and the wedding is to be the day after to-morrow, and we have got our promised trip to London, and those lovely brides-maid dressesmade by Valentine's own express desire at Elise'syou turn round and are grumpy and discontented. Don't you know, you foolish silly Lilias, that if Gerald had never fallen in love with Valentine Paget he'd have met someone else, and if he was father's curate, those horrid Mortimer girls and those ugly Pelhams would have one and all tried to get him. We can't keep Gerald to ourselves for ever, so there's no use fretting about the inevitable, say I."

Lilias' full red lips were pouting; she stooped, and recklessly gathering a handful of sweet-williams, flung them at her sister.

"I own to being inconsistent," she said, "I own to being crossI own to hating Valentine for this night at least, for it just tears my heart to give Gerald up."

There were real tears now in the bright, curly-fringed eyes and the would-be-defiant voice trembled.

Marjory shook the sweet-william petals off her dress.

"Come into the house," she said in a softened tone. "Father and Gerald must have finished that prosy discussion by now. Oh, do hark to those children's voices; what rampageous, excitable creatures they are. Lilly, did we ever shout in such shrill tones? That must be Augusta: no one else has a voice which sounds like the scraping of a coal-scoop in an empty coal-hod. Oh, of course that high laugh belongs to Joey. Aren't they feeding, and wrangling, and fighting? I am quite sure, Lil, that Betty is right, and they won't turn in for hours; we had better go and do our packing now."

"No, I see Gerald," exclaimed Lilias. And she flew up the narrow box-lined path to meet her brother.

CHAPTER II

Gerald Wyndham was not in the least like his rosy, fresh-looking sisters. He was tall and slenderly made, with very thick and rather light-brown hair, which stood up high over his low, white forehead—his eyes were large, but were deeply set, they were grey, not brown, in repose were dreaming in expression, but when he spoke, or when any special thought came to him, they grew intensely earnest, luminous and beautiful. The changing expression of his eyes was the chief charm of a highly sensitive and refined face—a face remarkable in many ways, for the breadth of his forehead alone gave it character, but with some weak lines about the finely cut lips. This weakness was now, however, hidden by a long, silken moustache. Lilias and Marjory thought Gerald's face the most beautiful in the world, and most people acknowledged him to be handsome, although his shoulders were scarcely broad enough for his height, and his whole figure was somewhat loosely hung together.

"Here you are at last," exclaimed Lilias, linking her hand in her brother's arm. "Here, take his other arm. Maggie. Oh, when, and oh, when, and oh, when shall we have him to ourselves again, I wonder?"

"You little goose," said Gerald. He shook himself as if he were half in a dream, and looked fondly down into Lilias' pretty dimpled, excitable face. "Well, girls, are the trunks packed, and have you put in plenty of finery? I promise you Mr. Paget will give a dinner-party every night—you'll want heaps of fine clothes while you stay at Queen's Gate."

Marjory began to count on her fingers.

"We arrive on Wednesday," she said. "On Wednesday evening, dinner number one, we wear our white Indian muslins, with the Liberty sashes, and flowers brought up from the dear old garden. Thursday evening, dinner number two, and evening of wedding day, our bridesmaids' toggery must suffice; Friday, dinner number three, those blue nun's veiling dresses will appear and charm the eyes. That's all. Three dresses for three dinners, for it's home, sweet home again on Saturday—isn't it, Lilias?"

"Of course," said Lilias, "that is, I suppose so," she added, glancing at her brother.

"Valentine wanted to know if you would stay in town for a week or ten days, and try to cheer up her father," said Gerald. "Mr. Paget and Valentine have scarcely been parted for a single day since she was born. Valentine is quite in a state at having to leave him for a month, and she thinks two bright little girls like you may comfort him somewhat."

"But we have our own father to see to," pouted Marjory; "and Sunday school, and choir practising, and the library books"

"And I don't see how Valentine can mind leaving her father—if he were the very dearest father in the world—when she goes away with you," interrupted Lilias.

Gerald sighed, just the faintest shadow of an impatient sigh, accompanied by the slightest shrug of his shoulders.

"Augusta can give out the library books," he said. "Miss Queen can manage the choir. I will ask Jones to take your class, Lilias, and Miss Peters can manage yours with her own, Marjory. As to the rector, what is the use of having five young daughters, if they cannot be made available for once in a way? And here they come, and there's the governor in the midst of them. He doesn't look as if he were likely to taste the sweets of solitude, eh. Marjory?"

Not at that moment, certainly, for a girl hung on each arm, and a smaller girl sat aloft on each square shoulder, while a fifth shouted and raced, now in front, now behind, pelting this moving pyramid of human beings with flowers, and screaming even more shrilly than her sisters, with eager exclamation and bubbling laughter.

"There's Gerry," exclaimed Augusta.

She was the tallest of the party, with a great stretch of stockinged legs, and a decided scarcity of skirts. She flew at her brother, flung her arms round his neck and kissed him rapturously.

"You darling old Gerry—don't we all just hate and detest that horrible Valentine Paget."

"Hush, Gussie," responded Gerald, in his quiet voice. "You don't know Valentine, and you pain me when you talk of her in that senseless fashion. Here, have a race with your big brother to the other end of the garden. Girls," turning to his elder sisters—"seriously speaking I should like you to spend about a fortnight with the Pagets. And had you not better go and pack, for we must catch the eleven o'clock train to-morrow morning. Now, Gussie—one, two, three, and away."

Two pairs of long legs, each working hard to come off victorious in the race, flew past the group—the rector and the little girls cheered and shouted—Marjory and Lilias, laughing at the sight, turned slowly and went into the house; Gerald won the race by a foot or two, and Gussie flung herself panting and laughing on the grass at the other end of the long walk.

"Well done, Augusta," said her brother. "You study athletics to a purpose. Now, Gussie, can't you manage to give away the library books on Sunday?"

"I? You don't mean it?" said Augusta. Her black eyes sparkled; she recovered her breath, and the full dignity of her five feet five and a-half of growth on the instant. "Am I to give away the library books, Gerry?"

"Yes, I want Lilias to stay in London for a few days longer than she intended."

"And Marjory too?"

"Of course. The girls would not like to be parted."

"Galuptions! Won't I have a time of it all round! Won't I give old Peters a novel instead of his favorite Sunday magazines? And won't I smuggle Pailey's Evidences of Christianity into the hand of Alice Jones, the dressmaker. She says the only books she cares for are Wilkie Collins 'Woman in White,' and the 'Dead Secret,' so she'll have a lively time of it with the Evidences. Then there's 'Butler's Analogy,' it isn't in the parish library, but I'll borrow it for once from father's study. That will exactly suit Rhoda Fleming. Oh, what fun, what fun. I won't take a single story-book with me, except the 'Woman in White,' for Peters. He says novels are 'rank poison,' so he shall have his dose."

"Now look here, Gussie," said Gerald, taking his sister's two hands in his, and holding them tight"you've got to please me about the library books, and not to play pranks, and make things disagreeable for Lilias when she comes back. You're thirteen now, and a big girl, and you ought to act like one. You're to make things comfortable for the dear old pater while we are all away, and you'll do it if you care for me, Gussie."

"Care for you!" echoed Augusta. "I love you, Gerry. I love you, and I hate"

"No, don't say that," said Gerald, putting his hand on the girl's mouth.

Gussie looked droll and submissive.

"It is so funny," she exclaimed at length.

"You can explain that as we walk back to the house," responded her brother.

"Why, Gerry, to see you so frightfully in love! You[ ] are, aren't you? You have all the symptomsoh, before I"

"I love Valentine," responded Gerald. "That is a subject I cannot discuss with you, Augusta. When you know her you will love her too. I am going to bring her here in the autumn, and then I shall want you all to be good to her, and to let her feel that she has a great number of real sisters at Jewsbury-on-the-Wold, who will be good to her if she needs them, by-and-bye."

"As if she ever could need us," responded Gussie. "She'll have you. Yes, I'll do my best about the booksgood-night. Gerald. Good-night, dear old darling king. That's Miss Queen's voice. Coming, Miss Queen, coming! Good-night, old Gerry. My love to that Val of yours. Oh, what a nuisance it is to have ever to go to bed."

Gussie's long legs soon bore her out of sight, and Gerald stepped into the silent and now empty study. To an initiated eye this room bore one or two marks of having lately witnessed a mental storm. Close to the rector's leather armchair lay a pile of carefully torn-up papersthe family Bible, which usually occupied a place of honor on his desk, had been pushed ruthlessly on one side, and a valuable work on theology lay wide open and face downwards on the floor. Otherwise the room was in perfect orderthe only absolutely neat apartment in the large old house. Not the most daring of all the young Wyndhams would disturb a volume here, or play any wild pranks in the sacred precincts of the rector's study. As Gerald now entered the room and saw these signs of mental disquiet round Mr. Wyndham's chair, the pleasant and somewhat cheerful look left his face, his eyes grew dark, earnest and full of trouble, and flinging himself on the sofa, he shaded them with his white long fingers. There was an oil painting of a lady over the mantel-piece, and this lady had Gerald's face. From her he inherited those peculiar and sensitive eyes, those somewhat hollow cheeks, and that noble and broad white brow. From her, too, came the lips which were curved and beautiful, and yet a little, a little wanting in firmness. In Mrs. Wyndham the expressive mouth only added the final touch of womanliness to a beautiful face. In her son it would have revealed, could it have been seen, a nature which might be led astray from the strictest paths of honor.

Wyndham sat motionless for a few moments, then springing to his feet, he paced restlessly up and down the empty study.

"Everything is fixed and settled now," he said, under his breath. "I'm not the first fellow who has sold himself for the sake of a year's happiness. If my mother were alive, though, I couldn't have done it, no, not even for Valentine. Poor mother! She felt sure I'd have taken Holy Orders, and worked on here with the governor in this sleepy little corner of the world. It's a blessing she can't be hurt by anything now, and as to the governor, he has seven girls to comfort him. No, if I'm sorry for anyone it's Lilias, but the thing's done now. The day after to-morrow Val will be mine. A whole year! My God, how short it is. My God, save and pity me, for afterwards comes hell."

CHAPTER III

The human face has been often spoken of as an index of the mind. There are people who boldly declare that they know a man by the height of his forehead, by the set of his eyes, by the shape of his head, and by the general expression of his countenance. Whether this rule is true or not, it certainly has its exceptions. As far as outward expression goes some minds remain locked, and Satan himself can now and then appear transformed as an angel of light.

Mortimer Paget, Esq., the head and now sole representative of the once great ship-broking firm of Paget Brothers, was one of the handsomest and most striking-looking men in the city. On more than one occasion sculptors of renown had asked to be permitted to take a cast of his head to represent Humanity, Benevolence, Integrity, or some other cardinal virtue. He had a high forehead, calm velvety brown eyes, perfectly even and classical features, and firm lips with a sweet expression. His lips were perfectly hidden by his silvery moustache, and the shape of his chin was not discernible, owing to his long flowing beard. But had the beard and moustache both been removed, no fault could have been found with the features now hiddenthey were firmly and well-moulded. On this beautiful face no trace of a sinister cast lurked.

Mortimer Paget in his business transactions was the soul of honor. No man in the city was more looked up to than he. He was very shrewd with regard to all money matters, but he was also generous and kind. The old servants belonging to the firm never cared to leave him; when they died off he pensioned their widows and provided for their orphans. He was a religious man, of the evangelical type, and he conducted his household in every way from a religious point of view. Family prayers were held night and morning in the great house in Queen's Gate, and the servants were expected each and all to attend church twice on Sundays. Mr. Paget had found a church where the ritual was sufficiently low to please his religious views. To this church he went himself twice on Sundays, invariably accompanied by a tall girl, richly dressed, who clung to his side and read out of the same book with him, singing when he sang, and very often slipping her little hand into his, and closing her bright eyes when he napped unconsciously during the prosy sermon.

This girl was his only child, and while he professed to be actuated by the purest love for both God and his fellow creatures, the one being for whom his heart really beat warmly, the one being for whom he could gladly have sacrificed himself was this solitary girl.

Valentine's mother had died at her birth, and since that day Valentine and her father had literally never been parted. She was his shadow, like him in appearance, and as far as those who knew her could guess like him in character.

The house in Queen's Gate was full of all the accompaniments of wealth. It was richly and splendidly furnished; the drawing-rooms were spacious, the reception rooms were all large. Valentine had her own boudoir, her own special school-room, her own bedroom and dressing-room. Her father had provided a suite of rooms for her, each communicating with the other, but except that she tossed off her handsome dresses in the dressing-room, and submitted at intervals during the day with an unwilling grace to the services of her maid, and except that she laid her bright little curling head each evening on the softest of down-pillows, Valentine's suite of rooms saw very little of their young mistress.

There was an old library in the back part of the house—an essentially dull room, with windows fitted with painted glass, and shelves lined with books, most of them in tarnished and worm-eaten bindings, where Mr. Paget sat whenever he was at home, and where in consequence Valentine was to be found. Her sunny head, with its golden wavy hair, made a bright spot in the old room. She was fond of perching herself on the top of the step-ladder, and so seated burrowing eagerly into the contents of some musty old volume. She devoured the novels of Smollett and Fielding, and many other books which were supposed not to be at all good for her, in this fashion—they did her no harm, the bad part falling away, and not touching her, for her nature was very pure and bright, and although she saw many shades of life in one way or another, and with all her expensive education, was allowed to grow up in a somewhat wild fashion, and according to her own sweet will, yet she was a perfectly innocent and unsophisticated creature.

When she was seventeen, Mr. Paget told her that he was going to inaugurate a new state of things.

"You must go into society, Val," he said. "In these days the daughters of city men of old standing like myself are received everywhere. I will get your mother's third cousin, Lady Prince, to present you at the next Drawing-room, and then you must go the usual round, I suppose. We must get some lady to come here to chaperon you, and you will go out to balls and assemblies, and during the London season turn night into day."

Val was seated on the third rung of the step-ladder when her father made this announcement. She sprang lightly from her perch now, and ran to his side.

"I won't go anywhere without you, dad; so that's settled. Poor old man!—dear old man!"

She put her arms round his neck, and his white moustache and beard swept across her soft, peach-like cheek.

"But I hate going out in the evening, Val. I'm getting an old man—sixty next birthday, my dear—and I work hard all day. There's no place so sweet to me in the evening as this worm-eaten, old armchair;—I should find myself lost in a crowd. Time was when I was the gayest of the gay. People used to speak of me as the life and soul of every party I went to, but that time is over for me. Val; for you it is beginning."

"You are mistaken, father. I perch myself on the arm of this wretched, worm-eaten, old chair, and stay here with you, or I go into society with you. It's all the same to me—you can please yourself."

"Don't you know that you are a very saucy lass, miss?"

"Am I? I really don't care—I go with you, or I stay with you—that's understood. Dad—father dear—that's always to be the way, you understand. You and I are to be always together—all our lives. You quite see what I mean?"

"Yes, my darling. But some day you will have a husband. Val. I want you to marry, and have a good husband, child; and then we'll see if your old father still comes first."

Valentine laughed gaily.

"We'll see," she repeated. "Father, if you are not awfully busy, I must read you this bit out of Roderick Random—listen, is not it droll?"

She fetched the volume with its old-fashioned type and obsolete s'es, and the two faces so alike and so beautiful, and so full of love for one another, bent over the page.

Valentine Paget had her way, and when she made her début in the world of fashion she was accompanied by no other chaperon than her handsome father. A Mrs. Johnstone, a distant relative of Valentine's mother had been asked to come to drive with the young lady in the Parks, and to exercise a very mild surveillance over her conduct generally, when she received her visitors at five o'clock tea, but in the evenings Mr. Paget alone took her into society. The pair were striking enough to make an instant success. Each acted as a foil and heightener to the beauty of the other. Mortimer Paget was recognized by some of his old cronies—fair ladies who had known him when he was young, reproached him gently for having worn so well, professed to take a great interest in his girl, and watched her with narrow, critical, but not unkindly eyes. The girl was fresh and naïve, perfectly free and untrammelled, a tiny bit reckless, a little out of the common. Her handsome face, her somewhat isolated position, and her reputed fortune, for Mortimer Paget was supposed to be one of the richest men in the city, soon made her the fashion. Valentine Paget, in her first season, was spoken about, talked over, acknowledged to be a beauty, and had, of course, plenty of lovers.

No one could have taken a daughter's success with more apparent calmness than did her father. He never interfered with herhe never curbed her light and graceful, although somewhat eccentric, ways; but when any particular young man had paid her marked attention for more than two nights running, had anyone watched closely they might have seen a queer, alert, anxious look come into the fine old face. The sleepy brown eyes would awake, and be almost eagle-like in the keenness of their glance. No one knew how it was done, but about that possible suitor inquiries of the closest and most delicate nature were instantly set on foot; and as these inquiries, from Mr. Paget's point of view, in each case proved eminently unsatisfactory, when next the ardent lover met the beautiful Miss Paget, a thin but impenetrable wall of ice seemed to have started up between them. Scarcely any of Valentine's lovers came to the point of proposing for her; they were quietly shelved, they scarcely knew how, long before matters arrived at this crisis. Young men who in all respects seemed eligible of the eligiblemen with good names and rent-rolls, alike were given a sort of invisible congé. The news was therefore received as a most startling piece of information at the end of Valentine's first season, that she was engaged, with the full consent and approval of her most fastidious father, to about the poorest man of her acquaintance.

Gerald Wyndham was the only son of a country clergymanhe was young, only twenty-two; he was spoken about as clever, but in the eyes of Valentine's friends seemed to have no one special thing to entitle him to aspire to the hand of one of the wealthiest and most beautiful girls of their acquaintance.

It was reported among Mr. Paget's friends that this excellent, honorable and worthy gentleman must surely have taken leave of his senses, for Gerald Wyndham had literally not a penny, and before his engagement to Valentine, the modest career opening up before him was that of Holy Orders in one of its humblest walks.

CHAPTER IV

Wyndham before his engagement was one of the most boyish of men. All the sunshine, the petting, the warmth, the love, which encircled him as the prime favorite of many sisters and an adoring father at Jewsbury-on-the-Wold, seemed to have grown into his face. His deep grey-blue changeful eyes were always laughinghe was witty, and he said witty and laughable things by the score. The young man had plenty of talent, and a public school and university education had developed these abilities to a fine point of culture. His high spirits, and a certain Irish way which he inherited from his mother, made him a universal favorite, but at all times he had his grave moments. A look, a word would change that beaming, expressive face, bring sadness to the eyes, and seriousness to the finely curved lips. The shadows passed as quickly as they came. Before Wyndham met Valentine they were simply indications of the sensitiveness of a soul which was as keenly strung to pain as to joy.

It is a trite saying that what is easily attained is esteemed of little value. Valentine found lovers by the score; in consequence, the fact of a man paying her attention, looking at her with admiration, and saying pretty nothings in her ear, gave her before her first season was over only a slightly added feeling of ennui. At this juncture in her life she was neither in love with her lovers nor with society. She was younger than most girls when they make their entrance into the world, and she would infinitely have preferred the sort of half school-room, half nursery existence she used to lead. She yawned openly and wished for bed when she was dragged out night after night, and when fresh suitors appeared she began really to regard them as a weariness to the flesh.

Gerald Wyndham did not meet Valentine in quite the ordinary fashion.

On a certain hot day in July, she had been absolutely naughty, the heat had enervated her, the languor of summer was over her, and after a late dinner, instead of going dutifully upstairs to receive some final touches from her maid, before starting for a great crush at the house of a city magnate near by, she had flown away to the library, turned on the electric light, and mounting the book-ladder perched herself on her favorite topmost rung, took down her still more favorite "Evelina," and buried herself in its fascinating pages. Past and present were both alike forgotten by the young reader, she hated society for herself, but she loved to read of Evelina's little triumphs, and Lord Orville was quite to her taste.

"If I could only meet a man like him," she murmured, flinging down her book, and looking across the old library with her starry eyes, "Oh, father, dear, how you startled me! Now, listen, please. I will not go out to-nightI am sleepyI am tiredI am yawning dreadfully. Oh, what have I said?how rude of you, sir, to come and startle me in that fashion!"

For Valentine's light words had not been addressed to Mr. Paget, but to a young man in evening dress, a perfect stranger, who came into the room, and was now looking up and actually laughing at her.

"How rude of you," said Valentine, and she began hastily to descend from her elevated position. In doing so she slipped, and would have fallen if Wyndham had not come to the rescue, coolly lifting the enraged young lady into his arms and setting her on the floor.

"Now I will beg your pardon as often as you like," he said. "I was shown in here by a servant. I am waiting for Mr. PagetI was introduced to him this morningmy father turns out to be an old friend, and he was good enough to ask me to go with you both to the Terrells to-night."

"Delightful!" said Valentine. "I'll forgive you, of course; you'll take the dear old man, and I'll stay snugly at home. I'm so anxious to finish 'Evelina.' Have you ever read the book?Don't you love Lord Orville?"

"No, I love Evelina best," replied Gerald.

The two pairs of eyes met, both were full of laughter, and both pairs of lips were indulging in merry peals of mirth when Mr. Paget entered the room.

"There you are, Val," he said. "You have introduced yourself to Wyndham. Quite right. Now, was there ever anything more provoking? I have just received a telegram." Here Mr. Paget showed a yellow envelope. "I must meet a business man at Charing Cross in an hour, on a matter of some importance. I can't put it off, and so. Val, I don't see how I am to send you to the Terrells all alone. It is too badwhy, what is the matter, child?"

"Too delightful, you mean," said Valentine. "I wasn't going. I meant to commit high treason to-night. I was quite determined tonow I needn't. Do you mean to go to the Terrells by yourself, Mr. Wyndham?"

"The pleasure held out was to go with you and your father," responded Wyndham, with an old-fashioned bow, and again that laughing look in his eyes.

Mr. Paget's benevolent face beamed all over.

"Go up to the drawing-room, then, young folks, and amuse yourselves," he said. "Our good friend, Mrs. Johnstone, will bear you company. Val, you can sing something to Wyndham to make up for his disappointment. She sings like a bird, and is vain of it, little puss. Yes, go away, both of you, and make the best of things."

"The best of things is to remain here," said Valentine. "I hate the drawing-room, and that dear, good Mrs. Johnstone, if she must act chaperon, can bring her knitting down here. I am so sorry for you, Mr. Wyndham, but I don't mean to sing a single song to-night. Had you not better go to the Terrells?"

"No, I mean to stay and read 'Evelina,'" replied the obdurate young man.

Mr. Paget laughed again.

"I will send our good friend, Mrs. Johnstone, to make tea for you," he said, and he hurried out of the room.

CHAPTER V

This was the very light and airy beginning of a friendship which was to ripen into serious and even appalling results. Wyndham was a man who found it very easy to make girls like him. He had so many sisters of his own that he understood their idiosyncrasies, and knew how to humor their little failings, how to be kind to their small foibles, and how to flatter their weaknesses. More than one girl had fallen in love with this handsome and attractive young man. Wyndham was aware of these passionate attachments, but as he could not feel himself particularly guilty in having inspired them, and as he did not in the slightest degree return them, he did not make himself unhappy over what could not be cured. It puzzled him not a little to know why girls should be so silly, and how hearts could be so easily parted withhe did not know when he questioned his own spirit lightly on the matter that the day of retribution was at hand. He lost his own heart to Valentine without apparently having made the smallest impression upon this bright and seemingly volatile girl.

On that very first night in the old library Wyndham left his heart at the gay girl's feet. He was seriously in love. Before a week was out he had taken the malady desperately, and in its most acute form. It was then that a change came over his face, it was then for the first time that he became aware of the depths of his own nature. Great abysses of pain were opened up to himhe found himself all sensitiveness, all nerves. He had been proud of his rather athletic bringing-up, of his intellectual training. He had thought poorly of other men who had given up all for the sake of a girl's smile, and for the rather doubtful possession of a girl's fickle heart. He did not laugh at them any longer. He spent his nights pacing his room, and his days haunting the house at Queen's Gate. If he could not go in he could linger near the house. He could lounge in the park and see Valentine as she drove past, and nodded and smiled to him brightly. His own face turned pale when she gave him those quick gay glances. She was absolutely heart-wholea certain intuition told him this, whereas hehe found himself drivelling into a state bordering on idiotcy.

Almost all men have gone through similar crises, but Wyndham at this time was making awful discoveries. He was finding out day by day the depths of weakness as well as pain within him.

"I'm the greatest fool that ever breathed," he would say to himself. "What would Lilias say if she saw me now? How often she and I have laughed over this great momentous matterhow often we have declared that we at least would never lose ourselves in so absurd a fashion. Poor Lilias, I suppose her turn will come as mine has comeI cannot understand myselfI really must be raving mad. How dare I go to Mr. Paget and ask him to give me Valentine? I have not got a halfpenny in the world. This money in my pocket is my father'sI have to come to him for every sixpence! I am no better off than my little sister Joan. When I am ordained, and have secured the curacy of Jewsbury-on-the-Wold, I shall have exactly £ a year. A large sum truly. And yet I want to marry Valentine Pagetthe youngest heiress of the seasonthe most beautifulthe most wealthy! Oh, of course I must be madquite mad. I ought to shun her like the plague. She does not in the least care for menot in the least. I often wonder if she has got a heart anywhere. She acts as a sort of siren to meluring me onweakening and enfeebling my whole nature. She is a little flirt in her way, but an unconscious one. She means nothing by that bright look in her eyes, and that sparkling smile, and that gay clear laugh. I wonder if any other man has felt as badly about her as I do. Oh, I ought to shun herI am simply mad to go there as I do. When I get an invitationwhen I have the ghost of a chance of seeing herit seems as if thousands of invisible ropes pulled me to her side. What is to come of it all? Nothingnothing but my own undoing. I can never marry herand yet I mustI will. I would go through fire and water to hold her to my heart for a moment. There, I must have been quite mad when I said thatI didn't mean it. I'm sane now, absolutely sane. I know what I'll do. I won't dine there to-night. I'll send an excuse, and I'll run down to the old rectory until Monday, and get Lilias to cure me."

The infatuated young man seized a sheet of notepaper, dashed off an incoherent and decidedly lame excuse to Mr. Paget, and trembling with fear that his resolution would fail him even at the eleventh hour, rushed out and dropped the letter into the nearest pillar-box. This action was bracing, he felt better, and in almost gay spirits, for his nature was wonderfully elastic. He took the next train to Jewsbury, and arrived unexpectedly at the pleasant old rectory late on Saturday evening.

The man who is made nothing of in one place, and finds himself absolutely the hero of the hour in another, cannot help experiencing a very soothed sensation. Valentine Paget had favored Gerald with the coolest of nods, the lightest of words, the most indifferent of actions. She met him constantly, she was always stumbling up against him, and when she wanted him to do anything for her she issued a brief and lordly command. Her abject slave flew to do her bidding.

Now at Jewsbury-on-the-Wold the slave was in the position of master, and he could not help enjoying the change.

"Augusta, wheel that chair round for Gerald. Sit there. Gerald, darlingoh, you are in a draught. Shut the door, please, Marjory. Joan, run to the kitchen, and tell Betty to make some of Gerald's favorite cakes for supper. Is your tea quite right, Gerry; have you sugar enoughandand cream?"

Gerald briefly expressed himself satisfied. Lilias was superintending the tea-tray with a delicate flush of pleasure on her cheeks, and her bright eyes glancing moment by moment in admiration at her handsome brother. Marjory had placed herself on a footstool at the hero's feet, and Augusta, tall and gawky, all stockinged-legs, and abnormally thin long arms, was standing at the back of his chair, now and then venturing to caress one of his crisp light waves of hair with the tips of her fingers.

"It is too provoking!" burst from Marjory, "you know, Lilias, we can't put Gerald into his old room, it is being papered, and you haven't half-finished decorating the door. Gerry, darling, you might have let us know you were coming and we'd have worked at it day and night. Do you mind awfully sleeping in the spare room? We'll promise to make it as fresh as possible for you?"

"I'llI'llI'llfill the vases with flowers" burst spasmodically from Augusta. "Do you like roses or hollyhocks best in the tall vases on the mantel-piece, Gerry?"

"By the way, Gerald," remarked the rector, who was standing leaning against the mantel-piece, gazing complacently at his son and daughters, "I should like to ask your opinion with regard to that notice on Herring's book in the Saturday. Have you read it? It struck me as over critical, but I should like to have your opinion."

So the conversation went on, all adoring, all making much of the darling of the house. Years afterwards, Gerald Wyndham remembered that summer's evening, the scent of the roses coming in at the open window, the touch of Marjory's little white hand as it rested on his knee, the kind of half-irritated, half-pleased thrill which went through him when Augusta touched his hair, the courteous and proud look on the rector's face when he addressed him, above all the glow of love in Lilias' beautiful eyes. He remembered that eveninghe was not likely ever to forget it, for it was one of the last of his happy boyhood, before he took upon him his manhood's burden of sin and sorrow and shame.

After tea Lilias and Gerald walked about the garden arm-in-arm.

"I am going to confess something to you," said the brother. "I want your advice, Lilly. I want you to cure me, by showing me that I am the greatest fool that ever lived."

"But you are not, Gerald; I can't say it when I look up to you, and think there is no one like you. You are first in all the world to meyou know that, don't you?"

"Poor Lil, that is just the pointthat is where the arrow will pierce you. I am going to aim a blow at you, dear. Take me down from your pedestal at onceI love someone else much, much better than I love you."

Lilias' hand as it rested on Gerald's arm trembled very slightly. He looked at her, and saw that her lips were moving, and that her eyes were looking downwards. She did not make any audible sound, however, and he went on hastily:

"And you and I, we always promised each other that such a day should not come—no wonder you are angry with me, Lil."

"But I'm not, dear Gerald—I just got a nasty bit of jealous pain for a minute, but it is over. I always knew that such a day would come, that it would have to come—if not for me, at least for you. Tell me about her, Gerry. Is she nice—is she half—or a quarter nice enough for you?"

Then Gerald launched into his subject, forgetting what he supposed could only be a very brief sorrow on Lilias' part in the enthralling interest of his theme. Valentine Paget would not have recognized the portrait which was drawn of her, for this young and ardent lover crowned her with all that was noble, and decked her with attributes little short of divine.

"I am absolutely unworthy of her," he said in conclusion, and when Lilias shook her head, and refused to believe this latter statement, he felt almost angry with her.

The two walked about and talked together until darkness fell, but, although they discussed the subject in all its bearings, Gerald felt by no means cured when he retired to rest, while Lilias absolutely cried herself to sleep.

Marjory and she slept in little white beds, side by side.

"Oh, Lil, what's the matter?" exclaimed the younger sister, disturbed out of her own sweet slumbers by those unusual tokens of distress.

"Nothing much," replied Lilias, "only—only—I am a little lonely—don't ask me any questions, Maggie, I'll be all right in the morning."

Marjory was too wise to say anything further, but she lay awake herself and wondered. What could ail Lilias?—Lilias, the brightest, the gayest of them all. Was she fretting about their mother. But it was seven years now since the mother had been taken away from the rectory children, and Lilias had got over the grief which had nearly broken her child-heart at the time.

Marjory felt puzzled and a little fearful, the evening before had been so sweet, Gerald had been so delightful. Surely in all the world there was not a happier home than Jewsbury-on-the-Wold. Why should Lilias cry, and say that she was lonely?

CHAPTER VI

On Monday morning Wyndham returned to town. His father had strained a point to give his only son the season in London, and Gerald was paying part of the expenses by coaching one or two young fellows for the next Cambridge term. He had just concluded his own University course, and was only waiting until his twenty-third birthday had passed, to be ordained for the curacy which his father was keeping for him. Gerald's birthday would be in September, and the rectory girls were looking forward to this date as though it were the beginning of the millennium.

"Even the cats won't fight, nor the dogs bark when Gerald is in the room," whispered little Joan. "I 'spect they know he don't like it."

Wyndham returned to London feeling both low and excited. His conversation with Lilias and the rather pallid look of her face, the black shadows under her eyes, and the pathetic expression which the shedding of so many tears had given to them, could not cure him nor extinguish the flame which was burning into his heart, and making all the other good things of life seem but as dust and ashes to his taste.

He arrived in town, went straight to his lodgings, preparatory to keeping his engagement with one of his young pupils, and there saw waiting for him a letter in the firm upright handwriting of Mortimer Paget. He tore the envelope open in feverish haste. The lines within were very few:

Dear Wyndham.

Val and I were disappointed at your not putting in an appearance at her dinner-party last night, but no doubt you had good reasons for going into the country. This note will meet you on your return. Can you come and lunch with me in the City on Monday at two o'clock? Come to my place in Billiter-square. I shall expect you and won't keep you waiting. I have a matter of some importance I should like to discuss with you.Yours, my dear Wyndham, sincerely,

"Mortimer Paget."
Wyndham put the letter into his pocket, flew to keep his appointment with his pupil, and at two o'clock precisely was inquiring for Mr. Paget at the offices of the shipping firm in Billiter-square.

Mortimer Paget was now head of the large establishment. He was the sole surviving partner out of many, and on him alone devolved the carrying out of one of the largest business concerns in the city.

Wyndham never felt smaller than when he entered those great doors, and found himself passed on from one clerk to another, until at last he was admitted to the ante-room of the chief himself.

Here there was a hush and stillness, and the young man sank down into one of the easy chairs, and looked around him expectantly. He was in the ante chamber of one of the great kings of commerce, the depressing influence of wealth when we have no share in it came over him. He longed to turn and fly, and but that his fingers, even now, fiddled with Mr. Paget's very pressing note he would have done so. What could the great man possibly want with him? With his secret in his breast, with the knowledge that he, a poor young expectant curate, had dared to lift up his eyes to the only daughter of this great house, he could not but feel ill at ease.

When Wyndham was not at home with any one he instantly lost his charm. He was painfully conscious of this himself, and felt sure that he would be on stilts while he ate his lunch with Mr. Paget. Nay more, he was almost sure that that astute personage would read his secret in his eyes.

A clerk came into the room, an elderly man, with reddish whiskers, small, deep-set eyes, and thin hair rapidly turning white. He stared inquisitively at young Wyndham, walked past him, drew up the blinds, arranged some papers on the table, and then as he passed him again said in a quick, half-frightened aside:

"If I was you, young man, I'd go."

The tone in which this was said was both anxious and familiar. Wyndham started aside from the familiarity. His face flushed and he gazed haughtily at the speaker.

"Did you address me?" he said.

"I did, young man, don't say nothing, for the good Lord's sake, don't say nothing. My name is Jonathan Helps. I have been here man and boy for close on forty years. I know the old house. Sound! no house in the whole city sounder, sound as a nut, or as an apple when it's rotten at the core. You keep that to yourself, young man—why I'd venture every penny I have in this yer establishment. I'm confidential clerk here! I'm a rough sort—and not what you'd expect from a big house, nor from a master like Mr. Paget. Now, young man, you go away, and believe that there ain't a sounder house in all the city than that of Paget, Brake and Carter. I, Jonathan Helps, say it, and surely I ought to know."

An electric bell sounded in the other room. Wiping his brow with his handkerchief as though the queer words he had uttered had cost him an effort, Helps flew to answer the summons.

"Ask Mr. Wyndham to walk in and have lunch served in my room," said an authoritative voice. "And see here. Helps, you are not to disturb us on any excuse before three o'clock."

Shutting the door behind him, Helps came back again to Gerald's side.

"If you don't want to run away at once you're to go in there," he said. "Remember, there isn't a sounder house in all London than that of Paget, Brake and Carter. Paget's head of the whole concern now. Don't he boss it over us though! Oh, you're going in?you've made up your mind not to run away. Surely in vain is the net spread in the sight of any bird. Good Lord, if that ain't the least true word that David ever writ. Well, here you are. Don't forget that this house is soundsound as an apple when it isMr. Wyndham, sir."

"You seem to have got a very extraordinary clerk," said Gerald, when he had shaken hands with his host, who had expressed himself delighted to see him.

"Helps?" responded Mr. Paget. "Yes, poor fellowhas he been entertaining youtelling you about the soundness of the house, eh? Poor Helpsthe best fellow in the world, but just a littlea very littletouched in the head."

"So I should think," said Gerald, laughing; "he compared me to a bird in the fowler's net, and all kinds of ridiculous similes. What a snug room you have here."

"I am glad you think it so. I have a still snugger room at the other side of this curtain, which I hope to introduce to you. Come along and see it. This was furnished at Val's suggestion. She comes here to have lunch with me once a week. Friday is her day. Will you come and join us here next Friday at two o'clock?"

"II shall be delighted," stammered Wyndham.

"She has good taste, hasn't she, little puss? All these arrangements are hers. I never saw any one with a better eye for color, and she has that true sympathy with her surroundings which teaches her to adapt rooms to their circumstances. Now, for instance, at Queen's Gate we are all cool greys and bluesplenty of sunshine comes into the house at Queen's Gate. Into this room the sun never shows his face. Val accordingly substitutes for his brightness golden tones and warm colors. Artistic, is it not? She is very proud of the remark which invariably falls from the lips of each person who visits this sanctum sanctorum, that it does not look the least like an office."

"Nor does it," responded Gerald. "It is a lovely room. What a beautiful portrait that is of your daughterhow well those warm greys suit her complexion."

"Yes, that is Richmond's, he painted her two years ago. Sit down at this side of the table, Wyndham, where you can have a good view of the saucy puss. Does she not look alive, as if she meant to say something very impertinent to us both. Thanks, Helps, you can leave us now. Pray see that we are not disturbed."

Helps withdrew with noiseless slippered feet. A curtain was drawn in front of the door, which the clerk closed softly after him.

"Excellent fellow, Helps," said Mr. Paget, "but mortal, decidedly mortal. If you will excuse me, Wyndham. I will take the precaution of turning the key in that door. This little room, Val's room, I call it, has often been privileged to listen to state secrets. That being the case one must take due precautions against eaves-droppers. Now, my dear fellow, I hope you are hungry. Help yourself to some of those cutletsI can recommend this champagne."

The lunch proceeded, the elder man eating with real appetite, the younger with effort. He was excited, his mind was full of troublehe avoided looking at Valentine's picture, and wished himself at the other side of those locked doors.

"You don't seem quite the thing," said Mr. Paget, presently. "I hope you have had no trouble at home. Wyndham. Is your father well? Let me see, he must be about my agewe were at Trinity College, Cambridge, some time in the forties."

"My father is very well, sir," said Gerald. "He is a hale man, he does not look his years."

"Have some more champagne? I think you told me you had several sisters."

"Yes, there are seven girls at home."

"Good heavensWyndham is a lucky man. Fancy seven Valentines filling a house with mirth! And you are the only sonand your mother is dead."

"My mother is not living," responded Wyndham with a flush. "Andyes, I am the only son. I won't have any more champagne, thank you, sir."

"Try one of these cigars—I can recommend them. Wyndham, I am going to say something very frank. I have taken a fancy to you. There, I don't often take fancies. Why, what is the matter, my dear fellow?"

Gerald had suddenly risen to his feet, his face was white. There was a strained, eager, pained look in his eyes.

"You wouldn't, if you knew," he stammered. "I—I have made a fool of myself, sir. I oughtn't to be sitting here, your hospitality chokes me. I—I have made the greatest fool of myself in all Christendom, sir."

"I think I know what you mean," said Mr. Paget, also rising to his feet. His voice was perfectly calm, quiet, friendly.

"I am not sorry you have let it out in this fashion, my poor lad. You have—shall I tell you that I know your secret, Wyndham?"

"No, sir; don't let us talk of it. You cannot rate me for my folly more severely than I rate myself. I'll go away now if you have no objection. Thank you for being kind to me. Try and forget that I made an ass of myself."

"Sit down again, Wyndham. I am not angry—I don't look upon you as a fool. I should have done just the same were I in your shoes. You are in love with Valentine—you would like to make her your wife."

"Good heavens, sir, don't let us say anything more about it."

"Why not? Under certain conditions I think you would make her a suitable husband. I guessed your secret some weeks ago. Since then I have been watching you carefully. I have also made private inquiries about you. All that I hear pleases me. I asked you to lunch with me, to-day, on purpose that we should talk the matter over."

Mr. Paget spoke in a calm, almost drawling, voice. The young man opposite to him, his face deadly white, his hands nervously clutching at a paper-knife, his burning eyes fixed upon the older man's face, drank in every word. It was an intoxicating draught, going straight to Gerald Wyndham's brain.

"God bless you!" he said, when the other had ceased to speak. He turned his head away, for absolute tears of joy had softened the burning feverish light in his eyes.

"No, don't say that, Wyndham," responded Mr. Paget, his own voice for the first time a little shaken. "We'll leave God altogether out of this business, if you have no objection. It is simply a question of how much a man will give up for love. Will he sell himself, body and soul, for it? That is the question of questions. I know all about you, Wyndham; I know that you have not a penny to bless yourself with; I know that you are about to embrace a beggarly profession. Oh, yes, we'll leave out the religious aspect of the question. A curacy in the Church of England is a beggarly profession in these days. I know too that you are your father's only son, and that you have seven sisters, who will one day look to you to protect them. I know all that; nevertheless I believe you to be the kind of man who will dare all for love. If you win Valentine, you have got to pay a price for her. It is a heavy one—I won't tell you about it yet. When you agree to pay this price, for the sake of a brief joy for yourself, for necessarily it must be brief; and for her life-long good and well-being, then you rise to be her equal in every sense of the word, and you earn my undying gratitude. Wyndham."

"I don't understand you, sir. You speak very darkly, and you hint at things which—which shock me."

"I must shock you more before you hold Valentine in your arms. You have heard enough for to-day. Hark, someone is knocking at the door."

Mr. Paget rose to open it, a gay voice sounded in the passage, and the next moment a brilliant, lovely apparition entered the room.

"Val herself!" exclaimed her father. "No, my darling. I cannot go for a drive with you just now, but you and Mrs. Johnstone shall take Wyndham. You will like a drive in the park, Wyndham. You have got to scold this young man, Val, for acting truant on Saturday night. Now go off, both of you, I am frightfully busy. Yes, Helps, coming, coming. Valentine, be sure you ask Mr. Wyndham home to tea. If you can induce him to dine, so much the better, and afterwards we can go to the play together."

CHAPTER VII

On a certain evening about ten days after the events related in the last chapter, Valentine Paget and her father were seated together in the old library. Good-natured Mrs. Johnstone had popped in her head at the door, but seeing the girl's face bent over a book, and Mr. Paget apparently absorbed in the advertisement sheet of the Times, she had discreetly withdrawn.

"They look very snug," soliloquized the widowed and childless woman with a sigh. "I wonder what Mortimer Paget will do when that poor handsome Mr. Wyndham proposes for Val? I never saw anyone so far gone. Even my poor Geoffrey long ago, who said his passion consumed him to tattersyes, these were poor dear Geoffrey's very wordswas nothing to Mr. Wyndham. Val is a desperately saucy girldoes not she see that she is breaking that poor fellow's heart? Such a nice young fellow, too. He looks exactly the sort of young man who would commit suicide. Dear me, what is the world coming to? That girl seems not in the very least troubled about the matter. How indifferent and easy-going she is! I know I could not calmly sit and read a novel when I knew that I was consuming the vitals out of poor dear Geoffrey. But it's all one to Val. I am very much afraid that girl is developing into a regular flirt. How she did go on and amuse herself with Mr. Carr at the cricket match to-day. Adrian Carr has a stronger face than poor young Wyndhamnot half as devoted to ValI doubt if he even admires her, and yet how white Gerald Wyndham turned when he walked her off across the field. Poor Valit is a great pity Mr. Paget spoils her so dreadfully. It is plain to be seen she has never had the advantage of a mother's bringing up."

Mrs. Johnstone entered the beautifully-furnished drawing-room, seated herself by the open window, and taking up the third volume of a novel, soon forgot Valentine's love affairs.

Meanwhile that young lady with her cheeks pressed on her hands, and her eyes devouring the final pages of "Jane Eyre," gave no thought to any uncomfortable combinations. Her present life was so full and happy that she did not, like most girls, look far aheadshe never indulged in day-dreams, and had an angel come to her with the promise of any golden boon she liked to ask for, she would have begged of him to leave her always as happy as she was now.

She came to the last page of her book, and, drumming with her little fingers on the cover, she raised her eyes in a half-dreaming fashion.

Mr. Paget had dropped his sheet of the Timeshis hand had fallen back in the old leathern armchairhis eyes were closedhe was fast asleep.

In his sleep this astute and careful and keen man of business dropped his mask—the smiling smooth face showed wrinkles, the gay expression was succeeded by a careworn look—lines of sadness were about the mouth, and deep crow's-feet wrinkled and aged the expression round the eyes.

The mantle of care had never yet touched Valentine. For the first time in all her life a pang of keen mental pain went through her as she gazed at her sleeping father. For the first time in her young existence the awful possibility stared her in the face that some time she might have to live in a cold and dreary world without him.

"Why, my father looks quite old," she half stammered. "Old, and—yes, unhappy. What does it mean?"

She rose very gently, moved her chair until it touched his, and then nestling up close to him laid her soft little hand on his shoulder.

Paget slept on, and the immediate contact of Valentine's warm, loving presence, made itself felt in his dreams—his wrinkles disappeared, and his handsome lips again half smiled. Val laid her hand on his—she noticed the altered expression, and her slightly roused fears slumbered. There was no one to her like her father. She had made a mistake just then in imagining that he looked old and unhappy. No people in all the world were happier than he and she. He was not old—he was the personification in her eyes of all that was manly and strong and beautiful.

The tired man slept on, and the girl, all her fears at rest, began idly to review the events of the past day. There had been gay doings during that long summer's afternoon, and Valentine, in the prettiest of summer costumes, had thoroughly enjoyed her life. She had spent some hours at Lords, and had entered with zest into the interest of the Oxford and Cambridge Cricket Match. She lay back in her chair now with her eyes half closed, reviewing in a lazy fashion the events of the bygone hours. A stalwart and very attractive young man in cricketing flannels mingled in these dreams. He spoke to her with strength and decision. His dark eyes looked keenly into her face, he never expressed the smallest admiration for her either by look or gesture, but at the same time he had a way of taking possession of her which roused her interest, and which secured her approbation. She laughed softly to herself now at some of the idle nothings said to her by Adrian Carr, and she never once gave a thought to Wyndham, who had also been at Lords.

CHAPTER VIII

"Val, child, what are you humming under your breath?" said her father, suddenly rousing himself from his slumbers and looking into his daughter's pretty face. "Your voice is like that of a bird, my darling. I think it has gained in sweetness a good deal lately. Have you and Wyndham been practising much together. Wyndham has one of the purest tenor voices I ever heard in an amateur."

"Oh, what a worry Mr. Wyndham is," said Valentine, rising from her seat and shaking out her muslin dress. "Everybody talks to me of his perfections. I'm perfectly tired of them. I wish he wouldn't come here so often. No, I was not thinking of any of his songs. I was humming some words Mr. Carr sings—'Bid me to Live'—you know the words—I like Mr. Carr so much—don't you, dad, dear?"

"Adrian Carryes," replied Mr. Paget in a slow deliberate voice. "Yes, a good sort of fellow, I've no doubt. I heard some gossip about him at my club yesterday—what was it? Oh, that he was engaged, or about to be engaged, to Lady Mabel Pennant. You know the Pennants, don't you, Val? Have you seen Lady Mabel? She is one of the youngest, I think."

"Yes, she's a fright," responded Valentine, with a decided show of temper in her voice.

Her face had flushed too, she could not tell why.

"I did not know Lady Mabel was such a plain girl," responded Mr. Paget drily. "At any rate it is a good connection for Carr. He seems a fairly clever fellow. Valentine, my child, I have something of importance to talk to you about. Don't let us worry about Carr just now—I have something to say to you, something that I'm troubled to have to say. You love your old father very much, don't you, darling?"

"Love you, daddy! Oh, you know—need you ask? I was frightened about you a few minutes ago, father. When you were asleep just now, your face looked old, and there were lines about it. It frightens me to think of you ever growing old."

"Sit close to me, my dear daughter. I have a great deal to say. We will leave the subject of my looks just at present. It is true that I am not young, but I may have many years before me yet. It greatly depends on you."

"On me, father?"

"Yes. I will explain to you by-and-bye. Now I want to talk about yourself. You have never had a care all your life, have you, my little Val?"

"I don't think so, daddyat least only pin-pricks. You know I used to hate my spelling lessons long ago, and Mdlle. Lacount used to worry me over the French irregular verbs. But such things were only pin-pricks. Yes, I am seventeen, and I have never had a real care all my life."

"You are seventeen and four months, Valentine. You were born on the th of February, and your mother and I called you after St. Valentine. Your mother died when you were a week old. I promised her then that her baby should never know a sorrow if I could help it."

"You have helped it, daddy; I am as happy as the day is long. I don't wish for a thing in the wide world. I just want us both to live together as we are doing now. Of course we willwhy not? Shall we go up to the drawing-room now, father?"

"My dear child, in a little time. I have not said yet what I want to say. Valentine, you were quite right when you watched my face as I slumbered. Child, I have got a care upon me. I can't speak of it to anybodyonly it could crush meandandpart us, Valentine. If it fell upon you, ititwould crush you, my child."

Mr. Paget rose. Valentine, deadly white and frightened, clung to him. She was half crying. The effect of such terrible and sudden words nearly paralyzed her; but when she felt the arm which her father put round her tremble, she made a valiant and brave effortthe tears which filled her brown eyes were arrested, and she looked up with courage in her face.

"You speak of my doing something," she whispered. "What is it? Tell me. Nothing shall part us. I don't mind anything else, but nothing shall ever part us."

"Val, I have not spoken of this care to any one but you."

"No, father."

"And I don't show it in my face as a rule, do I?"

"Oh, no! Oh, no! You always seem bright and cheerful."

Her tears were raining fast now. She took his hand and pressed it to her lips.

"But I have had this trouble for some time, my little girl."

"You will tell me all about it, please, dad?"

"No, my darling, you would not understand, and my keenest pain would be that you should ever know. You can remove this trouble, little Val, and then we need not be parted. Now, sit down by my side."

Mr. Paget sank again into the leathern armchair. He was still trembling visibly. This moment through which he was passing was one of the most bitter of his life.

"You will not breathe a word of what I have told you to any mortal, Valentine?"

"Death itself should not drag it from me," replied the girl.

She set her lips, her eyes shone fiercely. Then she looked at her trembling father, and they glowed with love and pity.

"I can save you," she whispered, going on her knees by his side. "It is lovely to think of saving you. What can I do?"

"My little Valmy little precious darling!"

"What can I do to save you, father?"

"Valentine, dearyou can marry Gerald Wyndham."

Valentine had put her arms round her father's neck, now they dropped slowly awayher eyes grew big and frightened.

"I don't love him," she whispered.

"Never mind, he loves youhe is a good fellowhe will treat you well. If you marry him you need not be parted from me. You and he can live together herehere, in this house. There need be no difference at all, except that you will have saved your father."

Paget spoke with outward calmness, but the anxiety under his words made them thrill. Each slowly uttered sentence fell like a hammer of pain on the girl's head.

"I don't understand," she said again in a husky tone. "I would, I will do anything to save you. But Mr. Wyndham is poor and young—in some things he is younger than I am. How can my marrying him take the load off your heart, father? Father, dear, speak."

"I can give you no reason, Valentine, you must take it on trust. It is all a question of your faith in me. I do not see any loophole of salvation but through you, my little girl. If you marry Wyndham I see peace and rest ahead, otherwise we are amongst the breakers. If you do this thing for your old father, Valentine, you will have to do it in the dark, for never, never, I pray, until Eternity comes, must you know what you have done."

Valentine Paget had always a delicate and bright color in her cheeks. It was soft as the innermost blush of a rose, and this delicate and lovely color was one of her chief charms. Now it faded, leaving her young face pinched and small and drawn. She sank down on the hearthrug, clasping her hands in her lap, her eyes looking straight before her.

"I never wanted to marry," she said at last. "Certainly not yet, for I am only a child. I am only seventeen, but other girls of seventeen are old compared to me. When you are only a child, it is dreadful to marry some one you don't care about, and it is dreadful to do a deed in the dark. If you trusted me, father—if you told me all the dreadful truth whatever it is, it might turn me into a woman—an old woman even—but it would be less bad than this. This seems to crush me—and oh, it does frighten me so dreadfully."

Mr. Paget rose from his seat and walked up and down the room.

"You shan't be crushed or frightened," he said. "I will give it up."

"And then the blow will fall on you?"

"I may be able to avert it. I will see. Forget what I said to-night, little girl."

Mortimer Paget's face just now was a good deal whiter than his daughter's, but there was a new light in his eyes—a momentary gleam of nobility.

"I won't crush you, Val," he said, and he meant his words.

"And I won't crush you," said the girl.

She went up to his side, and, taking his hand, slipped his arm round her neck.

"We will live together, and I will have perfect faith in you, and I'll marry Mr. Wyndham. He is good—oh, yes, he is good and kind; and if he did not love me so much, if he did not frighten me with just being too loving when I don't care at all, I might get on very well with him. Now dismiss your cares, father. If this can save you, your little Val has done it. Let us come up to the drawing-room. Mrs. Johnstone must think herself forsaken. Shall I sing to you to-night, daddy, some of the old-fashioned songs? Come, you have got to smile and look cheerful for Val's sake. If I give myself up for you, you must do as much for me. Come, a smile if you please, sir. 'Begone, dull care.' You and I will never agree."

CHAPTER IX

It was soon after this that Valentine Paget's world became electrified with the news of her engagement. Wyndham was congratulated on all sides, and those people who had hitherto not taken the slightest notice of a rather boyish and unpretentious young man, now found much to say in his favor.

Yes, he was undoubtedly good-looking—a remarkable face, full of interest—he must be clever too—he looked it. And then as to his youth—why was it that people a couple of months ago had considered him a lad, a boy—why, he was absolutely old for his two-and-twenty years. A grave thoughtful man with a wonderfully sweet expression.

It was plain to be seen that Wyndham, the expectant curate of Jewsbury-on-the-Wold, and Wyndham, the promised husband of Valentine Paget, were totally different individuals. Wyndham's prospects were changed, so was his appearance—so, in very truth, was the man himself.

Where he had been too young he was now almost too old, that was the principal thing outsiders noticed. But at twenty-two one can afford such a change, and his gravity, his seriousness, and a certain proud thoughtful look, which could not be classified by any one as a sad look, was vastly becoming to Wyndham.

His future father-in-law could not make enough of him, and even Valentine caught herself looking at him with a shy pride which was not very far removed from affection.

Wyndham had given up the promised curacy—this was one of Mr. Paget's most stringent conditions. On the day he married Valentine he was to enter the great shipping firm of Paget, Brake and Carter as a junior partner, and in the interim he went there daily to become acquainted—the world said—with the ins and outs of his new profession.

It was all a great step in the direction of fortune and fame, and the Rectory people ought, of course, to have rejoiced.

They were curious and unworldly, however, at Jewsbury-on-the-Wold, and somehow the news of the great match Gerald was about to contract brought them only sorrow and distress. Lilias alone stood out against the storm of woe which greeted the receipt of Wyndham's last letter.

"It is a real trouble," she said, her voice shaking a good deal; "but we have got to make the best of it. It is for Gerald's happiness. It is selfish for us just to fret because we cannot always have him by our side."

"There'll be no millennium," said Augusta in a savage voice. "I might have guessed it. That horrid selfish, selfish girl has got the whole of our Gerald. I suppose he'll make her happy, nasty, spiteful thing; but she has wrecked the happiness of seven other girlshorrid creature! I might have known there was never going to be a millennium. Where are the dogs? Let me set them fighting. Get out of that, madame pussyou and Rover and Drake will quarrel now to the end of the chapter, for Gerald is never coming home to live."

Augusta's sentiments were warmly shared by the younger girls, and to a great extent she even secured the sympathy of Marjory and the rector.

"I don't understand you, Lilias," said her pet sister. "I thought you would have been the worst of us all."

"Oh, don't," said Lilias, tears springing to her eyes. "Don't you see, Marjory, that I really feel the worst, so I must keep it all in? Don't let us talk it over, it is useless. If Valentine makes Gerald happy I have not a word to say, and if I am not glad I must pretend to be glad for his sake."

"Poor old Lil!" said Marjory.

And after this little speech she teased her sister no more.

A fortnight after his engagement Gerald came to the rectory for a brief visit. He was apparently in high spirits, and never made himself more agreeable to his sisters. He had no confidential talks, however, with Lilly, and they all noticed how grave and quiet and handsome he had grown.

"He's exactly like my idea of the god Apollo," remarked Augusta. "No wonder that girl is in love with him. Oh, couldn't I just pull her hair for her. I can't think how Lilly sits by and hears Gerald praise her! I'd like to give her a piece of my mind, and tell her what I think of her carrying off our ewe-lamb. Yes, she's just like David in the Bible, and I only wish I were the prophet Nathan, to go and have it out with her!"

Augusta was evidently mixed in her metaphors, for it was undoubtedly difficult to compare the same person to Apollo and a ewe-lamb. Nevertheless, she carried her audience with her, and when now and then Gerald spoke of Valentine he received but scant sympathy.

On the day he went away, the rector called Lilias into his study.

"My dear," he said, "I want to have a little talk with you. What do you think of all this? Has Gerald made you many confidences? You and he were always great chums. He was reserved with me, remarkably so, for he was always such an open sort of a lad. But of course you and he had it all out, my dear."

"No, father," replied Lilias. "That is just it. We hadn't anything out."

"What—nothing? And the boy is in love. Oh, yes, anyone can see that—in love, and no confidences. Then, my dear, I was afraid of it—now I am sure—there must be something wrong. Gerald is greatly changed. Lilias."

"Yes," said Lilias. "I can't quite define the change, but it is there."

"My dear girl, he was a boy—now he is a man. I don't say that he is unhappy, but he has a good weight of responsibility on his shoulders. He was a rather heedless boy, and in the matter of concealment or keeping anything back, a perfect sieve. Now he's a closed book. Closed?—locked I should say. Lilias, neither you nor I can understand him. I wish to God your mother was alive!"

"He told me," said Lilias, "that he had talked over matters with you—that—that there was nothing much to say—that he was perfectly satisfied, and that Valentine was like no other girl in the wide world. To all intents and purposes Gerald was a sealed book to me, father; but I don't understand your considering him so, for he said that he had spoken to you very openly."

"Oh, about the arrangements between him and Paget. Yes, I consider it a most unprecedented and extraordinary sort of thing. Gerald gives up the Church, goes into Paget's business—early next summer marries his daughter, and on the day of his wedding signs the deeds of partnership. He receives no salary—not so much as sixpence—but he and his wife take up their abode at the Pagets' house in Queen's Gate, Paget making himself responsible for all expenses. Gerald, in lieu of providing his wife with a fortune, makes a marriage settlement on her, and for this purpose is required to insure his life very heavily—for thousands, I am told—but the exact sum is not yet clearly defined. Paget undertakes to provide for the insurance premium. I call the whole thing unpleasant and derogatory, and I cannot imagine how the lad has consented. Liberty? What will he know of liberty when he is that rich fellow's slave? Better love in a cottage, with a hundred a year, say I."

"But, father, Mr. Paget would not have given Val to Gerald to live in a cottage with her—and Gerald, he has consented to this—this that you call degradation, because he loves Val so very, very much."

"I suppose so, child. I was in love once myself—your mother was the noblest and most beautiful of women; that lad is the image of her. Well, so he never confided in you. Lil? Very strange, I call it very strange. I tell you what. Lilias, I'll run up to town next week, and have a talk with Paget, and see what sort of girl this is who has bewitched the boy. That's the best way. I'll have a talk with Paget, and get to the bottom of things. I used to know him long ago at Trinity. Now run away, child. I must prepare my sermon for to-morrow."

CHAPTER X

At this period of her life Valentine was certainly not in the least in love with the man to whom she was engaged—she disliked caresses and what she was pleased to call honeyed words of flattery. Wyndham, who found himself able to read her moods like a book, soon learned to accommodate himself to her wishes. He came to see her daily, but he kissed her seldom—he never took her hand, nor put his arm round her slim waist; they sat together and talked, and soon discovered that they had many subjects of interest in common—they both loved music, they both adored novels and poetry. Wyndham could read aloud beautifully, and at these times Valentine liked to lie back in her easy chair and steal shy glances at him, and wonder, as she never ceased to wonder, from morning to night, why he loved her so much, and why her father wanted her to marry him.

If Valentine was cold to this young man, she was, however, quite the opposite to the rector of Jewsbury-on-the-Wold. Mr. Wyndham came to town, and of course partook of the hospitality of the house in Queen's Gate. In Valentine's eyes the rector was old, older than her father—she delighted for her father's sake in all old men, and being really a very loveable and fascinating girl soon won the rector's heart.

"I'm not a bit surprised, Gerald," the good man said to his son on the day of his return to his parish duties. "She's a wilful lass, and has a spirit of her own, but she's a good girl, too, and a sweet, and a young fellow might do worse than lose his heart to her. Valentine is open as the day, and when she comes to me as a daughter, I'll give her a daughter's place in my heart. Yes, Valentine is all right enough, and I'll tell Lilias so, and put her heart at rest, poor girl, but I'm not so sure about Paget. I think you are putting yourself in a very invidious position, if you will allow me to say so, my boy, coming into Paget's house as a sort of dependent, even though you are his girl's husband. I don't like the sound of it, and you won't care for the position, Gerald, when you've experienced it for a short time. However—oh, there's my train—yes, porter, yes, two bugs and a rag—I mean two bags and a rug—Here, this way, this way. Dear, dear, how confused one gets! Yes, Gerald, what was I saying? Oh, of course you're of age, my boy, you are at liberty to choose for yourself. Yes, I like the girl thoroughly. God bless you. Gerry; come down to the old place whenever you have a spare Saturday."

The younger Wyndham smiled in a very grave fashion, saw to his father's creature comforts, as regarded wraps, newspapers, etc., tipped the porter, who had not yet done laughing at the reverend gentleman's mistake, and left the station.

He hailed a cab and drove at once to his future father-in-law's business address. He was quite at home now in the big shipping office, the several clerks regarding him with mixed feelings of respect and envy. Gerald had a gracious way with everyone, he was never distant with his fellow-creatures, but there was also a slight indescribable touch about him which kept those who were beneath him in the social scale from showing the smallest trace of familiarity. He was sympathetic, but he had a knack of making those who came in contact with him treat him as a gentleman. The clerks liked Wyndham, and with one exception were extremely civil to him. Helps alone held himself aloof from the new-comer, watching him far more anxiously than the other clerks did, but, nevertheless, keeping his own counsel, and daring whenever he had the opportunity to use covert words of warning.

On his arrival, to-day, Wyndham sent a message to the chief, asking to see him as soon as convenient. While he waited in the ante-room, for in reality he had little or nothing to do in the place, the door was opened to admit another visitor, and then Adrian Carr, the young man whom Valentine had once spoken of with admiration, stepped across the threshold. The two young men were slightly acquainted, and while they waited they chatted together.

Carr was a great contrast to Wyndhamhe was rather short, but thin and wiry, without an atom of superfluous flesh anywherehis shoulders were broad, he was firmly knit and had a very erect carriage. Wyndham, tall, loosely built, with the suspicion of a stoop, looked frail beside the other man. Wyndham's dark grey eyes were too sensitive for perfect mental health. His face was pallid, but at times it would flush vividlyhis lips had a look of repression about themthe whole attitude of the man to a very keen observer was tense and watchful.

Carr had dark eyes, closely cropped hair, a smooth face but for his moustache, and a keen, resolute, bold glance. He was not nearly as handsome as Wyndham, beside Wyndham he might even have been considered commonplace, but his every gesture, his every glance betokened the perfection of mental health and physical vigor.

After a few desultory nothings had been exchanged between the two, Carr alluded to Wyndham's engagement, and offered him his congratulations. He did this with a certain guardedness of tone which caused Gerald to look at him keenly.

"Thank youyes, I am very lucky," he replied. "But can we not exchange good wishes, Carr? I heard a rumor somewhere, that you also were about to be married."

Carr laughed.

"These rumors are always getting about," he said, "half of them end in smoke. In my case you yourself destroyed the ghost of the chance of such a possibility coming about."

"I? What do you mean?" said Wyndham.

"Nothing of the least consequence. As matters have turned out I am perfectly heart-whole, but the fact is, the only girl I ever took the slightest fancy to is going to be your wife. Oh, I am not in love with her! You stopped me in time. I really only tell you this to show you how much I appreciate the excellence of your taste."

Wyndham did not utter a word, and just then Helps came to say that Mr. Paget would see Mr. Carr for a few moments. Carr instantly left the room, and Wyndham went over to the dusty window, leant his elbow against one of the panes, and peered out.

Apparently there was nothing for him to see—the window looked into a tiny square yard, in the centre of which was a table, which contained a dish of empty peapods, and two cabbages in a large basin of cold water. Not a soul was in the yard, and Wyndham staring out ought in the usual order of things soon to have grown weary of the objects of his scrutiny. Far from that, his fixed gaze seemed to see something of peculiar and intense interest. When he turned away at last, his face was ghastly white, and taking out his handkerchief he wiped some drops of moisture from his forehead.

"My master will see you now, sir," said Helps, in a quiet voice. He had been watching Wyndham all the time, and now he looked up at him with a queer significant glance of sympathy.

"Oh, ain't you a fool, young man?" he said. "Why, nothing ain't worth what you're a-gwine through."

"Is Carr gone?" asked Wyndham.

"Oh yes, sir, he's a gent as knows what he's after. No putting his foot into holes with him. He knows what ground he'll walk on. Come along, sir, here you are."

Helps always showed Wyndham into the chief's presence with great parade. Mr. Paget was in a genial humor. When he greeted the young man he actually laughed.

"Sit down, Gerald; sit down, my dear boy. Now, you'll never guess what our friend Adrian Carr came to see me about. 'Pon my word, it's quite a joke—you'll never guess it, Gerald."

"I'm sure of that, sir, I never guessed a riddle in my life."

Something in the hopeless tone in which these few words were uttered made Mr. Paget cease smiling. He favored Gerald with a lightning glance, then said quietly:

"I suppose I ought not to have laughed, but somehow I never thought Carr would have taken to the job. He wants me to introduce him to your father, Gerald. He is anxious to be ordained for the curacy which you have missed. Fancy a man like Carr in the Church! He says he never thought of such a profession until you put it into his head—now he is quite keen after it. Well, perhaps he will make an excellent clergyman—I rather fancy I should like to hear him preach."

"If I were you," said Gerald, "I would refuse to give him that introduction."

"Refuse to give it him! My dear boy, what do you mean? I am not quite such a churl. Why, I have given it him. I wrote a long letter to your excellent father, saying all sorts of nice things about Carr, and he has taken it away in his pocket. Her Majesty's post has the charge of it by this time, I expect. What is the matter, Wyndham? You look quite strange."

"I feel it, sir—I don't like this at all. Carr and I have got mixed somehow. He takes my curacy, and he confessed that but for me he'd have gone in for Val. Now you see what I mean. He oughtn't to have the curacy."

Mr. Paget looked really puzzled.

"You are talking in a strange way, Gerald," he said. "If poor Carr was unfortunate enough to fall in love with a girl whom you have won, surely you don't grudge him that poor little curacy too. My dear lad, you are getting positively morbid. There, I don't think I want you for anything special to day. Go home to Val—get her to cheer your low spirits."

"She cannot," replied Gerald. "You don't see, sir, because you won't. Carr is not in love with Valentine, and Valentine is not in love with him, but they both might be. I have heard Val talk of him—once. I heard him speak of her—to day. By-and-bye, sir—in the future, they may meet. You know what I mean. Carr ought not to go to Jewsbury-on-the-Wold—it is wrong. I will not allow it. I will myself write to the rector. I will take the responsibility, whoever gets my old berth it must not be Adrian Carr."

Wyndham rose as he spoke—he looked determined, all trace of weakness or irresolution left his face. Paget had never before seen this young man in his present mood. Somehow the sight gave him intense pleasure. A latent fear which he had scarcely dared to whisper even to his own heart that Wyndham had not sufficient pluck for what lay before him vanished now. He too rose to his feet, and laid his hand almost caressingly on the lad's shoulder.

"My boy, you have no cause to fear in this matter. In the future I myself will take care of Valentine, but I love you for your thoughtfulness, Gerald."

"You need not, sir. I have something on my mind which I must say now. I have entered into your scheme. I have"

"Yes, yeslet me shut and lock the door, my boy."

Wyndham, arrested in his speech, drew one or two heavy breaths.

He spoke again in a sort of panting way. His eyes grew bright and almost wild.

"I have promised you," he continued. "I'll go through with it. It's a million times worse fate for me than if I had killed someone, and then was hung up by the neck until I died. That, in comparison to this, would bewell, like the sting of a gnat. I'll go through with it, however, and you need not be afraid that I'll change my mind. I do it solely and entirely because I love your daughter, because I believe that the touch of dishonor would blight her, because unfortunately for herself she loves you better than any other soul in the world. If she did not, if she gave me even half of the great heart which she bestows upon you, then I would risk all, and feel sure that dishonor and poverty with me would be better than honor and riches with you. You're a happy man during these last six weeks. Mr. Paget. You have found your victim, and you see a way of salvation for yourself, and a prosperous future for Valentine. She won't grieve longoh, no, not long for the husband she never lovedbut look here, you have to guard her against the possibility in the future of falling in love with anotherof being won by another man, who will ask her to be his wife and the mother of his children. Though she does not love me, she must remain my widow all her days, for if she does not, if I hear that she, thinking herself free, is about to contract marriage with another, I will returnyes, I will return from the deadfrom the grave, and say that it shall not be, and I will show all the world that you arewhat you have proved yourself to be to mea devil. That is all. I wanted to say this to you. Carr has given me the opportunity. I won't see Val to-day, for I am upsetto-morrow I shall have regained my composure."

CHAPTER XI

Wyndham was engaged to Valentine Paget very nearly a year before their wedding. One of the young lady's stipulations was that under no circumstances would she enter into the holy estate of matrimony before she was eighteen. Paget made no objection to this proviso on Val's part. In these days he humored her slightest wish, and no happier pair to all appearance could have been seen driving in the Park, or riding in the Row, than this handsome father and daughter.

"What a beautiful expression he has," remarked many people. And when they said this to the daughter she smiled, and a sweet proud light came into her eyes.

"My father is a darling," she would say. "No one knows him as I do. I believe he is about the greatest and the best of men."

When Val made enthusiastic remarks of this kind. Wyndham looked at her sorrowfully. She was very fond of him by this timehe had learned to fit himself to her ways, to accommodate himself to her caprices, and although she frankly admitted that she could not for an instant compare him to her father, she always owned that she loved him next best, and that she thought it would be a very happy thing to be his wife.

No girl could look sweeter than Val when she made little speeches of this kind, but they had always a queer effect upon her lover, causing him to experience an excitement which was scarcely joy, for nothing could have more fatally upset Mr. Paget's plans than Valentine really to fall in love with Wyndham.

The wedding day was fixed for the first week in July, and Valentine was accompanied to the altar by no less than eight bridesmaids. It was a grand weddingquite one of the events of the season, and those who saw it spoke of the bride as beautiful, and of the bridegroom as a grave, striking-looking man.

If a man constantly practises self-repression there comes a time when, in this special art, he almost reaches perfection. Wyndham had come to this stage, as even Lilias, who read her brother like a book, could see nothing amiss with him on his wedding day. All, therefore, went merrily on this auspicious occasion, and the bride and bridegroom started for the continent amid a shower of blessings and good wishes.

"Gerald, dear, I quite forgive you," said Lilias, as at the very last minute she put her arms round her brother's neck.

"What for, Lilly?" he asked, looking down at her.

Then a shadow of great bitterness crossed the sunshine of his face. He stooped and kissed her forehead.

"You don't know my sin, so you cannot forgive it, Lilly," he continued.

"Oh, my darling, I know you," she said. "I don't think you could sin. I meant that I have learned already to love Valentine a little, and I am not surprised at your choice. I forgive you fully, Gerald, for loving another girl better than your sister Lilias. Good-bye, dear old Gerry. God bless you!"

"He won't do that, Lillyhe can't. Oh, forgive me, dear, I didn't mean those words. Of course I'm the happiest fellow in the world."

Gerald turned away, and Lilias kissed Valentine, and then watched with a queer feeling of pain at her heart as the bridal pair amid cheers and blessings drove away.

Gerald's last few words had renewed Lilias' anxiety. She felt restless in the great, grand house, and longed to be back in the rectory.

"What's the matter, Lil?" said Marjory; "your face is a yard long, and you are quite white and have dark lines under your eyes. For my part I did not think Gerald's wedding would be half so jolly, and what a nice unaffected girl Valentine is."

"Oh, yes, I'm not bothering my head about her," said Lilias. "She's all right, just what father said she was. I wish we were at home again, Maggie."

"Yes, of course, so do I," said Marjory. "But then we can't be, for we promised Gerald to try and make things bright for Mr. Paget. Isn't he a handsome man, Lilly? I don't think I ever saw anyone with such a beaming sort of benevolent expression."

"He is certainly very fond of Valentine, and she of him," answered Lilias. "No, I did not particularly notice his expression. The fact is I did not look at anyone much except our Gerald. Marjory, I think it is an awful thing for girls like us to have an only brotherhe becomes almost too precious. Marjory, I cannot sympathize with Mr. Paget. I wish we were at home. I know our dear old dad will want us, and there is no saying what mess Augusta will put things into."

"Father heard from Mr. Carr on the morning we left," responded Marjory. "I think he is coming to the rectory on Saturday. If so, father won't miss us: he'll be quite taken up showing him over the place."

"I shall hate him," responded Lilias, in a very tart voice. "Fancy his taking our Gerald's place. Oh. Maggie, this room stifles me—can't we change our dresses, and go out for a stroll somewhere? Oh, what folly you talk of it's not being the correct thing! What a hateful place this London is! Oh, for a breath of the air in the garden at home. Yes, what is it, Mrs. Johnstone?"

Lilias' pretty face looked almost grumpy, and a decidedly discontented expression lurked in the dark, sweet eyes she turned upon the good lady of the establishment.

"Lilly has an attack of the fidgets," said Marjory. "She wants to go out for a walk."

"You shall both come in the carriage with me, my dears. I was coming in to propose it to you. We won't dine until quite late this evening."

"Delightful," exclaimed Marjory, and the two girls ran out of the room to get ready. Mrs. Johnstone followed them, and a few moments later a couple of young men who were staying in the house sauntered lazily into the drawing-room.

"What do you think of Wyndham's sisters, Exham?" said one to the other.

Exham, a delicate youth of about nineteen, gave a long expressive whistle.

"The girls are handsome enough," he said. "But not in my style. The one they call Lilias is too brusque. As to Wyndham, well—"

"What a significant 'well,' old fellow—explain yourself."

"Nothing," returned Exham, who seemed to draw out of any further confidences he was beginning to make. "Nothing—only, I wouldn't be in Wyndham's shoes."

The other man, whose name was Power, gave a short laugh.

"You need not pretend to be so wise and close, Exham," he retorted. "Anyone can see with half an eye that Wyndham's wife is not in love with him. All the same. Wyndham has not done a bad thing for himself—stepping into a business like this. Why, he'll have everything by-and-bye. I don't see how he can help it."

"Did you hear that funny story," retorted Exham, "about Wyndham's life being insured?"

"No, what?—Most men insure their lives when they marry."

"Yes, but this is quite out of the common. At four offices, and heavily. It filtered to me through one of the clerks at the office. He said it was all Paget's doing."

"What a villain that clerk must be to let out family secrets," responded Power. "I don't believe there's anything in it, Exham. Ah, here comes the young ladies. Yes, Mrs. Johnstone, I should like to go for a drive very much."

CHAPTER XII

Some people concern themselves vey much with the mysteries of life, others take what good things fall into their way without question or wonder. These latter folk are not of a speculating or strongly reasoning turn; if sorrow arrives they accept it as wise, painful, inevitableif joy visits them they rejoice, but with simplicity. They are the people who are naturally endowed with faithfaith first of all in a guiding providence, which as a rule is accompanied by a faith in their fellow men. The world is kind to such individuals, for the world is very fond of giving what is expected of itto one hate and distrust, to another open-handed benevolence and cordiality. People so endowed are usually fortunate, and of them it may be said, that it was good for them to be born.

All people are not so constitutedthere is such a thing as a noble discontent, and the souls that in the end often attain to the highest, have nearly suffered shipwreck, have spent with St. Paul a day and a night in the deepbeing saved in the end with a great deliverancethey have often on the road been all but lost. Such people often sin very deeplytemptation assails them in the most subtle forms, many of them go down really into the deep, and are never in this life heard of againthey are spoken of as "lost," utterly lost, and their names are held up to others as terrible warnings, as examples to be shunned, as reprobates to be spoken of with bated breath.

It may be that some of these so-called lost souls will appear as victors in another state; having gone into the lowest depths of all they may also attain to the highest heights; this, however, is a mystery which no one can fathom.

Gerald Wyndham was one of the men of whom no one could quite say it was good for him to have been born. His nature was not very easily read, and even his favorite sister Lilias did not quite know him. From his earliest days he was so far unfortunate as never to be able to take things easily; even in his childhood this characteristic marked him. Sorrows with Gerald were never trivial; when he was six years old he became seriously ill because a pet canary died. He would not talk of his trouble, nor wail for his pet like an ordinary child, but sat apart, and refused to eat, and only his mother at last could draw him away from his grief, and show him it was unmanly to be rebellious.

His joys were as intense as his woeshe was an intense child in every sense of the word; eager, enthusiastic, with many noble impulses. All might have gone well with him but for a rather strange accompaniment to his special character; he was as reserved as most such boys would be open. It was only by the changing expression of his eyes that on many occasions people knew whether a certain proposition would plunge him in the depths of woe or raise him to the heights of joy. He was innately very unselfish, and this characteristic must have been most strongly marked in him, for his father and his mother and his seven sisters did their utmost to make him the reverse. Lilias said afterwards that they failed ignobly. Gerald would never see it, she would say. Talk of easy-chairshe would stand all the evening rather than take one until every other soul in the room was comfortably provided. Talk of the best in anything,you might give it to Gerald, but in five minutes he would have given it away to the person who wanted it least. It was aggravating beyond words, Lilias Wyndham often exclaimed, but before you could even attempt to make old Gerry decently comfortable you had to attend to the wants of even the cats and dogs.

Wyndham carrying all his peculiarities with him went to school and then to Cambridge. He was liked in both places, and was clever enough to win distinction, but for the same characteristic which often caused him at the last moment to fail, because he thought another man should win the honor, or another schoolboy the prize.

His mother wished him to take holy orders, and although he had no very strong leaning in that direction he expressed himself satisfied with her choice, and decided for the first few years of his life as deacon and priest to help his father at the dear old parish of Jewsbury-on-the-Wold.

Then came his meeting with Valentine Paget, the complete upheaval of every idea, the revolution which shook his nature to its depths. His hour had come, and he took the malady of young lovefirst, earnest, passionate loveas anyone who knew him thoroughly, and scarcely anyone did know the real Wyndham, might have expected.

One pair of eyes, however, looked at this speaking face, and one keen mental vision pierced down into the depths of an earnest and chivalrous soul. Mortimer Paget had been long looking for a man like Wyndham. It was not a very difficult matter to make such a lad his victim, hence his story became one of the most sorrowful that could be written, as far as this life is concerned. Had his mother, who was now in her grave for over seven years, known what fate lay before this bright beautiful boy of hers, she would have cursed the day of his birth. Fortunately for mothers, and sisters too, the future lies in darkness, for knowledge in such cases would make daily life unendurable.

Valentine and her husband extended their wedding tour considerably over the original month. They often wrote home, and nothing could exceed the cheerfulness of the letters which Mr. Paget read with anxiety and absorbing interestthe rectory folks with all the interest minus the anxiety. Valentine frankly declared that she had never been so happy in her life, and it was at last, at her father's express request, almost command, that the young couple consented to take up their abode in Queen's Gate early in the November which followed their wedding. They spent a fortnight first at the old rectory, where Valentine appeared in an altogether new character, and commenced her career by swearing an eternal friendship with Augusta. She was in almost wild spirits, and they played pranks together, and went everywhere arm-in-arm, accompanied by the entire bevy of little sisters.

Lilias and Marjory began by being rather scandalized, but ended by thoroughly appreciating the arrangement, as it left them free to monopolize Gerald, who on this occasion seemed to have quite recovered his normal spirits. He was neither depressed nor particularly exultant, he did not talk a great deal either about himself or his wife, but was full of the most delighted interest in his father's and sisters' concerns. The new curate, Mr. Carr, was now in full force, and Gerald and he found a great deal to say to one another. The days were those delicious ones of late autumn, when nature quiet and exhausted, as she is after her time of flower and fruit, is in her most soothing mood. The family at the rectory were never indoors until the shades of night drove them into the long, low, picturesque, untidy drawing-room.

Then Gerald sang with his sisters—they had all sweet voices, and his was a pure and very sympathetic tenor. Valentine's songs were not the same as those culled from old volumes of ballads, and selected from the musical mothers' and grandmothers' store, which the rectory folk delighted in. Hers were drawing-room melodies of the present day, fashionable, but short-lived.

The first night the young bride was silent, for even Augusta had left her to join the singers round the piano. Gerald was playing an accompaniment for his sisters, and the rector, standing in the back ground, joined the swell of harmony with his rich bass notes. Valentine and Carr, who was also in the room, were the silent and only listeners. Valentine wore a soft white dress, her bright wavy locks of golden hair were a little roughened, and her starry eyes were fixed on her husband. Carr, who looked almost monastic in his clerical dress, was gazing at her—her lips were partly open, she kept gentle time to the music with her little hand. A very spirited glee was in full tide, when there came a horrid discordant crash on the piano—everyone stopped singing, and Gerald, very white, went up to Val, and took her arm.

"Come over here and join us," he said almost roughly.

"But I don't know any of that music, Gerald, and it is so delicious to listen."

"Folly," responded her husband. "It looks absurd to see two people gaping at one. I beg your pardon, Carr—I am positively sensitive, abnormally so, on the subject of being stared at. Girls, shall we have a round game? I will teach Val some of Bishop's melodies to-morrow morning."

"I am going home," said Carr, quietly. "I did not know that anyone was looking at you except your wife. Wyndham. Good-night?"

It was an uncomfortable little scene, and even the innocent, unsophisticated rectory girls felt embarrassed without knowing why. Marjory almost blamed Gerald afterwards, and would have done so roundly, but Lilias would not listen to her.

At the next night's concert, Valentine sang almost as sweetly as the others, but Carr did not come back to the rectory for a couple of days.

"I evidently acted like a brute, and must have appeared one," said Gerald to himself. "But God alone knows what all this means to me."

It was a small jar, the only one in that happy fortnight, when the girls seemed to have quite got their brother back, and to have found a new sister in pretty, bright Valentine.

It was the second of November when the bride and bridegroom appeared at a big dinner party made in their honor at the house in Queen's Gate.

All her friends congratulated Valentine on her improved looks, and told Wyndham frankly that matrimony had made a new man of him. He was certainly bright and pleasant, and took his part quite naturally as the son of the house. No one could detect the shadow of a care on his face, and as to Val, she sat almost in her father's pocket, scarcely turning her bright eyes away from his face.

"I always thought that dear Mr. Paget the best and noblest and most Christian of men," remarked a certain Lady Valery to her daughter as they drove home that evening. "I am now more convinced of the truth of my views than ever."

"Why so, mother?" asked her daughter.

"My dear, can you not see for yourself? He gave that girl of histhat beautiful girl, with all her fortuneto a young man with neither position nor money, simply and entirely because she fell in love with him. Was there ever anything more disinterested? Yes, my dear, talk to me of every Christian virtue embodied, and I shall invariably mention my old friend, Mortimer Paget."

CHAPTER XIII

"Valentine," said her husband, as they stood together by the fire in their bedroom that night, "I have a great favor to ask of you."

"Yes, Geralda favor! I like to grant favors. Is it that I must wear that soft white dress you like so much to-morrow evening? Or that I must sing no songs but the rectory songs for father's visitors in the drawing-room. How solemn you look, Gerald. What is the favor?"

Gerald's face did look careworn. The easy light-hearted expression which had characterized it downstairs had left him. When Valentine laid her hand lovingly on his shoulder, he slipped his arm round her waist, however, and drew her fondly to his side.

"Val, the favor is this," he said. "You can do anything you like with your father. I want you to persuade him to let us live in a little house of our own for a time, until, say next summer."

Valentine sprang away from Gerald's encircling arm.

"I won't ask that favor," she said, her eyes flashing. "It is mean of you, Gerald. I married you on condition that I should live with my father."

"Very well, dear, if you feel it like that, we won't say anything more about it. It is not of real consequence."

Gerald took a letter out of his pocket, and opening the envelope began leisurely to read its contents. Valentine still, however, felt ruffled and annoyed.

"It is so queer of you to make such a request," she said. "I wonder what father would say. He would think I had taken leave of my senses, and just now too when I have been away from him for months. And when it is such a joy, such a deep, deep joy, to be with him again."

"It is of no consequence, darling. I am sorry I mentioned it. See, Valentine, this letter is from a great friend of mine, a Mrs. Priceshe wants to call on you; she is coming to-morrow. You will be at home in the afternoon, will you not?"

Valentine nodded.

"I will be in," she said. Then she added, her eyes filling with tears"You don't really want to take me away from my father, Gerald?"

"I did wish to do so, dear, but we need not think of it again. The one and only object of my life is to make you happy, Val. Now go to bed, and to sleep, dearest. I am going downstairs to have a smoke."

The next morning, very much to her surprise, Mr. Paget called his daughter into his study, and made the same proposition to her which Gerald had made the night before.

"I must not be a selfish old man, Val," he said. "And I think it is best for young married folks to live alone. I know how you love me, my child, and I will promise to pay you a daily visit. Or at least when you don't come to me, I will look you up. But all things considered, it is best for your husband and you to have your own house. Why, what is it, Valentine, you look quite queer, child."

"This is Gerald's doing," said Valentine—her face had a white set look—never before had her father seen this expression on it. "No, father, I will not leave you; I refuse to do so; it is breaking our compact; it is unfair."

She went up to him, and put her arms round his neck, and again her golden locks touched his silvered head, and her soft cheek pressed his.

"Father darling, you won't break your own Val's heart—you couldn't; it would be telling a lie. I won't live away from you—I won't, so there."

Just at this moment Wyndham entered the room.

"What is it, sir?" he said, almost fiercely. "What are you doing with Val? Why, she is crying. What have you been saying to her?"

"My father said nothing," answered Valentine for him. "How dare you speak to my father in that tone? It is you. Gerald; you have been mean and shabby. You went to my father to try to get him on your side—to try and get him—to try and get him to aid you in going away—to live in another house. Oh, it was a mean, cowardly thing to do, but you shan't have your way, for I'm not going; only I'm ashamed of you, Gerald, I'm ashamed of you."

Here Valentine burst into a tempest of angry, girlish tears.

"Don't be silly, Val," said her husband, in a quiet voice. "I said nothing about this to Mr. Paget. I wished for it, but as I told you last night, when you disapproved, I gave it up. I don't tell lies. Will you explain to Valentine, please, sir, that I'm guiltless of anything mean, or, as she expresses it, shabby, in this matter."

"Of course, Wyndhamof course, you are," said Paget. "My dear little Val, what a goose you have made of yourself. Now run away, Wyndham, there's a good fellow, and I'll soothe her down. You might as well go to the office for me. Ask Helps for my private letters, and bring them back with you. Now, Valentine, you and I are going to have a drive together. Good-bye, Wyndham."

Wyndham slowly left the roomValentine's head was still on her father's shoulderas her husband went away he looked back at her, but she did not return his glance.

"The old man is right," he soliloquized bitterly. "I have not a chance of winning her heart. No doubt under the circumstances this is the only thing to be desired, and yet it very nearly maddens me."

Wyndham did not return to Queen's Gate until quite late; he had only time to run up to his room and change his dress hastily for dinner. Valentine had already gone downstairs, and he sighed heavily as he noticed this, or he felt that unwittingly he had managed to hurt her in her tenderest feelings that morning.

"If there is much of this sort of thing," he said to himself. "I shall not be so sorry when the year is up. When once the plunge is over I may come up another man, and anything is better than perpetually standing on the brink." Yet half an hour later Wyndham had completely changed his mind, for when he entered the drawing-room, a girlish figure jumped up at once out of an easy-chair, and ran to meet him, and Valentine's arms were flung about his neck and several of her sweetest kisses printed on his lips.

"Forgive me for being cross this morning, dear old darling. Father has made me see everything in quite a new light, and has shown me that I acted quite like a little fiend, and that you are very nearly the best of men. And do you know, Gerry, he wishes us so much to live alone, and thinks it the only right and proper thing to do, that I have given in, and I quite agree with him, quite. And we have almost taken the sweetest, darlingest little bijou residence in Park-lane that you can imagine. It is like a doll's house compared to this, but so exquisite, and furnished with such taste. It will feel like playing in a baby-house all day long, and I am almost in love with it already. You must come with me and see it the first thing in the morning. Gerry, for if we both like it, father will arrange at once with the agent, and then, do you know the very first thing I mean to do for you, Gerry? Oh, you need not guess, I'll tell you. Lilias shall come up to spend the winter with us. Oh, you need not say a word. I'm not jealous, but I can see how you idolize Lilias, Gerry."

CHAPTER XIV

At the end of a week the Wyndhams were settled in their new home, and Valentine began her duties as wife and housekeeper in earnest. She, too, was more or less impulsive, and beginning by hating the idea she ended by adopting it with enthusiasm. After all it was her father's plan, not Gerald's, and that in her heart of hearts made all the difference.

For the first time in her life, Valentine had more to get through than she could well accomplish. Her days, therefore, just now were one long delight to her, and even Gerald felt himself more or less infected by her high spirits. It was pretty to see her girlish efforts at housekeeping, and even her failures became subjects of good-humored merriment. Mr. Paget came over every day to see her, but he generally chose the hours when her husband was absent, and Wyndham and his young wife were in consequence able to spend many happy evenings alone.

By-and-bye this girlish and thoughtless wife was to look back on these evenings, and wonder with vain sighs of unavailing regret if life could ever again bring her back such sweetness. Now she enjoyed them unthinkingly, for her time for wakening had not come.

When the young couple were quite settled in their own establishment, Lilias Wyndham came up from the country to spend a week with them. Nothing would induce her to stay longer away from home. Although Valentine pleaded and coaxed, and even Gerald added a word or two of entreaty, she was quite firm.

"No," she said, "nothing would make me become the obnoxious sister-in-law, about whom so much has been written in all the story books I have ever read."

"Oh, Lilias, you darling, as if you could!" exclaimed Val, flying at her and kissing her.

"Oh, yes, my dear, I could," calmly responded Lilly "and I may just as well warn you at once that my ways are not your ways in a great many particulars, and that you'd find that out if I lived too long with you. No, I'm going home to-morrow to my own life, and you and Gerald must live yours without me. I am ready to come, if ever either of you want me, but just now no one does that as much as Marjory and my father."

Lilias returned to Jewsbury-on-the-Wold, and Valentine for some days continued to talk of her with enthusiasm, and to quote her name on all possible occasions.

"Lilias says that I'll never make a good housekeeper, unless I bring my wants into a fixed allowance, Gerald. She says I ought to know what I have got to spend each week, and not to exceed it, whether it is a large or small sum. She says that's what she and Marjory always do. About how much do you think I ought to spend a week on housekeeping, Gerry?"

"I don't know, darling. I have not the most remote idea."

"But how much have we to spend altogether? We are very rich, are we not?"

"No, Valentine, we are very poor. In fact we have got nothing at all."

"Why, what a crease has come between your brows; let me smooth it out—there, now you look much nicer. You have got a look of Lilias, only your eyes are not so dark. Gerald, I think Lilias so pretty. I think she is the very sweetest girl I ever met. But what do you mean by saying we are poor? Of course we are not poor. We would not live in a house like this, and have such jolly, cosy, little dinners if we were poor. Why, I know that champagne that we have a tiny bottle of every evening is really most costly. I thought poor people lived in attics, and ate bread and American cheese. What do you mean by being poor, Gerald?"

"Only that we have nothing of our own, dearest; we depend on your father for everything."

"You speak in quite a bitter tone. It is sweet to depend on my father. But doesn't he give us an allowance?"

"No, Valentine, I just take him all the bills, and he pays them."

"Oh, I don't like that plan. I think it is much more important and interesting to pay one's own bills, and I can never learn to be a housekeeper if I don't understand the value of money. I'll speak to father about this when he comes to-morrow. I'll ask him to give me an allowance."

"I wouldn't," replied Gerald. He spoke lazily, and yawned as he uttered the words.

"There's no use in taking up things that one must leave off again," he added, somewhat enigmatically. Then he opened a copy of Browning which lay near, and forgot Valentine and her troubles, at least she thought he forgot her.

She looked at him for a moment, with a half-pleased, half-puzzled expression coming into her face.

"He is very handsome and interesting," she murmured under her breath. "I like him, I certainly do like him, not as well as my father of course—I'm not sorry I married him now. I like him quite as well as I could ever have cared for the other man—the man who wore white flannels and had a determined voice, and now has been turned into a dreadful prosy curate. Yes, I do like Gerald. He perplexes me a good deal, but that is interesting. He is mysterious, and that is captivating—yes, yes—yes. Now, what did he mean by that queer remark about my housekeeping—'that it wasn't worth while?' I hope he's not superstitious—if anything could be worth while it would be well for a young girl like me to learn something useful and definite. I'll ask him what he means."

She drew a footstool to her husband's side, and taking one of his hands laid her cheek against it. Wyndham dropped his book and smiled down at her.

"Gerry, do you believe in omens?" she asked.

Gerald gave a slight start. Circumstances inclined him to superstition—then he laughed. He must not encourage his wife in any such folly.

"I don't quite understand you, my love," he replied.

"Only you said it was not worth my while to learn to housekeep. Why do you say that? I am very young, you are young. If we are to go on always together, I ought to become wise and sensible. I ought to have knowledge. What do you mean, Gerald? Have you had an omen? Do you think you will die? Or perhaps that I shall die? I should not at all like it. I hope—I trust—no token of death has been sent to you about me."

"None, my very dearest, none. I see before you a life of—of peace. Peace and plenty—and—and—honor—a good life, Valentine, a guarded life."

"How white you are, Gerald. And why do you say 'you' all the time? The life, the peaceful life, and it sounds rather dull, is for us both, isn't it?"

"I don't know—I can't say. You wouldn't care, would you, Val—I mean—I mean—"

"What?"

Valentine had risen, her arms were thrown round Gerald's neck.

"Are you trying to tell me that I could be happy now without you?" she whispered. "Then I couldn't, darling. I don't mind telling you I couldn't. II"

"What, Val, what?"

"I like you, Gerald. Yes, I know itI do like youmuch."

It ought to have been the most dreadful sound to him, and yet it wasn't. Wyndham strained his wife to his heart. Then he raised his eyes, and with a start Valentine and he stepped asunder.

Mr. Paget had come into the room. He had come in softly, and he must have heard Valentine's words, and seen that close embrace.

With a glad cry the girl flew to his side, but when he kissed her his lips trembled, he sank down on the nearest chair like a man who had received a great shock.

CHAPTER XV

"I'm afraid I can't help it, sir," said Wyndham.

Mr. Paget and his son-in-law were standing together in the very comfortable private room before alluded to in the office of the former.

Wyndham was standing with his back to the mantel-piece; Valentine's lovely picture was over his head. Her eyes, which were almost dancing with life, seemed to have something mocking in them to Mr. Paget, as he encountered their gaze now. As eyes will in a picture, they followed him wherever he moved. He was restless and ill at ease, and he wished either that the picture might be removed, or that he could take up Wyndham's position with his back to it.

"I tell you," he said, in a voice that betrayed his perturbation, "that you must help it. It's a clear breaking of contract to do otherwise."

"You see," said Wyndham, with a slow smile, "you under-rated my attractions. I was not the man for your purpose after all."

"Sit down for God's sake, Wyndham. Don't stand there looking so provokingly indifferent. One would think the whole matter was nothing to you."

"I am not sure that it is much; that is, I am not at all sure that I shall not take my full meed of pleasure out of the short time allotted to me."

"Sit down, take that chair, no, not that one—that—ah, that's better. Valentine's eyes are positively uncomfortable the way they pursue me this evening. Wyndham, you must feel for me—you must see that it will be a perfectly awful thing if my—my child loses her heart to you."

"Well, Mr. Paget, you can judge for yourself how matters stand. I—I cannot quite agree with you about what you fear being a catastrophe."

"You must be mad, Wyndham—you must either be mad, or you mean to cheat me after all."

"No, I don't. I have a certain amount of honor left—not much, or I shouldn't have lent myself to this, but the rag remaining is at your service. Seriously now, I don't think you have grave cause for alarm. Valentine is affectionate, but I am not to her as you are."

"You are growing dearer to her every day. I am not blind, I have watched her face. She follows you with her eyes—when you don't eat she is anxious, when you look dismal—you have an infernally dismal face at times, Wyndham—she is puzzled. It wasn't only what I saw last night. Valentine is waking up. It was in the contract that she was not to wake up. I gave you a child for your wife. She was to remain a child when"

"When she became my widow," Wyndham answered calmly.

"Yes. My God, it is awful to think of it. We must go in, we daren't turn back, and she may suffer, she may suffer horribly, she has a great heart—a deep heart. It is playing with edged tools to make it live."

"Can't you shorten the time of probation?" asked Wyndham.

"I wish to heaven I could, but I am powerless. Wyndham, my good friend, my son—something must be done."

"Don't call me your son," said the younger man, rising and shaking himself. "I have a father who besides you is—there, I won't name what I think of you. I have a mother—through your machinations I shall never see her face any more. Don't call me your son. You are very wise, you have the wisdom of a devil, but even you can overreach yourself. You thought you had found everything you needed, when you found me—the weak young fool, the despairing idiotic lover. Poor? Yes, cursedly poor, and with a certain sense of generosity, but nothing at all in myself to win the heart of a beautiful young girl. You should have gone down to Jewsbury-on-the-Wold for a little, before you summed up your estimate of my character, for the one thing I have always found lying at my feet is—love. Even the cats and dogs loved me—those to whom I gave nothing regarded me with affection. Alack—and alas—my wife only follows the universal example."

"But it must be stopped, Wyndham. You cannot fail to see that it must be stopped. Can you not help me—can you not devise some plan?"

Wyndham dropped his head on his hands.

"Hasten the crisis," he said. "I want the plunge over; hasten it."

There came a tap at the room door. Mr. Paget drew back the curtain which stood before it, slipped the bolts, and opened it.

"Ah, I guessed you were here!" said Valentine's gay voice; "yes, and Gerald too. This is delightful," added she, as she stepped into the room.

"What is it, Val?" asked her father. "I was busy—I was talking to your husband. I am very much occupied this afternoon. I forgot it was the day you generally called for me. No, I'm afraid I can't go with you, my pet."

Valentine was looking radiant in winter furs.

"I'll go with Gerald, then," she said. "He's not too busy."

She smiled at him.

"No, my dear, I'll go with you," said the younger man. "I don't think, sir," he added, turning round, with a desperately white but smiling face, "that we can advance business much by prolonging this interview, and if you have no objection, I should like to take a drive with my wife as she has called."

Valentine instinctively felt that these smoothly spoken words were meant to hide something. She glanced from the face of one man to another; then she went up to her father and linked her hand in his arm.

"Come, too, daddy," she said. "You used always to be able to make horrid business wait upon your own Valentine's pleasure."

Mr. Paget hesitated for a moment. Then he stooped and lightly kissed his daughter's blooming cheek.

"Go with your husband, dear," he said, gently. "I am really busy, and we shall meet at dinner time."

"Yes, we are to dine with you to-night—I've a most important request to make after dinner. You know what it is, Gerry. Won't father be electrified? Promise beforehand that you'll grant it, dad."

"Yes, my child, yes. Now run away both of you. I am really much occupied."

Valentine and her husband disappeared. Mr. Paget shut and locked the door behind them—he drew the velvet curtains to insure perfect privacy. Then he sank down in his easy-chair to indulge in anxious meditation.

He thought some of those hard thoughts, some of those abstruse, worrying, almost despairing thoughts, which add years to a man's life.

As he thought the mask dropped from his handsome face; he looked old and wicked.

After about a quarter-of-an-hour of these meditations, he moved slightly and touched an electric bell in the wall. His signal was answered in about a minute by a tap at the room door. He slipped the bolts again, and admitted his confidential clerk, Helps.

"Sit down, Helps. Yes, bolt the door, quite right. Now, sit down. Helps, I am worried."

"I'm sorry to observe it, sir," said Helps. "Worries is nat'ral, but not agreeable. They come to the good and they come to the bad alike; worries is like the sun—they shines upon all."

"A particularly agreeable kind of glare they make," responded Mr. Paget, testily. "Your similes are remarkable for their aptitude, Helps. Now, have the goodness to confine yourself to briefly replying to my questions. Has there been any news from India since last week?"

"Nothing fresh, sir."

"No sign of stir; no awakening of interest—of—of—suspicion?"

"Not yet, sir. It isn't to be expected, is it?"

"I suppose not. Sometimes I get impatient, Helps."

"You needn't now, sir. Your train is, so to speak, laid. Any moment you can apply the match. Any moment, Mr. Paget. Sometimes, if you'll excuse me for speaking of that same, I have a heart in my bosom that pities the victim. You shouldn't have done it from among the clergy. Mr. Paget, and him an only son, too."

"Hush, it's done. There is no help now. Helps, you are the only soul in the world who knows everything. Helps, there may be two victims."

Helps had a sallow face. It grew sickly now.

"I don't like it," he muttered. "I never did approve of meddling with the clergy—he was meant for the Church, and them is the Lord's anointed."

"Don't talk so much," thundered Mr. Paget. "I tell you there are two victims—and one of them is my child. She is falling in love with her husband. It is true—it is awful. It must be prevented. Helps, you and I have got to prevent it."

Helps sat perfectly still. His eyes were lowered; they were following the patterns of the carpet. He moved his lips softly.

"It must be prevented," said Mr. Paget. "Why do you sit like that? Will you help me, or will you not?"

Helps raised his greeny-blue eyes with great deliberation.

"I don't know that I will help you, Mr. Paget," he replied; and then he lowered them again.

"You won't help me? You don't know what you are saying, Helps. Did you understand my words? I told you that my daughter was falling in love with that scamp Wyndham."

"He ain't a scamp," replied the clerk. "He's in the conspiracy, poor lad, he's the victim of the conspiracy, but he's no scamp. Now I never liked it. I may as well own to you, Mr. Paget, that I never liked your meddling with the clergy. I said, from the first, as no good would come of it. It's my opinion, sir" here Helps rose, and raising one thin hand shook it feebly at his employer, "it's my opinion as the Lord is agen you—agen us both for that matter. We can't do nothing if He is, you know. I had a dream last night—I didn't like the dream, it was a hominous dream. I didn't like your scheme, Mr. Paget, and I don't think I'll help you more'n I have done."

"Oh, you don't? You are a wicked old scoundrel. You think you can have things all your own way. You are a thief. You know the kind of accommodation thieves get when their follies get found out. Of course, it's inexpensive, but it's scarcely agreeable."

Helps smiled slightly.

"No one could lock me up but you, and you wouldn't dare," he replied.

These words seemed somehow or other to have a very calming effect on Mr. Paget. He did not speak for a full moment, then he said quietly

"We won't go into painful scenes of the past, Helps. Yes; we have both committed folly, and must stand or fall together. We have both got only daughters—it is our life's work to shield them from dishonor, to guard them from pain. Suppose, Helps, suppose your

Esther was in the position of my child? Suppose she was learning to love her husband, and you knew what that husband had before him, how would you feel, Helps? Put yourself in my place, and tell me how you'd feel."

"It 'ud all turn on one point," said Helps. "Whether I loved the girl or myself most. Ef I saw that the girl was going deep in love with her husbanddeep, mind youmortal deepso I was nothing at all to her beside him, why then, maybe, I'd save the young man for her sake, and go under myself. I might do that, it 'ud depend on how much I loved."

"Nonsense; you would bring dishonor and ruin on her. How could she ever hold up her head again?"

"Maybe he'd comfort her through it. There's no saying. Love, deep love, mind you, does wonders."

Mr. Paget began to pace up and down the room.

"You are the greatest old fool I ever came across," he said. "Now, mind you, your sentiments with regard to your low-born daughter are nothing at all to me. Noblesse oblige doesn't come into the case with you as it does with my child. Dishonor shall never touch her; it would kill her. She must be guarded against it. Listen, Helps. We have talked folly and sentiment enough. Now to business. That young man must not rise in my daughter's esteem. There is such a thinglisten, Helps, come closesuch a thing as blackening a man's character. You think it overyou're a crafty old dog. Go home and look at Esther, and think it over. God bless me, I'd not an idea how late it was. Here's a five pound note for your pretty girl, Helps. Now go home and think it over."

CHAPTER XVI

Helps buttoned on his great coat, said a few words to one of the clerks, and stepped out into the foggy night. He hailed a passing omnibus, and in the course of half-an-hour found himself fumbling with his latch-key in the door of a neat little house, which, however, was at the same moment thrown wide open from within, and a tall girl with a pale face, clear grey eyes, and a quantity of dark hair coiled about her head stood before him.

"It's father, Cherry," she said to a little cousin who popped round the corner. "Put the sausages on, and dish up the potatoes. Now don't be awkward. I'm glad you're in good time, father—here, give us a kiss. Do I look nice in this dress? I made it all myself. Here, come up to the gas, and have a good look at it. How does it fit? Neat, eh?"

The dress was a dark green velveteen, made without attempt at ornament, but fitting the slim and lissom figure like a glove.

"It's neat, but plain, surely," replied Helps, looking puzzled, proud, and at the same time dissatisfied. "A bit more color now,—more flouncing—Why, what's the matter, Essie? How you do frown, my girl."

"Come in out of the cold, father. Oh, no, not the kitchen, I've ordered supper to be laid in the dining-room. Well, perhaps the room it does smoke, but that will soon clear off. Now, father, I want to ask you an important question. Do I look like a lady in this dress?"

She held herself very erect, the pure outline of her grand figure was shown to the best advantage, her massive head had a queenly pose, and the delicate purity of her complexion heightened the effect. Her accent was wrong, her words betrayed her—could she have become dumb, she might have passed for a princess.

"Do I look like a lady?" she repeated.

Little Helps stepped back a pace or two—he was puzzled and annoyed.

"You look all right, Essie," he said. "A lady? Oh, well—but you ain't a lady, my girl. Look here, Esther, this room is mortal cold—I'd a sight rather have my supper cosy in the kitchen."

"You can't then, father. You must take up with the genteel ways. After supper we're going into the drawing-room, and I'll play to you on the pianner, pa; I have been practising all day. Perhaps, too, we'll have company—there's no saying."

"Company?" repeated Helps. "Who—what?"

"Oh, I'm not going to say, maybe he won't come. I met him in the park—I was skating with the Johnsons, and I fell, and he picked me up. I might have been hurt but for him. Then he heard George Johnson calling me by my name, and it turned out that he knew you. Oh, wasn't he a swell, and didn't he look it! And hadn't he a name worth boasting of! 'Mr. Gerald Wyndham.' Why, what's the matter, father? He said that he had often promised to look you up some evening, to bring you some stupid book or other. He said maybe he would come to-night. That's why I had the drawing-room and dining-room all done up. He said perhaps he'd call, and took off his hat most refined. I took an awful fancy to him—his ways was so aspiring. He said he might come to-night, but he wasn't sure. I didn't know you had young men like that at your office, father. And what is the matter?—why, you're quite white!"

"I never talk of what goes on at the place of business," replied Helps, in quite a brusque voice for him. "And as to that young gent, Esther, he's our Miss Valentine's husband."

"Married? Oh, lor, he didn't look it! And who is 'our Miss Valentine?' if I may be bold enough to ask."

"Mr. Paget's daughter. I said I didn't mention matters connected with the place of business."

"You always were precious close, father. But you're a dear, good, old dad, all the same, and Cherry and I would sooner die than have you scolded about anything. Cherry, my fine beau's a married man—pity, aint it? I thought maybe he'd suit me."

"Then you needn't have lit the fire in the drawing-room," answered Cherry, a very practical and stoutly-built little maid of fifteen.

"Maybe I needn't, but there's no harm done. I suppose I can talk to him, even if he is married. Won't I draw him out about Miss Valentine, and tell him how father always kept her a secret from us."

"Supper's ready, uncle," said Cherry. "Oh, bother that fire! It's quite out. Don't the sausages smell good, uncle? I cooked them myself."

The three sat down to the table, poor Helps shivering not a little, and casting more than one regretful glance at the warm and cosy kitchen. He was feeling depressed for more than one reason this evening, and a sense of dismay stole over him at Esther's having accidentally made Wyndham's acquaintance.

"It's a bad omen," he said, under his breath, "and Esther's that contrary, and so taken up with making a lady of herself, and she's beautiful as a picter, except when she talks folly.

"I liked that young man from the first," he murmured. "I took, so to speak, a fancy to him, and warned him, and I quoted scripter to him. All to no good. The glint of a gel's eye was too much for him, he sold himself for herbody and soul he sold himself for her. Still, I went on keeping up a fancy for him, and I axed him to look me up some evening, and have a pipehe's wonderful on words toohe can derivate almost as many as I can. I'm sorry now I asked himEsther's that wilful, and as beautiful as a picter. She talks too much to young men that's above her. She's set on being a lady. Mr. Wyndham's married, of course, but Esther wouldn't think nothing of trying to flirt with him for all that."

"Esther," he said, suddenly, raising his deep-set eyes, and fixing them on his daughter, "ef the young man calls, it's to see me, mind youhe's a married man, and he has got the most beautiful wife in the world, and he loves her. My word, I never heard tell of nobody loving their wife so much!"

Esther's big grey eyes opened wide.

"How you look at me, dad," she said. "One would think I wanted to steal Mr. Wyndham from his wife! I'm glad he loves her, it's romantic, it pleases me."

"And there's his ring at the door," suddenly exclaimed Cherry. "Esther was right to prepare the drawing-room. I'm glad he have come. I like to look at handsome gents, particular when they are in love."

Gerald's arrival was accidental after all. He and his wife were dining in Queen's Gate, and after dinner he remembered his adventure on the ice, and told the story in an amusing way.

"A most beautiful girl, but with such an accent and manner," he said. "And who do you think she turned out to be, sir?" he added, turning to his father-in-law. "Why, your cracked clerk's daughter. She told me her name was Esther Helps, and I found they were father and daughter."

"Has old Helps got a daughter?" exclaimed Valentine.

"How funny that I should never have known it. I have always been rather fond of old Helps."

"He has an only daughter, as I have an only daughter," replied Mr. Paget. Valentine was sitting close to him; he put his arm around her waist as he spoke.

"How queer that I should never have known," continued Valentine. "And her name is Esther? It is a pretty name. And you say that she is handsome, Gerry? What is she like?"

"Tall and pale, with an expressive face," replied Wyndham, lightly. "She is lady-like, and even striking-looking until she opens her lips—then" he made an expressive grimace.

"Poor girl, as if she could help that," replied Val. "She has never been educated, you know. Her father is poor, and he can't give her advantages. Does old Helps love his daughter very much, dad?"

"I suppose so, Val. Yes, I think I may say I am sure he does."

"I am so interested in only girls with fathers," continued Mrs. Wyndham. "I wish I had seen Esther Helps. I hope you were kind to her, Gerald."

"I picked her up, dear, and gave her to her friends. By-the-way, I said I'd call to see old Helps this evening. He has a passion for the derivation of words, and I have Trench's book on the subject. Shall I take Esther a message from you, Val?"

"Yes, say something nice. I am not good at making up messages. Tell her I am interested in her, and the more she loves her father, the greater my interest must be. See, this is much better than any mere message—take her this bunch of lilies—say I sent them. Now, Gerald, is it likely I should be lonely? Father and I are going to have two hours all to ourselves."

But as Valentine said these light words, her hand lingered on her husband's shoulder, and her full brown eyes rested on his face. Something in their gaze made his heart throb. He put his arm round her neck and kissed her forehead.

"I shan't be two hours away," he said.

He took up the flowers, put "Trench on Words" into his pocket, and went out.

Wyndham had a pleasant way with all people. His words, his manner, his gentle courteous smile won for him hearts in all directions. He was meant to be greatly beloved; he was born to win the most dangerous popularity of all—that which brought to him blind and almost unreasoning affection.

He was received at No. Acadia Terrace with enthusiasm. Esther and Cherry were open-eyed in their admiration, and Helps, a little sorrowful—somehow Helps if he wasn't cynical was always sorrowful—felt proud of the visit.

Gerald insisted on adjourning to the kitchen. He and Helps had a long discussion on words—Cherry moved softly about, putting everything in order—Esther sat silent and lovely, glancing up now and then at Gerald from under her black eyelashes. Valentine's flowers lay in her lap. They were dazzlingly white, and made an effective contrast to her dark green dress. It was a peaceful little scene—nothing at all remarkable about it. Gerald fell more contented than he had done for many a day. Who would have thought that out of such innocent materials mischief of the deadliest sort might be wrought to him and his.

CHAPTER XVII

When Wyndham came back to Queen's Gate his wife met him with sparkling eyes.

"How much time can you give me to-morrow?" she said. "I want to go out with you. I have been speaking to father, and he accedes to all our wisheshe will give us an income. He says he thinks a thousand a year will be enough. Oh, he is kind, and I feel so excited. Don't let us drive, let us walk home, Gerry. I know the night is fine. I feel that everything is bright just now, and you will come with me to-morrow, won't you, Gerry? Father, could you spare Gerald from business to-morrow? You know it is so important."

Mr. Paget was standing a little in the shadow, his face was beaming, his eyes smiling. When Valentine turned to him, he laid his hand lightly on her shoulder.

"You are an inconsistent little girl," he said. "You want to become a business woman yourself. You want to be practical, and clever, and managing, and yet you encourage that husband of yours to neglect his work."

Gerald flushed.

"I don't neglect my work," he said. "My heavy work has never a chance of being neglected, it is too crushing."

Valentine looked up in alarm, but instantly Mr. Paget's smiling face was turned to the young man, and his other hand touched his arm.

"Your work to-morrow is to go with your wife," he said gently. "She wants to shopto spendto learn saving by expenditure. You have to go with her to give her the benefit of your experience. Look out for cheap sales, my dear childgo to Whiteley's, and purchase what you don't want, provided it is a remnant, and sold under cost price. Save by learning, Val, and, Gerald, you help her to the best of your ability. Now good-night, my children, good-night, both of you, bless you."

"It almost seemed to me," said Valentine, as they walked home togetherit was a starry night and she clung affectionately to her husband's arm"it almost seemed to me that father was put out with you, and you with him. He was so sweet while you were out, but although he smiled all the time after you returned I don't think he was really sweet, and you didn't speak nicely to him, Gerald, about the work I mean. Is the work at the office very heavy. Gerald? You never spend more than about two hours a day there."

"The work is heavy, Val, and it will grow more so. I don't complain, however—I have not the shadow of a right to complain. I am sorry I spoke to your father so as to vex you, dearest- I won't do so again."

"I want you to love him, Gerry; I want you to feel for him a little bit, as I do, as if he were the first of men, you understand. Don't you think you could try. I wish you would."

"You see I have my own father, darling."

"Oh yes, but really now—the rector is a nice old man, but, Gerry, if you were to speak from your inmost heart, without any prejudice, you know; if you could detach from your mind the fact that you are the son of the rector, you would not compare them, Gerry, you could not."

"As you say, Valentine, I could not. They stand on different pedestals. Now let us change the subject. So you are the happy possessor of a thousand a year."

"We both possess that income, Gerry. Is not it sweet of father—he felt for me at once. He said he was proud of me, that I was going to make a capital wife—he said you were a lucky fellow, Gerry."

"Yes, darling, so I am, so I am."

"Then he spoke of a thousand a year to begin with. He mentioned a lot more, but he said a thousand was an income on which I might begin to learn to save. And he gave me a cheque for the first quarter to-night. He said we had better open a banking account. As soon as we get in, I'm going to give you the cheque, I'm afraid to keep it. Father said we might open a separate account in his bank."

"My father has always banked at the Westminster," said Gerald. "It would suit me best to take the money there."

They had reached the house by this time. Gerald opened the door with a latch-key, and the two went into the pretty, cosy drawing-room. Valentine threw off her white fur wrap, and sank down into an easy-chair. Her dinner dress was white, and made in a very simple girlish fashion—her hair, which was always short and curled in little rings about her head and face, added to the extreme youth of her appearance. She raised her eyes to her husband, who stood by the mantel-piece. The expression she wore was that of a happy, excited, half-spoiled child, a creature who had been somebody's darling from her birth. This was the predominating expression of her face, and yet—and yet—Gerald seemed to read something more in the gaze of the sweet eyes to-night; a question was half coming into them, the dawn of a possible awakening might even be discerned in them.

"My darling," he said, suddenly coming up to her, putting his arm about her, and kissing her with passion, "I love you better than my life—better than my hope of heaven. Can you love me a little, Valentine—just a little?"

"I do love you, Gerald." But she spoke quietly, and without any answering fire.

His arms dropped, the enthusiasm went out of his face; he went back again to his old position with his back to the fire.

"What kind of girl is Esther Helps, Gerald?"

"A beautiful girl."

"As beautiful as I am?"

"In her way quite as beautiful."

"Why do you say 'in her way?' Beauty must always be beauty."

"It has degrees, Esther Helps is not a lady."

Valentine was silent for half a minute.

"I should like to know her," she said then. "I wonder how much she cares for old Helps."

"Look here, Valentine, Esther Helps is not the least like you. I don't know that she has any romantic attachment for that old man. She is a very ordinary girl—a most commonplace person with just a beautiful face."

"How queerly you speak, Gerald. As if it were something strange for an only daughter to be attached to her father."

"The amount of attachment you feel, darling, is uncommon."

"Is it? Well, I have got a very uncommon father."

"My dear Valentine, God knows you have."

Gerald sank down into a chair by the fire. He turned his face, dreary, white and worn, to the blaze. Valentine detected no hidden sarcasm in his tones. After a time she took the cheque out of her purse and handed it to him.

"Here, Gerry, you will put this into your bank to-morrow, won't you? We will open an account in our joint names, won't we? And then we can calculate how much we are to spend weekly and monthly. Oh, won't it be interesting and exciting. So much for my clothes, so much for yours, so much for servants, so much for foodwe need not spend so much on food, need we? So much for pleasuresI want to go to the theatre at least twice a weekoh, we can manage it all and have something to spare. And no debts, remember, Gerryready money will be our system. We'll go in omnibuses, too, to save cabsI shall love to feel that I am doing for a penny what might cost a shilling. Gerald darling, do you know that just in one way you have vexed my father a little?"

"Vexed himhow, Valentine?"

"He says it is very wrong of you to croak, and have gloomy prognostications. You know you said it was not worth while for me to learn to housekeep. Just as if you were going to die, or I were going to die. Father was quite vexed when I told him. Now you look vexed, Gerry. Really between such a husband and such a father, a poor girl may sometimes feel puzzled. Well, have you nothing to say?"

"I'm afraid I have nothing to say, Valentine."

"Then you won't croak any more."

"Not for youI have never croaked for you."

"Nor for yourself."

"I cannot promise. Sometimes fits of depression come over me. There, good-night, sweet. Go to bed. I am not sleepy. I shall read for a time. Your future is all right, Valentine."

CHAPTER XVIII

"I don't like it," said Lilias.

She was sitting in the sunny front parlor, the room which was known as the children's room at the rectory. An open letter lay on her dark winter dress; her sunny hair was piled up high on her shapely head, and her eyes, wistful and questioning, were raised to Marjory's brisker, brighter face, with a world of trouble in them.

The snow lay thick outside, covering the flower beds and the grassy lawn, and laying in piles against the low rectory windows. Marjory was standing by a piled up fire, one of those perfect fires composed of great knobs of sparkling coal and well dried logs of wood. She, too, had on a dark dress, but it was nearly covered by a large holland apron with a bib. Her sleeves were protected by cuffs of the same, on her hands she wore chamois leather gloves with the tips cut off. She looked all bright, and active, and sparkling, and round her on the table and on the floor lay piles and bales of unbleached calico, of coarse red flannel, of bright dark blue and crimson merino. In one of Marjory's capable hands was a large pair of cutting-out scissors, and she paused, holding this implement slightly open, to listen to Lilias' lugubrious words.

"If you must croak to-day," she said, "get it over quickly, and come and help me. Twenty-four blue frocks and twenty-four red to be ready by the time the girls come at four o'clock, besides the old women's flannel and this unlimited supply of unbleached calico. If there is a thing which ruffles my equanimity it is unbleached calico, it fluffs so, and makes one so messy. Now, what do you want to say, Lilias?"

"I'm troubled," said Lilias, "it's about Gerald. I've the queerest feeling about him three times lately I've dreamt intangible dreams, of course, but all dark and foreboding."

"Is that a letter from Gerry in your lap, Lilias?"

"No, it is from Vala nice little letter, too, poor child. I am sure she is doing her best to be a good wife to Gerald. Do you know that she has taken up housekeeping in real earnest."

"Does she say that Gerald is ill?"

"No, she scarcely mentions his name at all."

"Then what in the name of goodness are you going into the dismals for on this morning of all mornings. Twenty-four blue frocks and twenty-four red between noon and four o'clock, and the old women coming for them to the moment. Really, Lilias, you are too provoking. You are not half the girl you were before Gerald's marriage. I don't know what has come to you. Oh, there's Mr. Carr passing the window, I'll get him to come in and help us. Forgive me, Lil, I'll just open this window a tiny bit and speak to him. How do you do, Mr. Carr? You can step in this way—you need not go round through all the slush to the front door. There, you can wipe your feet on that mat. Lilias, say 'how do you do' to Mr. Carr, that is if you are not too dazed."

"How do you do, Miss Wyndham? How do you do. Miss Lilias?" said Carr in a brisk tone. "It is very good of you both to let me into this pleasant room after the cold and snow outside. And how busy you are! Surely, Miss Wyndham, your family don't require such a vast amount of re-clothing."

"Yes," said Marjory, "these bales of goods are for my shivering widows," and she pointed to the red flannel and unbleached calico. "And those are for my pretty orphans—our pretty orphans, Lilly darling, twenty-four in the West Refuge, twenty-four in the East; the Easterns are apparelled in red, the Westerns in blue. Now, Mr. Carr, I'll put it to you as our spiritual pastor, is it right for Lilias to sit and croak instead of helping me with all this prodigious work?"

"But croaking for nothing is not Miss Lilias' way," said Carr, favoring her with a quick glance, a little anxious, a little surprised.

Lilias sprang up with almost a look of vexation. Valentine's letter fell unheeded on the floor.

"You are too bad, Maggie," she said, with almost a forced laugh. "I suppose there are few people in this troublesome world who are not now and then attacked with a fit of the blues. But here goes. I'll shake them off. I'll help you all I can."

"You must help, too," said Marjory in a gay voice, turning to Carr. "Please take off your great coat—put it anywhere. Now then, are your hands strong? are your arms steady? You have got to hold this bale of red merino while Lilly cuts dress lengths from it. Don't forget. Lil, nine lengths of three-and-a-half yards each, nine lengths of four yards each, and six lengths of five yards each. Oh, thank you, Mr. Carr, that will be a great assistance."

Carr was a very energetic, wide-awake, useful man. He could put his hands to anything. No work, provided it was useful, was derogatory in his eyes—he was always cheerful, always bright and obliging. Even Gerald Wyndham could scarcely have made a more popular curate at Jewsbury-on-the-Wold than did this young man.

"If anything could provoke me about him, it is that he is too sunny," Marjory said one day to her sister.

Lilias was silent. It occurred to her, only she was not sure, that in those dark, quick, keen eyes there could come something which might sustain and strengthen on a day of clouds as well as sunshine.

It came now, when Marjory suddenly left the room, and Carr abruptly let the great bale of merino drop at his feet.

"Are you worried about anything?" he asked, in that direct fashion of his which made people trust him very quickly.

Lilias colored all over her face.

"I suppose I ought not to be silly," she said, "but my brotheryou see he is my only brotherhis marriage has made a great gulf between us."

Carr looked at her sharply.

"You are not jealous?" he said.

"I don't knowwe used to be great chums. I think if I were sure he was happy I should not be jealous?"

Carr walked to the fireplace.

"It would not be folly if you were," he said. "All sisters must face the fact of their brothers taking to themselves wives, and, of course, loving the wives best. It is the rule of nature, and it would be foolish of you to fret against the inevitable."

He spoke abruptly, and with a certain coldness, which might have offended some girls. Lilias' slow earnest answer startled him.

"I don't fret against the inevitable," she said. "But I do fret against the intangible. There is a mystery about Gerald which I can't attempt to fathom. I know it is there, but I can't grapple with it in any direction."

"You must have some thought about it, though, or it would not have entered into your head."

"I have many thoughts, but no clues. Oh, it would take me a long, long time to tell you what I fear, to bring my shadowy dread into life and being. I have just had a letter from Valentine, a sweet nice letter, and yet it seems to me full of mystery, although I am sure she does not know it herself. Yes, it is all intangibleit is kind of you to listen to me. Marjory would say I was talking folly."

"You are talking as if your nerves were a little out of sorts. Could you not have a change? Even granted that there is trouble, and I don't suppose for an instant that anything of the kind is in store for your brother, it is a great waste of life to meet it half way."

Lilias smiled faintly.

"I am silly," she said. And just then Marjory came into the room, followed by Augusta, and the cutting out proceeded briskly.

Carr was an invaluable help. Some people would have said that he was a great deal too gay and cheerfula great deal too athletic and well-knit and keen-eyed for a curate.

This was not the case; he made an excellent clergyman, but he had a great sense of the fitness of things, and he believed fully in a time for everything.

Helping three merry girls to cut out red and blue merino frocks, on a cold day in January, seemed to him a very cheerful occupation. Gay laughter and light and innocent chatter filled the room, and Lilias soon became one of the merriest of the party.

In the midst of their chatter the rector entered.

"I want you, Carr," he said, abruptly; he was usually a very polite man, almost too ceremonious. Now his words came with a jerk, and the moment he had uttered them he vanished.

As Carr left the room in obedience to this quick summons. Lilias' face became once more clouded.

The rector was pacing up and down his study. When Carr entered he asked him to bolt the door.

"Is anything the matter, sir?" asked the young man.

Mr. Wyndham's manner was so perturbed, so unlike himself, that it was scarcely wonderful that Carr should ask this question. It received, however, a short and sharp reply.

"I hope to goodness, Carr, you are not one of those imaginative people who are always foreboding a lion in the path. What I sent for you was—well" the rector paused. He raised his eyes slowly until they rested upon the picture of Gerald's mother; the face very like Gerald's seemed to appeal to him; his lips trembled.

"I can't keep it up, Carr," he said, with an abandon which touched the younger man to the heart. "I'm not satisfied about my son. Nothing wrong, oh, no—and yet—and yet—you understand, Carr, I have only one son—a lot of girls, God bless them all!—and only one son."

Carr came over and stood by the mantel-piece. If he felt any surprise, he showed none. His words came out gently, and in a matter-of-fact style.

"If you have any cause to be worried, Mr. Wyndham—and—and—you think I can help you, I shall be proud to be trusted." Then his thoughts flew to Lilias, and his firm, rather thin lips, took a faint smile.

"I have no doubt I am very foolish," replied the rector. "I had a letter this morning from Gerald. He tells me in it that he is going to Australia in March, on some special business for his father-in-law's firm—you know he is a partner in the firm. His wife is not to accompany him."

The rector paused.

Carr made no answer for a moment. Then he said, feeling his way—

"This will be a trial for Mrs. Wyndham."

"One would suppose so. Gerald doesn't say anything on the subject."

"Well," said the rector, "how does it strike you? Perhaps I'm nervous—Lilly, poor girl, is the same, and Marjory laughs at us both. How does this intelligence strike you as an outsider, Carr? Pray give me your opinion."

"Yes," said Carr, simply. "I do not think my opinion need startle anyone. Doubtless, sir, you know facts which throw a different complexion on the thing. It all seems to me a commonplace affair. In big business houses partners have often to go away at short notice. It will certainly be a trial for Mrs. Wyndham to do without her husband. I don't like to prescribe change of air for you, Mr. Wyndham, as I did for Miss Lilias just now, but I should like to ask you if your nerves are quite in order?"

The rector laughed.

"You are a daring fellow to talk of nerves to me, Carr," he said. "Have not I prided myself all my life on having no nerves? Well, well, the fact is, a great change has come over the lad's face. He used to be such a boy, too light-hearted, if anything, too young, if anything, for his years—the most unselfish fellow from his birth. Give away? Bless you, there was nothing Gerald wouldn't give away. Why, look here, Carr, we all tried to spoil the boy amongst us—he was the only one—and his mother taken away when he so young—and he the image of her. Yes, all the girls resemble me, but Gerald is the image of his mother. We all tried to teach him selfishness, but we couldn't. Now. Carr, you will be surprised at what I am going to say, but if a man can be unselfish to a fault, to a fault mind you—to the verge of a crime—it's my son Gerald. I know this. I have always seen it in him. Now my boy's father-in-law. Mortimer Paget, is as selfish as my lad is the reverse. Why did he want a poor lad like mine to marry his rich and only daughter? Why did he make him a partner in his house of business, and why did he insure my boy's life? Insure it heavily? Answer me that. My boy would have taken your place here, Carr; humbly but worthily would he have served the Divine Master, no man happier than he. Is he happy now? Is he young for his years now? Tell me, Carr, what you really think?"

"I don't know, sir. I have not looked at things from your light. You are evidently much troubled, and I am deeply troubled for you. I don't know Wyndham very well but I know him a little. I think that marriage and the cares of a house of business and all his fresh responsibilities may be enough to age your son's face. As to the insurance question, all business is so fluctuating that Mr. Paget was doubtless right in securing his daughter and her children from possible want in the future. See here, Mr. Wyndham, I am going up to town this evening for two or three days. Shall I call at Park-lane and bring you my own impressions with regard to your son?"

"Thank you, Carr, that is an excellent thought, and what is more you shall escort Lilias or Marjory up to town. They have a standing invitation to my boy's house, and a little change just now would do—shall I say Lilias?—good."

"Miss Lilias wants a change, sir. She is affected like yourself with, may I call it, an attack of the nerves."

CHAPTER XIX

Valentine really made an excellent housekeeper. Nobody expected it of her; her friends, the ladies, old and young, the girls, married or otherwise, who knew Valentine as they supposed very intimately, considered the idea of settling this remarkably ignorant young person down with a fixed income and telling her to buy with it, and contrive with it, and make two ends meet with it, quite one of the best jokes of the day.

Valentine did not regard it as a joke at all. She honestly tried, honestly studied, and honestly made a success as housekeeper and household manager.

She was a most undeveloped creature, undeveloped both in mind and heart; but she not only possessed intense latent affections, but latent capacities of all sorts. She scarcely knew the name of poverty, she had no experience with regard to the value of money, but nature had given her an instinct which taught her to spend it wisely and well. She found a thousand a year a larger income than she and Gerald with their modest wants needed. She scarcely used half of what she received, and yet her home was cheerful, her servants happy, her table all that was comfortable.

When she brought her housekeeping books to her husband to balance at the end of the first month, he looked at her with admiration, and then said in a voice of great sadness:

"God help me, Valentine, have I made a mistake altogether about you? Am I dreaming, Valentine, are you meant for a poor man's wife after all?"

"For your wife, whether rich or poor," she said; and she knelt down by his side, and put her hand into his.

She had always possessed a sweet and beautiful face, but for the last few weeks it had altered; the sweetness had not gone, but resolution had grown round the curved pretty lips, and the eyes had a soft happiness in them.

"Pretty, charming creature!" people used to say of her. "But just a trifle commonplace and doll-like."

This doll-like expression was no longer discernible in Valentine.

Gerald touched her hair tenderly.

"My little darling!" he said. His voice shook. Then he rose abruptly, with a gesture which was almost rough. "Come upstairs, Val; the housekeeping progresses admirably. No, my dear, you made a mistake, you were never meant for a poor man's wife."

Valentine kissed his brow: she looked at him in a puzzled way.

"Do you know," she said, laying her hands on his, with a gesture half timid, half appealing; "don't go up to the drawing-room for a moment, Gerald, I want to say a thing, something I have observed. I am loved by two men, by my father and by you. I am loved by them very muchby both of them very much. Oh, yes, Gerald, I know what you feel for me, and yet I can't make either of them happy. My father is not happy. Oh, yes, I can seelove isn't blind. I never remembered my father quite, quite happy, and he is certainly less so than ever now. He tries to look all right when people are by; even succeeds, for he is so unselfish, and brave, and noble. But when he is aloneah, then. Once he fell asleep when I was in the room, he looked terrible in that sleep; his face was haggardhe sighedthere was moisture on his brow. When he woke he asked me to marry you. I didn't care for you then, Gerald, but I said yes because of my father. He said if I married you he would be perfectly happy. I did sohe is not happy."

Gerald did not say a word.

"And you aren't happy, dear," she continued, coming a little nearer to him. "You used to be; before we were engaged you had such a gay face. I could never call you gay since, Gerald. You are so thin, and sometimes at night I lie awake, and I hear you sigh. Why, what is the matter. Gerald? You look ghastly now. Am I hurting you? I wouldn't hurt you, darling."

Wyndham turned round quickly. He had been white almost to fainting, now a great light seemed to leap out of his eyes.

"What did you say? What did you call me? Say it again."

"Darling."

"Then I thank my Godeverything has not been in vain."

He sank down on the nearest chair and burst into tears. Tragedies go on where least expected. The servants in the servants' hall thought their young master and mistress quite the happiest people in the world. Were they not gay, young, rich? Did they not adore one another? Gerald's devotion to Valentine was almost a joke with them, and Valentine's increasing regard for him was very observable to those watchful outsiders.

Certainly the pair stayed in a good deal in the evenings, and why to-night in particular did they linger so long in the dining-room, rather to the inconvenience of the kitchen regime. But presently their steps were heard going upstairs, and then Valentine accompanied Gerald's violin on the piano.

Wyndham played very well for an amateur, so well that with a little extra practice he might almost have taken his place as a professional of no mean ability. He had exquisite taste and a sensitive ear. Music always excited him, and perhaps was not the safest recreation for such a highly strung nature.

Valentine could accompany well; she, too, loved music, but had not her husband's facility nor grace of execution. In his happiest moments Gerald could compose, and sometimes even improvise with success.

During their honeymoon it seemed to him one day as he looked at the somewhat impassive face of the girl for whom he had sold himself body and soulas he looked and felt that not yet at least did her heart echo even faintly to any beat of his, it occurred to him that he might tell his story in its pain and its longing best through the medium of music. He composed a little piece which, for want of another title, he called "Waves." It was very sweet in melody, and had some minor notes of such pathos that when Valentine first heard him play it on the violin she burst into tears. He told her quite simply then that it was his story about her, that all the sweetness was her share, all the graceful melody, the sparkling joyous notes which coming from Gerald's violin seemed to speak like a gay and happy voice, represented his ideal of her. The deeper notes and the pain belonged to him; pain must ever come with love when it is strongest, she would understand this presently.

Then he put his little piece awayhe only played it once for her when they were in Switzerland; he forgot it, but she did not.

To-night, after her confession, when they went up to the drawing-room, his heart immeasurably soothed and healed, and hers soft with a wonderful joy which the beginning of true love can give, he remembered "Waves," and thought he would play it for her again. It did not sound so melancholy this time, but strange to say the gay notes were not quite so gay, the warble of a light heart had deepened. As Wyndham played and Valentine sat silent, for she offered no accompaniment to this little fugitive piece, he found that he must slightly reconstruct the melody. The minor keys were still minor, but there was a ring of victory through them now; they were solemn, but not despairing.

"He that loseth his life shall find it," Wyndham said suddenly, looking full into her eyes.

The violin slipped from his hand, coming down with a discordant crash, the door was flung open by the servant, as Lilias Wyndham and Adrian Carr came into the room.

In a minute all was gay bustle and confusion. Gerald forgot his cares, and Valentine was only too anxious to show herself as the hospitable and attentive hostess.

A kind of improvised meal between dinner and tea was actually brought up into the drawing-room. Lilias ate chicken and ham holding her plate on her lap. Carr, more of a stranger, was not allowed to feel this fact. In short, no four could have looked merrier or more free from trouble.

"It is delightful to have you here—delightful, Lilias," said Valentine, taking her sister-in-law's hand and squeezing it affectionately.

"Do you know, Lil," said Gerald, "that this little girl-wife of mine, with no experience whatever, makes a most capable housekeeper. With all your years of knowledge I should not like you to enter the lists with her."

"With all my years of failure, you mean," answered Lilias. "I always was and always will be the most incompetent woman with regard to beef and mutton and pounds, shillings and pence who walks this earth."

She laughed as she spoke; her face was cloudless, her dark eyes serene. For one moment before he went away Carr found time to say a word to her.

"Did I not tell you it was simply a case of nerves?" he remarked.

CHAPTER XX

Esther Helps was certainly neither a prudent nor a careful young woman. She meant no harm, she would have shuddered at the thought of actual sin, but she was reckless, a little defiant of all authority, even her father's most gentle and loving control, and very discontented with her position in life.

Morning, noon, and night, Esther's dream of dreams, longing of longings, was to be a lady. She had some little foundation for this desire. The mother who had died at her birth had been a poor half-educated little governess, whose mother before her had been a clergyman's daughter. Esther quickly discovered that she was beautiful, and her dream of dreams was to marry a gentleman, and so go back to that station in life where her mother had moved.

Esther had no real instincts of ladyhood. She spoke loudly, her education had been of a very flashy and superficial order. From the time she left the fourth-rate boarding-school where her father alone had the means to place her, she had stayed at home and idled. Idling was very bad for a character like hers; she was naturally active and energeticshe had plenty of ability, and would have made a capital shopwoman or dressmaker. But Esther thought it quite beneath her to work, and her father, who could support her at home, was only too delighted to have her there. He was inordinately proud of hershe was the one sunbeam in his dull, clouded timorous life. He adored her beauty, he found no fault with her Cockney twang, and he gave her in double measure the love which had lain buried for many years with his young wife.

Esther, therefore, when she left school, sat at home, and made her own dresses, and chatted with her cousin Cherry, who was an orphan, and belonged to Helps' side of the house. Cherry was a very capable, matter-of-fact hearty little girl, and Esther thought it an excellent arrangement that she should live with them, and take the drudgery and the cooking, and in short all the household work off her hands. Esther was very fond of Cherry, and Cherry, in her turn, thought there was never anyone quite so grand and magnificent as her tall, stately cousin.

"Well, Cherry," said Esther, as the two were going to bed on the night after Wyndham's visit, "what do you think of him? Oh, I needn't ask, there's but one thing to be thought of him."

"Elegant, I say," interrupted Cherry. She was looking particularly round and dumpy herself, and her broad face with her light grey eyes was all one smile. "An elegant young man, Essiea sort of chevalier, now, wouldn't you say so?"

"It's just like you, Cherry, you take up all your odd moments with those poetry books. Mr. Wyndham ain't a chevalierhe's just a gentleman, neither more nor lessa real gentleman, oh dear. I call it a cruel disappointment. Cherry," and she heaved a profound sigh.

"What's a disappointment?" asked unsuspicious Cherry, as she tumbled into bed.

"Why, that he's married, my dear. He'd have suited me fine. Well, there's an end of that."

Cherry thought there was sufficiently an end to allow her to drop off to sleep, and Esther, after lying awake for a little, presently followed her example.

The next day she was more restless than ever, once or twice even openly complaining to Cherry of the dullness of her lot, and loudly proclaiming her determination to become a lady in spite of everybody.

"You can't, Essie," said her father, in his meek, though somewhat high-pitched voice, when he overheard some of her words that evening. "It ain't your lot, childyou warn't born in the genteel line; there's all lines and all grooves, and yours is the narrowing one of the poverty-struck clerk's child."

"I think it's mean of you to talk like that, father," said Esther, her eyes flashing. "It's mean of you, and unkind to my poor mother, who was a lady born."

"I don't know much about that," replied Helps, looking more despondent than ever. "She was the best of little wives, and if she was born a lady, which I ain't going to deny, for I don't know she warn't a lady bred, I mind me she thought it a fine bit of a rise to leave off teaching the baker's children, and come home to me. Poor little Essiepoor, dear little Essie. You don't take much after her, Esther, my girl."

"If she was spiritless, and had no mind for her duties, which were in my opinion to uphold her station in life, I don't want to take after her," answered Esther, and she flounced out of the room.

Helps looked round in an appealing way at Cherry.

"I don't want to part with her," he said, "but it will be a good thing for us all when Essie is wed. I must try and find some decent young fellow who will be likely to take a fancy to her. Her words fret me on account of their ambition. Cherry, child."

"I wouldn't be put out if I was you, uncle," responded Cherry in her even, matter-of-fact voice. "Esther is took up with a whim, and it will pass. It's all on account of the chevalier."

"The what, child?"

"The chevalier. Oh, my sakes alive, there's the milk boiling all over the place, and my hearth done up so beautiful. Here, catch hold of this saucepan, uncle, while I fetch a cloth to wipe up. My word, ain't this provoking. I thought to get time to learn a verse or two out of the poetry book to-night; but no such luckI'll be brushing and blacking till bed-time."

In the confusion which ensued, Helps forgot to ask Cherry whom she meant by the chevalier.

A few days after this, as Helps was coming home late, he was rather dismayed to find his daughter returning also, accompanied by a young man who was no better dressed than half the young men with whom she walked, but who had a certain air and a certain manner which smote upon the father's heart with a dull sense of apprehension.

"Essie, my girl," he said, when she had bidden her swain good-bye, and had come into the house, with her eyes sparkling and her whole face looking so bright and beautiful, that even Cherry dropped her poetry book to gaze in admiration. "Essie," said Helps, all the tenderness of the love he bore her trembling in his voice, "come here. Kiss your old father. You love him, don't you?"

"Why, dad, what a question. I should rather think I did."

"You wouldn't hurt him now, Essie? You wouldn't break his heart, for instance?"

"I break your heart, dad? Is it likely? Now, what can the old man be driving at?" she said, looking across at Cherry.

"It's this," responded Helps, "I want to know the name of the fellowyes, thethe fellow, who saw you home just now?"

"Now, father, mightn't he be Mr. Gray, or Mr. Jones, or Mr. Abbott; some of those nice young men you bring up now and then from the city? Why mightn't he be one of them, father?"

"But he wasn't, my dear. The young men you speak of are honest lads, every one of them. I wouldn't have no sort of objection to your walking with them, Esther. It wasn't none of my friends from the city I saw you with to-night. Essie."

"And why shouldn't this be an honest fellow, too?" answered Esther, her eyes sparkling dangerously.

"I don't know, my dear. I didn't like the looks of him. What's his name, Essie, my love?"

"Captain Herriot, of the Hussars."

"There! Esther, you're not to walk with Captain Herriot any more. You're not to know him. I won't have itso now."

"Highty-tighty!" said Esther. "There are two to say a word to that bargain, father. And pray, why may I walk with Mr. Jones and not with Captain Herriot? Captain Herriot's a real gentleman, and Mr. Jones ain't."

"And that's the reason, my child. If Jones walked with you, he'd maybeyes, I'm sure of ithe'd want all his heart and soul to make you his honest wife some day. Do you suppose Captain Herriot wants to make you his wife. Essie?"

"I don't say. I won't be questioned like that." Her whole pale face was in a flame. "Maybe we never thought of such a thing, but just to be friends, and to have a pleasant time. It's cruel of you to talk like that, father."

"Well, then, I won't, my darling, I won't. Just promise you'll have nothing more to say to the fellow. I'd believe your word against the world, Essie."

"Against the world? Would you really, dad? I wouldn't, though, if I were you. No, I ain't going to make a promise I might break." She went out of the room, she was crying.

A short time after this, indeed the very day after Lilias Wyndham's visit to London, Gerald noticed that Helps followed his every movement as he came rather languidly in and out of the office, with dull imploring eyes. The old clerk was particularly busy that morning, he was kept going here, there, and everywhere. Work of all kinds, work of the most unexpected and unlooked for nature seemed to descend to-day with the force of a sledge hammer on his devoted head.

Gerald saw that he was dying to speak to him, and at the first opportunity he took him aside, and asked him if there was anything he could do for him.

"Oh, yes, Mr. Wyndham, you can, you can. Oh, thank the good Lord for bringing you over to speak to me when no one was looking. You can save Esther for me—that's what you can do, Mr. Wyndham. No one can save her but you. So you will, sir; oh, you will. She's my only child, Mr. Wyndham."

CHAPTER XXI

"I will certainly do what I can," responded Wyndham, in his grave, courteous voice.

He was leaning against the window-ledge in a careless attitude; Helps, looking up at him anxiously, noticed how pale and wan his face was.

"Ah," he responded, rising from his seat, and going up to the younger man. "'Tis them as bears burdens knows how to pity. Thank the Lord there's compensation in all things. Now look here, Mr. Wyndham, this is how things are. You have seen my Essie, she's troublesome and spiritedoh, no one more so."

Helps paused.

"Yes," answered Gerald, in a quiet, waiting voice. He was not particularly interested in the discussion of Esther Helps' character.

"And she's beautiful, Mr. Wyndham. Aye, there's her curse. Beautiful and hambitious and not a lady, and dying to be one. You understand, Mr. Wyndhamyou must understand."

Wyndham said nothing.

"Well, a month or so ago I found out there was a gentlemanat least a man who called himself a gentlemanwalking with her, and filling her head with nonsense. His name was Herriot, a captain in the Hussars. I told her she was to have nought to say to him, but I soon found that she disobeyed me. Then I had to spy on heryou may think how I felt, but it had to be done. I found that she walked with him, and met him at all hours. I made inquiries about his character, and I found he was a scoundrel, a bad fellow out and out. He'd be sure to break my Essie's heart if he did no worse. Then I was in a taking, for the girl kept everything in, and would scarcely brook me so much as to look at her. I was that upset that I took Cherry into my confidence. She's a very good girl, is Cherrythe Lord hasn't cursed her with no beauty. Last week she brought me word that Esther was going to the Gaiety with Captain Herriot, that he had taken two stalls and they were to have a fine time. She said Esther was almost out of her mind with delight, as it was always her dream to be seen at the theatre, beautifully dressed, with a real gentleman. She had shown the tickets to Cherry, and Cherry was smart enough to take the numbers and keep them in the back of her head. She told me, and I can tell you, Mr. Wyndham, I was fit to kill someone. I went straight off to the Gaiety office, and by good luck or the grace of God, I found there was a vacant stall next to Esther'sjust one, and no more. I paid for that stall, here's the ticket in my pocket."

"Yes," said Wyndham, "and you mean to go with Esther to-night? A very good ideaexcellent. But how will she take it?"

"How will she take it, Mr. Wyndham? I feel fit to pull my grey hairs out. How would she have taken it, you mean? For it's all a thing of the past, sir. Oh, I had it all planned fine. I was to wait until she and that fellow had taken their places, and then I'd come in quite natural, and sit down beside her, and answer none of her questions, only never leave her, no, not for a quarter of a minute. And if he spoke up, the ruffian, I had my reply for him. I'd stay quiet enough till we got outside, and then just one blow in the middle of his faceyes, just one, to relieve a father's feelings. Then home with my girl, and I think it's more than likely we wouldn't have been troubled with no more of Captain Herriot's attentions."

Helps paused again.

"You speak in the past tense," said Gerald. "Why cannot you carry out this excellent programme?"

"That's it, sir, that's what about maddens me. I came to the office this morning, and what has happened hasn't happened this three months past. There's business come in of a nature that no one can tackle but myself. Business of a private character, and yet what may mean the loss or gain of thousands. Oh, I can't explain it, Mr. Wyndham, even though you are a partner; there are things that confidential clerks know that are hid from junior partners. I can't leave here till eleven o'clock to-night, Mr. Wyndham, and if you don't help me Esther may be a lost girl. Yes, there's no mincing matterslost, beyond hope. Will you help me, Mr. Wyndham? I'll go mad if my only girl, my beautiful girl, comes to that."

"I? Can I help you?" asked Wyndham. There was hesitation and distress in his voice. He saw that he was going to be asked to do something unpleasant.

"You can do this, sir. You can make it all right. Bless you, sir, who's there to see? And you go with the best intentions. You go in a noble cause. You can afford to risk that much, Mr. Wyndham. I want you to take my place at the Gaiety to-night; take my ticket and go there. Talk pleasant to Esther: not much, but just a little, nothing to rouse her suspicions. Let her think it was just a coincidence your being there. Then, just at the end, give her this letter from me. I've said a thing in it that will startle her. She'll get a fright and turn to you. Put her into a cab then, and bring her here. You can sit on the box if you like. That's all. Put her into my arms and your task is done. Here's the ticket and the letter. Do it, Mr. Wyndham, and God will bless you. Yes, yes, my poor young sirHe'll bless you."

"Don't talk of God when you speak of me," said Wyndham. "Something has happened which closes the door of religion for me. The door between God and me is closed. I am still open, however, to the call of humanity. You want me to go to the Gaiety to-night to save your daughter. It is very probable that if I went I should save her. I am engaged, however, for to-night. My sister is in town. We are going to make a party to the Haymarket."

"Oh, sir, what of that? Send a telegram to say you have an engagement. Think of Esther. Think what it means if you fail me now."

"I do think of it, Helps. I will do what you want. Give me the letter and the theatre ticket."

CHAPTER XXII

Valentine was delighted to have Lilias as her companion. She was in excellent spirits just now, and Lilias and she enjoyed going about together. They had adventures which pleased them both, such simple adventures as come to poorer girls every day—a ride in an omnibus to Kew, an excursion up the river to Battersea in a penny steamer, and many other mild intoxicants of this nature. Sometimes Gerald came with them, but oftener they went alone. They laughed and chatted at these times, and people looked at them, and thought them two particularly merry good-looking school-girls.

Valentine was very fond of going to the theatre, and of course one of the principal treats in store for Lilias was a visit to the play. Valentine decided that they would go to some entertainment of a theatrical character nearly every evening. On the day of Helps' strange request to Wyndham they were to see Captain Swift at the Haymarket. Mr. Paget had taken a box for the occasion, and Valentine's last injunction to her husband was to beg of him to be home in good time so that they might have dinner in peace, and reach the Haymarket before the curtain rose.

Lilias and she trotted about most of the morning, and sat cosily now in the pretty drawing-room in Park-Lane, sipping their tea, examining their purchases, or chatting about dress, and sundry other trivial matters after the fashion of light-hearted girls.

Presently Valentine pulled a tiny watch out of her belt.

"Gerald is late," she said. "He promised faithfully to be in to tea, and it is now six o'clock. We dine at half-past. Had we not better go and dress, Lilias?"

Lilias was standing on the hearthrug, she glanced at the clock, then into the ruddy flames, then half-impatiently towards the door.

"Oh, wait a moment or two," she said. "If Gerald promised to come he is safe to be here directly. I never met such a painfully conscientious fellow; he would not break his word even in a trifle like this for all the world. Give him three minutes longer. You surely will not take half-an-hour to dress."

"How solemnly you speak, Lilias," responded Valentine. "If Gerald is late, that could scarcely be considered a breaking of his word. I mean in a promise of that kind one never knows how one may be kept. That is always understood, of course."

There came a pealing ring and a double knock at the door, and a moment after the page entered with a telegram which he handed to his mistress. Valentine tore the yellow envelope open, and read the contents of the pink sheet.

"No answer, Masters," she said to the boy. Then she she turned to Lilias. "Gerald can't go with us to-night. He is engaged. You see, of course, he would not break his word, Lilias. He is unavoidably prevented coming. It is too bad."

Some of the brightness went out of her face, and her spirits went down a very little.

"Well, it can't be helped," she said, "only I am disappointed."

"So am I, awfully disappointed," responded Lilias.

Then the two went slowly upstairs to change their dresses.

When they came down again, Mr. Paget, who was to dine with them, was waiting in the drawing-room. There was a suppressed excitement, a suppressed triumph in his eyes, which, however, only made him look more particularly bright and charming.

When Valentine came in in the pure white which gave her such a girlish and even pathetically innocent air, he went up and kissed her almost fiercely. He put his arm round her waist and drew her close to him, and looked into her eyes with a sense of possession which frightened her. For the first time in all her existence she half shrank from the father whom she idolized. She was scarcely conscious of her own shrinking, of the undefinable something which made her set herself free, and stand on the hearthrug by Lilias' side.

"I don't see your husband, my pet," said Mr. Paget. "He ought to have come home long before now, that is, if he means to come with us to-night."

"But he doesn't, father," said Valentine. "That's just the grief. I had a telegram from him, half-an-hour ago; he is unavoidably detained."

Mr. Paget raised his eyebrows.

"Not at the office," he said, in a markedly grave voice, and with another significant raise of his brows. "That I know, for he left before I did. Ah, well, young men will be young men."

Neither Valentine nor Lilias knew why they both flushed up hotly, and left a wider space between them and Valentine's handsome father.

He did not take the least notice of this movement on both their parts, but went on in a very smooth, cheerful voice.

"Perhaps Gerald does not miss as much as he thought," he said. "Since I saw you this morning, Val, our programme has been completely altered. We go to Captain Swift to-morrow night. I went to the office and exchanged the box. To-night we go to the Gaiety. I have been fortunate in securing one of the best boxes in the whole house, and Monte Christo Junior is well worth seeing."

"I don't know that I particularly care for the Gaiety, father," said Valentine. "How very funny of you to change our programme."

"Well, the fact is, some business friends of mine who were just passing through town were particularly anxious to see Captain Swift, so as I could oblige them, I did. It is all the better for your husband, Valentine; he won't miss this fine piece of drama."

"No, that is something to be thankful for," responded Valentine. "But I'm sorry you selected the Gaiety as an exchange. I don't think Lilias will care for Monte Christo. However, it can't be helped now, and dinner waits. Shall we go downstairs?"

Mr. Paget and his party were in good time in their places. Valentine took a seat rather far back in the box, but her father presently coaxed her to come to the front, supplied both her and Lilias with opera glasses, and encouraged both girls to look about them, and watch the different people who were gradually filing into their places in the stalls.

Mr. Paget himself neither wore glasses nor aided his vision with an opera glass. His face was slightly flushed, and his eyes, keen and bright, travelled round the house, taking in everything, not passing over a single individual.

Valentine was never particularly curious about her neighbors, and as Lilias knew no one, they both soon leant back in their chairs, and talked softly to one another.

The curtain rose, and each girl bent forward to see and enjoy. The rest of the house was now comparatively dark, but just before the lights were lowered, Mr. Paget might have been heard to give a faint quick sigh of relief.

A tall girl in cream-color and soft furs walked slowly down the length of stalls, and took her place in such a position that Valentine could scarcely look down without seeing her. This girl's beauty was so marked that many eyes were turned in her direction as she appeared. She was very regal looking, very quiet and dignified in manner. Her features were classical and pure in outline, and her head, with its wealth of raven black hair, was splendidly set.

She was accompanied by a tall, fairly good-looking man who sat next to her.

When the curtain rose and the lights were lowered the stall at her other side was vacant.

Mr. Paget felt his heart beat a trifle too fast. Would that stall be full or empty when the curtain dropped at the close of the first act? Would his heart's desire, his wicked and treacherous heart's desire be torn from him in the very moment of apparent fruition. Suppose Gerald did not put in an appearance at the Gaiety? Suppose at the eleventh hour he changed his mind and resolved to leave Esther Helps to her fate? Supposepshaw!where was the use of supposing? To leave a girl to her fate would not be his chivalrous fool of a son-in-law's way. No, it was all right; even now he could dimly discern a faint commotion in the neighborhood of Esther Helpsthe kind of commotion incident on the arrival of a fresh person, the gentle soft little movement made by the other occupants of the stalls to let the new comer, who was both late and tiresome, take his reserved seat in comfort. Mr. Paget sank back in his seat with a sensation of relief; he had not listened for nothing behind an artfully concealed curtain that morning.

The play proceeded. Much as he had said about it beforehand, it had no interest for Mr. Paget. He scarcely troubled to look at the stage. There was no room in his heart that moment for burlesque: he was too busily engaged over his own terrible life's drama. On the result of this night more or less depended all his future happiness.

"If she turns back to me after what she sees to-night then I can endure," he said to himself. "I can go on to the bitter endif notwell, there are more expedients than one for a ruined man to throw up the sponge."

The curtain fell, the theatre was in a blaze of light; Valentine and Lilias sank back in their seats and began to fan themselves. They had been pleased and amused. Lilias, indeed, had laughed so heartily that the tears came to her eyes.

"I hate to cry when I laugh," she said, taking out her handkerchief to wipe them away. "It's a tiresome trick we all have in our family, Gerald and all."

She had a habit of bringing in Gerald's name whenever she spoke of her family, as if he were the topmost stone, the crowning pride and delight.

Mr. Paget had his back slightly turned to the girls. Once more he was devouring the stalls with his eager bright eyes. Yes, Gerald Wyndham was in his stall. He was leaning back, not exerting himself much; he looked nonchalant and strikingly handsome. Mr. Paget did not wish him to appear too nonchalant when Valentine first caught sight of him. Noah, that was better. Esther was turning to speak to him. By Jove, what a face the girl had!

Mr. Paget had often seen Helps' only daughter, for he found it convenient occasionally to call to see Helps at Acadia Villa. But he had never before seen her dress becomingly, and he was positively startled at the pure, high type of her beauty. At this distance her common accent, her poor uneducated words, could not grate. All her gestures were graceful; she looked up at Gerald, said something, smiled, then lowered her heavy black lashes.

It was at that moment, just as Wyndham was bending forward to reply to her remark, and she was leaning slightly away from her other cavalier, so that he scarcely seemed to belong to her party, that Valentine, tired of doing nothing, came close to her father, and allowed her eyes to wander round the house. Suddenly she uttered a surprised exclamation.

"Look, father, look! Is that Gerald? Who is with him? Who is he talking to? How is it that he comes to be here? Yes, it is Gerald! Oh, what a lovely girl he is talking to!"

Valentine's words were emphatic and slightly agitated, for she was simply overpowered with astonishment, but they were spoken in a low key. Lilias did not hear them. She was reading her programme over for the twentieth time, and wondering when the curtain would rise and the play go on.

"Look, father," continued Valentine, clutching her father's arm. "Isn't that Gerald? How strange of him to be here. Who can he be talking to? I don't know herdo you? Do you see him, father? Won't you go down and tell him we are here, and bring him upandthe lady who is with him. Go, please, father, you see where he is, don't you?"

"I do, my child. I have seen him for some time past. Would you like to come home, Valentine?"

"Home! What in the world do you mean? How queer you look! Is there anything wrong? Who is with Gerald? Who is he talking to? How lovely she is. I wish she would look up again."

"That girl is not a lady, Valentine. She is Esther Helpsyou have heard of her. Yes, now I understand why your husband could not come with us to the Haymarket to-night. My poor child! Don't look at them again. Valentine, my darling."

Valentine looked full into her father's eyes; full, long, and steadily she gazed. Then slowly, very slowly, a crimson flood of color suffused her whole face; it receded, leaving her deathly pale. She moved away from her father and took a back seat behind Lilias.

The curtain rose again, the play continued. Lilias was excited, and wanted to pull Valentine to the front.

"No," she said. "My head aches; I don't care to look any more."

She sat back in her seat, very white and very calm.

"Would you like to come home?" said her father, bending across to her, and speaking in a voice which almost trembled with the emotion he felt.

"No," she said in reply, and without raising her eyes. "I will sit the play out till the end."

When the curtain fell again she roused herself with an effort and coaxed Lilias to come into the back of the box with her. The only keen anxiety she was conscious of was to protect her husband from Lilias' astonished eyes.

Mr. Paget felt well satisfied. He had managed to convey his meaning to his innocent child's heart; an insinuation, a fall of the voice, a look in the eyes, had opened up a gulf on the brink of which Valentine drew back shuddering.

"I was only beginning to love him; it doesn't so much matter," she said many times to herself. Even now she thought no very bad things of her husband; that is no very bad things according to the world's code. To her, however, they were black. He had deceived herhe had made her a promise and broken it. Why? Because he liked to spend the evening with another girl more beautiful than herself.

"Oh, no, I am not jealous," said Valentine, softly under her breath. "I won't say anything to him either about it, poor fellow. It does not matter to me, not greatly. I was only beginning to love him. Thank God there is always my dear old father."

When the curtain rose for the final act of the play. Valentine moved her chair so that she could slightly lean against Mr. Paget. He took her hand and squeezed it. He felt that he had won the victory.

CHAPTER XXIII

Gerald had found his task most uncongenial. In the first place he was disappointed at not spending the evening with Valentine and Lilias. In the second the close proximity of such a girl as Esther Helps could not but be repugnant to him. Still she was a woman, a woman in danger, and her father had appealed to him to save her. Had he been ordained for the Church, such workah, no, he must not think of what his life would have been then. After all, it was good of the distracted father to trust him, and he must not betray the trust.

He went to the theatre and acquitted himself with extreme tact and diplomacy. When Gerald chose to exert himself his manner had a quieting effect, a compelling, and almost a commanding effect on women. Esther became quiet and gentle; she talked to Captain Herriot, but not noisily; she laughed, her laugh was low and almost musical. Now and then her quick eyes glanced at Wyndham; she felt thirsty for even his faintest approvalhe bestowed it by neither word nor movement.

As they were leaving the theatre, however, and the gallant captain, who inwardly cursed that insufferable prig who happened to have a slight acquaintance with his beautiful Esther, grew cheerful under the impression that now his time for enjoyment was come, Gerald said in a low, grave voice:

"Your father has given me a letter for you. Pray be quiet, don't excite yourself. It is necessary that you should go to your father directly. Allow me to see you into a cab. Your father is waiting for youit is urgent that you should join him at once."

Scarcely knowing why she did it, Esther obeyed. She murmured some eager agitated words to Captain Herriot; she was subdued, frightened, shaken; as Gerald helped her into a cab he felt her slim fingers tremble in his. He took his seat upon the box beside the driver, and ten minutes later had delivered Esther safely to her father. His task was done, he did not wait to hear a word of Helps' profuse thanks. He drew a sigh of relief as he hurried home. Soon he would be with his wifethe wife whom he idolizedthe wife who was beginning to return his love. Suppose her passion went on and deepened? Suppose a day came when to part from him would be a sorer trial than poverty or dishonor! Oh, if such a day camehe mightah, he must not think in that direction. He pushed his hand through his thick hair, leant back in his cab, and shut his eyes.

When he reached the little house in Park-lane he found that the lights in the drawing-room were out, and the gas turned low in the hall. He was later even than he had intended to be. The other theatre-goers had returned home and gone to bed. He wondered how they had enjoyed Captain Swift. For himself he had not the least idea of what he had been looking at at the Gaiety.

He let himself in with a latch-key, and ran up at once to his room. He wanted to kiss Valentine, to look into her eyes, which seemed to him to grow sweeter and softer every day. He opened the door eagerly and looked round the cheerful bedroom.

Valentine was not there.

He called her. She was not in the dressing-room.

"She is with Lilias," he said to himself. "How these two young things love to chatter."

He sat down in an easy chair by the fire, content to wait until his wife should return. He was half inclined to tell her what he had been doing; he had a great longing to confide in her in all possible ways, for she had both brains and sense, but he restrained himself. The subject was not one he cared to discuss with his young wife, and, besides, the secret belonged to Esther and to her father.

He made up his mind to say nothing about it. He had no conception then what this silence was to cost him, and how different all his future life might have been had he told his wife the truth that night.

Presently Valentine returned. Her face was flushed, and her eyes had an unquiet troubled expression. She had been to Lilias with a somewhat strange request.

"Lilias, I want you to promise me something, to ask no questions, but just like a kind and truthful sister to make me a faithful promise."

"You look strange, Valentine; what do you want me to promise?"

"Will you promise it?"

"If I can, I will promise, to please you; but I never make promises in the dark."

"Oh, there's Gerald's step, I must go. Lilias, I've a very particular reason, I cannot explain it to you. I want you not to tell Gerald, now or at any time, that we were at the Gaiety to-night."

"My dear Val, how queer! Why shouldn't poor Gerald know? And you look so strange. You are trembling."

"I am. I'm in desperate earnest. Will you promise?"

"Yes, yes, you silly child, if you set such store on an utterly ridiculous promise you shall have it. Only if I were you, Valentine, I wouldn't begin even to have such tiny little secrets as that from my husband. I wouldn't, Val; it isn't wiseit isn't really."

Valentine neither heard nor heeded these last words. She gave Lilias a hasty, frantic kiss, and rushed back to her own room.

"Now," she said to herself, "nownownowif he tells me everything, every single thing, all may be well. I won't ask him a question; but if he tells, tells of his own accord, all may be quite well yet. Oh, how my heart beats! It is good I have not learned to love him any better."

Gerald rose up at her entrance and went to meet her eagerly.

"Ah, here's my bright little wife," he said. "Give me a kiss, Valentine."

She gave it, and allowed him to fold her in his arms. She was almost passive, but her heart beat hardshe was so eagerly waiting for him to speak.

"Sit down by the fire, darling. I don't like long evenings spent away from you, Val. How did you enjoy Captain Swift?"

"We didn't go to the Haymarket; no, we are going to-morrow. Father thought it a pity you should miss such a good play."

"Then where did you go? You and Lil did not stay at home the whole evening?"

"No, father took us to another theatre. I can't tell you the name; don't ask me. I hate theatresI detest them. I never want to go inside one again as long as I live!"

"How strongly you talk, my dear little Val. Perhaps you found it dull to-night because your husband was not with you."

She moved away with a slight little petulant gesture. When would he begin to speak?

Gerald wondered vaguely what had put his sweet-tempered Valentine out. He stirred the fire, and then stood with his back to it. She looked up at him, his face was very grave, very calm. Her own Geraldhe had a nice face. Surely there was nothing bad behind that face. Why was he silent? Why didn't he begin to tell his story? Well she would—she would—help him a little.

She cleared her throat, she essayed twice to find her voice. When it came out at last it was small and timorous.

"Was it—was it business kept you from coming with me to-night, Gerry?"

"Business? Yes, my darling, certainly."

Her heart went down with a great bound. But she would give him another chance.

"Was it—was it business connected with the office?"

"You speak in quite a queer voice, Valentine. In a measure it was business connected with the office—in a measure it was not. What is it, Valentine? What is it, my dear?"

She had risen from her seat, put her arms round his neck, and laid her soft young head on his shoulder.

"Tell me the business, Gerry, Tell your own Val."

He kissed her many times.

"It doesn't concern you, my dear wife," he said. "I would tell you gladly, were I not betraying a trust. I had some painful work to do to-night, Valentine. Yes, business, certainly. I cannot tell it, dear. Yes, what was that you said?"

For she had murmured "Hypocrite!" under her breath. Very low she had said it, too faintly for him to catch the word. But he felt her loving arms relax. He saw her face grow grave and cold, something seemed to go out of her eyes which had rendered them most lovely. It was the wounded soul going back into solitude, and hiding its grief and shame in an inmost recess of her being.

Would Gerald ever see the soul, the soul of love, in his wife's eyes again?

CHAPTER XXIV

A few days after the events related in the last chapter Mr. Paget asked his son-in-law to have a few minutes' private conversation with him. Once more the young man found himself in that inner room at the rich merchant's office which represented more or less a torture-chamber to him. Once more Valentine's untroubled girlish innocent eyes looked out of Richmond's beautiful picture of her.

Wyndham hated this room, he almost hated that picture; it had surrounded itself with terrible memories. He turned his head away from it now as he obeyed Mr. Paget's summons.

"It's this, Gerald," said his father-in-law. "When a thing has to be done the sooner the better. I mean nobody cares to make a long operation of the drawing of a tooth for instance!"

"An insufficient metaphor," interrupted Wyndham roughly. "Say, rather, the plucking out of a right eye, or the cutting off a right hand. As you say, these operations had better be got quickly over."

"I think so—I honestly think so. It would convenience me if you sailed in the Esperance on the th of March for Sydney. There is a bonâ fide reason for your going. I want you to sample—"

"Hush," interrupted Wyndham. "The technicalities and the gloss and all that kind of humbug can come later. You want me to sail on the th of March. That is the main point. When last you spoke of it, I begged of you as a boon to give me an extension of grace, say until May or June. It was understood by us, although there was no sealed bond in the matter, that my wife and I should spend a year together before this—this temporary parting took place. I asked you at one time to shorten my season of grace, but a few weeks ago I asked you to extend it."

"Precisely, Wyndham, and I told you I would grant your wish, if possible. I asked you to announce to your own relatives that you would probably have to go away in March, for a time; but I said I would do my utmost to defer the evil hour. I am sorry to say that I cannot do so. I have had news from India which obliges me to hasten matters. Such a good opportunity as the business which takes you out in the Esperance will probably not occur again. It would be madness not to avail ourselves of it. Do not you think so? My dear fellow, do take a chair."

"Thank you, I prefer to stand. This day—what is this day?" He raised his eyes; they rested on the office calendar. "This day is the th of February. A spring-like day, isn't it? Wonderful for the time of year. I have, then, one month and one day to live. Are these Valentine's violets? I will help myself to a few. Let me say good-morning, sir."

He bowed courteously—no one could be more courteous than Gerald Wyndham—and left the room.

His astonished father in-law almost gasped when he found himself alone.

"Upon my word," he said to himself, "there's something about that fellow that's positively uncanny. I only trust I'll be preserved from being haunted by his ghost. My God! what a retribution that would be. Wyndham would be awful as a ghost. I suppose I shall have retribution some day. I know I'm a wicked man. Hypocritical, cunning, devilish. Yes, I'm all that. Who'd have thought that soft-looking lad would turn out to be all steel and venom. I hate him—and yet, upon my soul, I admire him. He does more for the woman he loves than I do—than I could do. The woman we both love. His wife—my child."

"There, I'll get soft myself if I indulge in these thoughts any longer. Now is the time for him to go. Valentine has turned from him; any fool can see that. Now is the time to get him out of the way. How lucky that I overheard Helps that day. Never was there a more opportune thing."

Mr. Paget went home early that evening. Valentine was dining with him. Lately, within the last few weeks, she often came over alone to spend the evening with her father.

"Where's your husband, my pet?" the old man used to say to her on these occasions.

And she always answered him in a bright though somewhat hard little voice.

"Oh, Gerald is such a book-worm—he is devouring one of those abstruse treatises on music. I left him buried in it," or, "Gerald is going out this evening," or, "Gerald isn't well, and would like to stay quiet, so"—the end was invariably the same—"I thought I'd come and have a cosy chat with you, dad."

"And no one more welcome—no one in all the wide world more welcome," Mortimer Paget would answer, glancing, with apparent pleased unconcern, but with secret anxiety, at his daughter's face.

The glance always satisfied him; she looked bright and well—a little hard, perhaps—well, the blow must affect her in some way. What had taken place at the Gaiety would leave some results even on the most indifferent heart. The main result, however, was well. Valentine's dawning love had changed to indifference. Had she cared for her husband passionately, had her whole heart been given into his keeping, she must have been angry; she must have mourned.

As, evening after evening, Mr. Paget came to this conclusion, he invariably gave vent to a sigh of relief. He never guessed that if he could wear a mask, so also could his child. He never even suspected that beneath Valentine's gay laughter, under the soft shining of her clear eyes, under her smiles, her light easy words, lay a pain, lay an ache, which ceased not to trouble her day and night.

Mr. Paget came home early. Valentine was waiting for him in the drawing-room.

"We shall have a cosy evening, father," she said. "Oh, no, Gerald can't come. He says he has some letters to write. I think he has a headache, too. I'd have stayed with him, only he prefers being quiet. Well, we'll have a jolly evening together. Kiss me, dad."

He did kiss her, then she linked his hand in her arm, and they went downstairs and dined together, as they used to do in the old days before either of them had heard of Gerald Wyndham.

"Let us come into the library to-night," said Valentine. "You know there is no room like the library to me."

"Nor to me," said Mr. Paget brightly. "It reminds me of when you were a child, my darling."

"Ah, well, I'm not a child now, I'm a woman."

She kept back the sigh which rose to her lips.

"I think I like being a child best, only one never can have the old childish time back again."

"Who knows, Val? Perhaps we may. If you have spoiled your teeth enough over those filberts, shall we go into the library? I have something to tell you—a little bit of news."

"All right, you shall tell it sitting in your old armchair."

She flitted on in front, looking quite like the child she more or less still was.

"Now isn't this perfect?" she said, when the door was shut, Mr. Paget established in his armchair, and the two pairs of eyes fixed upon the glowing fire. "Isn't this perfect?"

"Yes, my darling—perfect. Valentine, there is no love in all the world like a father's for his child."

"No greater love has come to me," replied Valentine slowly; and now some of the pain at her heart, notwithstanding all her brave endeavors, did come into her face. "No greater love has come to me, but I can imagine, yes. I can imagine a mightier."

"What do you mean, child?"

"For instance—if you loved your husband perfectly, and he—he loved you, and there was nothing at all between—and the joy of all joys was to be with him, and you were to feel that in thought—in word—in deed—you were one, not two. There, what am I saying? The wildest nonsense. There isn't such a thing as a love of that sort. What's your news, father?"

"My dear child, how intensely you speak!"

"Never mind! Tell me what is your news, father."

Mr. Paget laughed, his laugh was not very comfortable.

"Has Gerald told you anything, Valentine?"

"Gerald? No, nothing special; he had a headache this evening."

"You know, Val—at least we often talked the matter over—that Gerald might have to go away for a time. He is my partner, and partners in such a firm as mine have often to go to the other side of the world to transact important business."

"Yes, you and Gerald have both spoken of it. He's not going soon, is he?"

"That's it, my pet. The necessity has arisen rather suddenly. Gerald has to sail for Sydney in about a month."

Valentine was sitting a little behind her father. He could not see the pallor of her face; her voice was quite clear and quiet.

"Poor old Gerry," she said; "he won't take me, will he, father?"

"Impossible, my dear—absolutely. You surely don't want to go."

"No, not particularly."

Valentine yawned with admirable effect.

"She really can't care for him at all. What a wonderful piece of luck," muttered her father.

"I daresay Gerald will enjoy Sydney," continued his wife. "Is he likely to be long away?"

"Perhaps six months—perhaps not so long. Time is always a matter of some uncertainty in cases of this kind."

"I could come back to you while he is away, couldn't I, dad?"

"Why, of course, my dear one, I always intended that. It would be old times over again—old times over again for you and your father, Valentine."

"Not quite, I think," replied Valentine. "We can't go back really. Things happen, and we can't undo them. Do you know, father, I think Gerald must have infected me with his headache. If you don't mind, I'll go home."

Mr. Paget saw his daughter back to Park-lane, but he did not go into the house. Valentine rang the bell, and when Masters opened the door she asked him where her husband was.

"In the library, ma'am; you can hear him can't you? He's practising of the violin."

Yes, the music of this most soul-speaking, soul-stirring instrument filled the house. Valentine put her finger to her lips to enjoin silence, and went softly along the passage which led to the library. The door was a little ajar—she could look in without being herself seen. Some sheets of music were scattered about on the table, but Wyndham was not playing from any written score. The queer melody which he called Waves was filling the room. Valentine had heard it twice before—she started and clasped her hands as its passion, its unutterable sadness, its despair, reached her. Where were the triumph notes which had come into it six weeks ago?

She turned and fled up to her room, and locking the door, threw herself by her bedside and burst into bitter weeping.

"Oh, Gerald, I love you! I do love you; but I'll never show it. No, never, until you tell me the truth."

CHAPTER XXV

"Yes," said Augusta Wyndham, "if there is a young man who suits me all round it's Mr. Carr. Yes," she said, standing very upright in her short skirts, with her hair in a tight pigtail hanging down her back, and her determined, wide open, bright eyes fixed upon an admiring audience of younger sisters. "He suits me exactly. He's a kind of hail-fellow-well-met; he has no nonsensical languishing airs about him; he preaches nice short sermons, and never bothers you to remember what they are about afterwards; he's not bad at tennis or cricket, and he really can cannon quite decently at billiards; but for all that, if you think, you young 'uns, that he's going to get inside of Gerry, or that he's going to try to pretend to know better than Gerry what I can or can't do, why you're all finely mistaken, so there!"

Augusta turned on her heel, pirouetted a step or two, whistled in a loud, free, unrestrained fashion, and once more faced her audience.

"Gerry said that I could give out the library books. Now is it likely that Mr. Carr knows more of my capacities after six months' study than Gerry found out after fifteen years?"

"But Mr. Carr doesn't study you, Gus. It's Lilias he's always looking at," interrupted little Rosie.

"You're not pretty, are you, Gus?" asked Betty. "Your cheeks are too red, aren't they? And nurse says your eyes are as round as an owl's!"

"Pretty!" answered Augusta, in a lofty voice. "Who cares for being pretty? Who cares for being simply pink and white? I'm for intellect. I'm for the march of mind. Gerry believes in me. Hurrah for Gerry! Now, girls, off with your caps, throw them in the air, and shout hurrah for Gerry three times, as loud as you can!"

"What an extraordinary noise the children are making on the lawn," said Lilias to Marjory. "I hear Gerald's name. What can they be saying about Gerald? One would almost think he was coming down the avenue to see the state of excitement they are in! Do look, Meg, do."

"It's only one of Gussie's storms in a tea-cup," responded Marjory, cheerfully. "I am so glad, Lil, that you found Gerald and Val hitting it off so nicely. You consider them quite a model pair for affection and all that, don't you, pet?"

"Quite," said Lilias. "My mind is absolutely at rest. One night Val puzzled me a little. Oh, nothing to speak of—nothing came of it, I mean. Yes, my mind is absolutely at rest, thank

God! What are all the children doing. Maggie? They are flying in a body to the house. What can it mean?"

"We'll know in less than no time," responded Marjory, calmly. And they did.

Four little girls, all out of breath, all dressed alike, all looking alike, dashed into the drawing-room, and in one breath poured out the direful intelligence that Augusta had mutinied.

"Mr. Carr forbade her to give away the library books," they said, "and she has gone up now to the school-room in spite of him. She's off; she said Gerry said she might do it, long ago. Isn't it awful of her? She says beauty's nothing, and she's only going to obey Gerry," continued Betty. "What shall we do? She'll give all the books away wrong, and Mr. Carr will be angry."

They all paused for want of breath. Rosie went up and laid her fat red hand on Lilias' knee.

"I said it was you he stared at," she remarked. "You wouldn't like him to be vexed, would you?"

The words had scarcely passed her lips before the door was opened, and the object of the children's universal commiseration entered. A deep and awful silence took possession of them. Lilias clutched Rosie's hand, and felt an inane desire to rush from the room with her.

Too late. The terrible infant flew to Adrian Carr, and clasping her arms around his legs, looked up into his face.

"Never mind," she said, "it is wrong of Gussie, but it isn't Lilias' fault. She wouldn't like to vex you, 'cause you stare so at her."

"Nursie says that you admire Lilias; do you?" asked Betty.

"Oh, poor Gussie!" exclaimed the others, their interest in Lilias and Carr being after all but a very secondary matter. "We all do hope you won't do anything dreadful to her. You can, you know. You can excommunicate her, can't you?"

"But what has Augusta done?" exclaimed Carr, turning a somewhat flushed face in the direction not of Lilias, but of Marjory. "What a frightful confusion—and what does it mean?"

Marjory explained as well as she was able. Carr had lately taken upon himself to overhaul the books of the lending library. He believed in literature as a very elevating lever, but he thought that books should not only be carefully selected in the mass, but in lending should be given with a special view to the needs of the individual who borrowed. Before Gerald's marriage Marjory had given away the books, but since then, for various reasons, they had drifted into Augusta's hands, and through their means this rather spirited and daring young lady had been able to inflict a small succession of mild tyrannies. For instance, poor Miss Yates, the weak-eyed and weak-spirited village dressmaker, was dosed with a series of profound and dull theology; and Macallister, the sexton and shoemaker, a canny Scot, who looked upon all fiction as the "work of the de'il," was put into a weekly passion with the novels of Charles Reade and Wilkie Collins.

These were extreme cases, but Augusta certainly had the knack of giving the wrong book to the wrong person. Carr heard mutterings and grumbling. The yearly subscriptions of a shilling a piece diminished, and he thought it full time to take the matter in hand. He himself would distribute the village literature every Saturday, at twelve o'clock.

The day and the hour arrived, and behold Miss Augusta Wyndham had forestalled him, and was probably at this very moment putting "The Woman in White" into the enraged Macallister's hand. Carr's temper was not altogether immaculate; he detached the children's clinging hands from his person, and said he would pursue the truant, publicly take the reins of authority from her, and send her home humiliated. He left the rectory, walking fast, and letting his annoyance rather increase than diminish, for few young men care to be placed in a ridiculous situation, and he could not but feel that such was his in the present instance.

The school-house was nearly half a mile from the rectory, along a straight and dusty piece of road; very dusty it was to-day, and a cutting March east wind blew in Carr's face and stung it. He approached the school-houseno, what a reliefthe patient aspirants after literature were most of them waiting outside. Augusta, then, could not have gone into the school-room.

"Has Miss Augusta Wyndham gone upstairs?" he asked of a rosy-cheeked girl who adored the "Sunday At Home."

"No, please, sir. Mr. Gerald's come, please, Mr. Carr, sir," raising two eyes which nearly blazed with excitement. "He shook 'ands with me, he did, and with Old Ben, there; and Miss Augusta, she give a sort of a whoop, and she had her arms round his neck, and was a-hugging of him before us all, and they has gone down through the fields to the rectory."

"About the books," said Carr; "has Miss Augusta given you the books?"

"Bless your 'eart, sir," here interrupted Old Ben, "we ain't of a mind for books to-day. Mr. Gerald said he'd come up this evening to the Club, and have a chat with us all, and Sue and me, we was waiting here to tell the news. Litteratoor ain't in our line to-day, thank you, sir."

"Here's Mr. Macallister," said Sue. "Mr. Macallister. Mr. Gerald's back. He is, truly. I seen him, and so did Old Ben."

"And he'll be at the Club to-night," said Ben, turning his wrinkled face upwards towards the elongated visage of the canny Scot.

"The Lord be praised for a' His mercies," pronounced Macallister, slowly, with an upward wave of his hand, as if he were returning thanks for a satisfying meal. "Na, na. Mr. Carr, na books the day."

Finding that his services were really useless, Carr went away. The villagers were slowly collecting from different quarters, and all faces were broadening into smiles, and all the somewhat indifferent sleepy tones becoming perceptibly brighter, and Gerald Wyndham's name was passed from lip to lip. Old Miss Bates wiped her tearful eyes, as she hurried home to put on her best cap. Widow Simpkins determined to make up a good fire in her cottage, and not to spare the coals; the festive air was unmistakeable. Carr felt smitten with a kind of envy. What wonders could not Wyndham have effected in this place, he commented, as he walked slowly back to his lodgings. Later in the day he called at the rectory to find the hero surrounded by his adoring family, and bearing his honors gracefully.

Gerald was talking rather more than his wont; for some reason or other his face had more color than usual, his eyes were bright, he smiled, and even laughed. Lilias ceased to watch him anxiously, a sense of jubilation filled the breast of every worshipping sister, and no one thought of parting or sorrow.

Perhaps even Gerald himself forgot the bitterness which lay before him just then; perhaps his efforts were not all efforts, and that he really felt some of the old home peace and rest with its sustaining power.

You can know a thing and yet not always realize it. Gerald knew that he should never spend another Saturday in the old rectory of Jewsbury-on-the-Wold. That Lilias' bright head and Lilias' tender, steadfast earnest eyes would be in future only a memory. He could never hope again to touch that hair, or answer back the smile on that beloved and happy face. The others, too—but Lilias, after his wife, was most dear of all living creatures to Gerald. Well, he must not think; he resolved to take all the sweetness, if possible, out of this Saturday and Sunday. He resolved not to tell any of his people of the coming parting until just before he left.

The small sisters squatted in a semicircle on the floor round their hero; Augusta, as usual, stood behind him, keeping religious guard of the back of his head.

"If there is a thing I simply adore," that vigorous young lady was often heard to say, "it's the back of Gerry's head."

Lilias sat at his feet, her slim hand and arm lying across his knee; Marjory flitted about, too restless and happy to be quiet, and the tall rector stood on the hearthrug with his back to the fire.

"It is good to be home again," said Gerald. Whereupon a sigh of content echoed from all the other throats, and it was at this moment that Carr came into the room.

"Come in, Carr, come in," said the rector. "There's a place for you, too. You're quite like one of the family, you know. Oh, of course you are, my dear fellow, of course you are. We have got my son back, unexpectedly. Gerald, you know Carr, don't you."

Gerald stood up, gave Carr's hand a hearty grip, and offered him his chair.

"Oh, not that seat, Gerry," groaned Augusta, "it's the only one in the room I can stand at comfortably. I can't fiddle with your curls if I stand at the back of any other chair."

Gerald patted her cheek.

"Then perhaps, Carr, you'll oblige Augusta by occupying another chair. I am sorry that I am obliged to withhold the most comfortable from you."

Carr was very much at home with the Wyndhams by now. He pulled forward a cane chair, shook his head at Augusta, and glanced almost timidly at Lilias. He feared the eight sharp eyes of the younger children if he did more than look very furtively, but she made such a sweet picture just then that his eyes sought hers by a sort of fascination. For the first time, too, he noticed that she had a look of Gerald. Her face lacked the almost spiritualized expression of his, but undoubtedly there was a likeness.

The voices, interrupted for a moment by the curate's entrance, soon resumed their vigorous flow.

"Why didn't you bring my dear little sister Valentine down, Gerald?" It was Lilias who spoke.

He rewarded her loving speech by a flash, half of pleasure, half of pain in his eyes. Aloud he said:

"We thought it scarcely worth while for both of us to come. I must go away again on Monday."

A sepulchral groan from Augusta. Rosie, Betty and Joan exclaimed almost in a breath:

"And we like you much better by yourself."

"Oh, hush, children," said Marjory. "We are all very fond of Val."

"You have brought a great deal of delight into the village. Wyndham," said Carr, and he related the little scene which had taken place around the school-house. "I'd give a good deal to be even half as popular," he said with a sigh.

"You might give all you possessed in all the world, and you wouldn't succeed," snapped Gussie.

"Augusta, you really are too rude," said Lilias with a flush on her face.

"No, I'm not, Lil. Oh, you needn't stare at me. I like him, and he knows it," nodding with her head in the direction of Adrian Carr; "but you have to be born in a place, and taught to walk in it, and you have had to steal apples in it and eggs out of birds' nests, and to get nearly drowned when fishing, and to get some shot in your ankle, and you've got to know every soul in all the country round, and to come back from school to them in the holidays, and for them first to see your moustache coming; and then, beyond and above all that, you've got just to be Gerry, to have his way of looking, and his way of walking, and his way of shaking your hand, and to have his voice and his heart, to be loved as well. So how could Mr. Carr expect it?"

"Bravo, Augusta," said Adrian Carr. "I'd like you for a friend better than any girl I know."

"Please, Gerry, tell us a story," exclaimed the younger children. They did not want Augusta to have all the talking.

"Let it be about a mouse, and a cricket on the hearth, and a white elephant, and a roaring bull, and a grizzly bear."

"And let the ten little nigger-boys come into it," said Betty.

"And Bo-Peep," said Rosie.

"And the Old Man who wouldn't say his prayers," exclaimed Joan.

"And let it last for hours," exclaimed they all.

Gerald begged the rest of the audience to go away, but they refused to budge an inch. So the story began. All the characters appeared in due order; it lasted a long time, and everybody was delighted.

CHAPTER XXVI

Lilias Wyndham never forgot that last Sunday with Gerald spent at Jewsbury-on-the-Wold. The day in itself was perfect, the air blew softly from the west, the sun shone in a nearly cloudless heaven; the gentle breezes, the opening flowers, the first faint buds of spring on tree and hedge-row seemed all to give a foretaste of summer. Nobody knew, none could guess, that in one sense they foretold the desolation of dark winter.

It was in this light that Wyndham himself regarded the lovely day.

"I leap from calm to storm," he said to himself. "Never mind, I will enjoy the present bliss!"

He did enjoy it, really, not seemingly. He took every scrap of sweetness out of it, almost forgetting Valentine for the time being, and living over again the days when he was a light-hearted boy.

He went to church twice, and sat in the corner of the square family pew which had always been reserved for him. As of old, Lilias sat by his side, and when the sermon came he lifted little Joan into his arms, and she fell asleep with her golden head on his breast. The rector preached and Gerald listened. It was an old-fashioned sermon, somewhat long for the taste of the present day. It had been carefully prepared, and was read aloud, for the benefit of the congregation, in a clear, gentlemanly voice.

Gerald almost forgot that he was a man with an unusual load of suffering upon him, as he listened to the time-honored softly-flowing sentences.

"Blessed are the pure in heart," was the rector's text, and it seemed to more than one of that little village congregation that he was describing his own son when he drew his picture of the man of purity.

In the evening Carr preached. He was as modern as the rector was the reverse. He used neither M.S. nor notes, and his sermon scarcely occupied ten minutes.

"To die is gain" was his text. There were some in the congregation who scarcely understood the vigorous words, but they seemed to one weary man like the first trumpet notes of coming battle. They spoke of a fight which led to a victory. Wyndham remembered them by-and-bye.

It was the custom at the rectory to have a kind of open house on Sunday evening, and tonight many of Gerald's friends dropped in. The large party seemed a happy one. The merriment of the night before had deepened into something better. Lilias spoke of it afterwards as bliss.

"Do you remember," she said to Marjory, in the desolate days which followed, "how Gerald looked when he played the organ in the hall? Do you remember his face when we sang 'Sun of my soul?'"

The happiest days come to an end. The children went to bed, the friends one by one departed. Even Lilias and Marjory kissed their brother and bade him good-night. He was to leave before they were up in the morning. This he insisted on, against their will.

"But we shall see you soon in London," they both said, for they were coming up in a few weeks to stay with an aunt. Then they told him to kiss Valentine for them, and went upstairs, chatting lightly to one another.

The rector and his son were alone.

"We have had a happy day," said Gerald, abruptly.

"We have, my son. It does us all good to have you with us, Gerald. I could have wished—but there's no good regretting now. Each man must choose his own path, and you seem happy, my dear son; that is the main thing."

"I never thought primarily of happiness," responded Gerald. "Did you listen to Carr's sermon to-night? He proved his case well. To die is sometimes gain."

The rector, who was seated by the fire, softly patted his knee with one hand.

"Yes, yes," he said, "Carr proved his case ably. He's a good fellow. A little inclined to the broad church, don't you think?"

"Perhaps so."

Gerald stood up. His face had suddenly grown deadly white.

"Father, I kept a secret from you all day. I did not wish to do anything to mar the bliss of this perfect Sunday. You—you'll break it to Lilias and Maggie, and the younger children. I'm going to Sydney on Wednesday. I came down to say good-bye."

He held out his hand. The rector stood up and grasped it.

"My dear lad—my boy. Well—well—you'll come back again. Of course, I did know that you expected to go abroad on business for your firm. My dear son. Yes, my boy—aye—you'll come back again soon. How queer you look, Gerald. Sit down. I'm afraid you're a little overdone."

"Good-bye, father. You're an old man, and Sydney is a long way off. Good-bye. I have a queer request to make. Grant it, and don't think me weak or foolish. Give me your blessing before I go."

Suddenly Wyndham fell on his knees, and taking his father's hand laid it on his head.

"I am like Esau," he said. "Is there not one blessing left for me?"

The rector was deeply moved.

"Heaven above bless you, my boy," he said. "Your mother's God go with you. There, Gerald, you are mor bid. You will be back with me before the snows of next winter fall. But God bless you, my boy, wherever you are and whatever you do!"

CHAPTER XXVII

Valentine was sitting in her pretty drawing-room. It was dinner time, but she had not changed her dress. She was too young, too fresh, and unused to trouble, for it yet to leave any strong marks on her face. The delicate color in her cheeks had slightly paled, it is true, her bright hair was in confusion, and her eyes looked larger and more wistful than their wont, but otherwise no one could tell that her heart was beating heavily and that she was listening eagerly for a footstep.

Seven o'clock came—half-past seven. This was Gerald's last night at home; he was to sail in the Esperance for Sydney to-morrow. Valentine felt stunned and cold, though she kept on repeating to herself over and over:

"This parting is nothing. He's sure to be home in six months at the latest. Six months at the very latest. In these days there is really no such thing as distance. What is a six months' parting? Besides, it is not as if I were really in love with him. Father asked me the question direct last night, and I said I wasn't. How could I love him with all my heart when I remember that scene at the Gaiety? Oh, that scene! It burns into me like fire, and father's look—I almost hated father that night. I did really. Fancy, Valentine hating her father! Oh, of course it passed. There is no one like my father. Husbands aren't like fathers, not in the long run. Oh, Gerald, you might have told me the truth? I'd have forgiven you, I would really, if you had told me the truth. Oh, why don't you come? Why don't you come? You might be in time this last evening. It is a quarter to eight now. I am impatient—I am frightened. Oh, there's a ring at the hall door. Oh, thank God. No, of course, Gerald, I don't love you—not as I could have loved—and yet I do—I do love you—I do!"

She clasped her hands—a footstep was on the stairs. The door was opened, Masters brought her a thick letter on a salver.

"Has not Mr. Wyndham come? Was not that ring Mr. Wyndham's?"

"No, madam, a messenger brought this letter. He said there was no answer."

The page withdrew, and Valentine tore open the envelope. A letter somewhat blotted, bearing strong marks of agitation, but in her husband's writing, lay in her hand. Her eager eyes devoured the contents.

"I can't say good-bye, my darling—there are limits even to my endurance—I can't look at you and hear you say 'Good-bye, Gerald.' I bade you farewell this morning when you were asleep. I am not coming home to-night, but your father will spend the evening with you. You love him better than me, and I pray the God of all mercy that he may soften any little pang that may come to you in this separation. When you are reading this I shall be on my way to Southampton. I have bid your father good-bye, and he will tell you everything there is to tell about me. The Esperance sails at noon to-morrow, and it is a good plan to be on board in good time. I cannot tell you. Valentine, what my own feelings are. I cannot gauge my love for you. I don't think anything could probe it to its depths. I am a sinful man, but I sometimes hope that God will forgive me, because I have loved as much as the human heart is capable of loving. You must remember that, dear. You must always know that you have inspired in one man's breast the extreme of love!

"Good-bye, my darling. It is my comfort to know that the bitterness of this six months' separation falls on me. If I thought otherwise, if I thought even for a moment that you cared more for your husband than you do for the world's opinion, or for riches, or for honor, that you would rather have him with poverty and shame, that he was more to you even than the father who gave you your being, then I would say even now, at the eleventh hour, 'fly to me, Valentine. Let us go away together on board the Esperance, and forget all promises and all honor, and all truth.' Yes, I would say it. But that is a mad dream. Forget this part of my letter. Valentine. It has been wrung from a tortured and almost maddened heart. Good-bye, my wife. Be thankful that you have not it in you to love recklessly.

"Your husband,

"Gerald Wyndham."

"But I have!" said Valentine. She raised her eyes. Her father was in the room.

"Yes, I can loveI too can give back the extreme of love. Father, I am going to my husband. I am going to Southampton. What's the matter? What are you looking at me like that for? Why did you send Gerald away without letting him come to say good-bye? Not that it matters, for I am going to him. I shall take the very next train to Southampton."

"My darling," began Mr. Paget.

"Oh, yes, father, yes. But there's no time for loving words just now. I've had a letter from my husband, and I'm going to him. I'm going to Sydney with him. Yesyou can't prevent me!"

"You are talking folly, Valentine," said Mr. Paget. "You are excited, my child; you are talking wildly. Going with your husband? My poor little girl. There, dear, there. He'll soon be back. You can't go with him, you know, my love. Show me his letter. What has he dared to say to excite you like this?"

"No, you shan't see a word of his dear letter. No, not for all the world. I understand him at last, and I love him with all my heart and soul. Yes, I do. Oh, no, I don't love you as I love my husband."

Mr. Paget stepped back a pace or two. There was no doubting Valentine's words, no doubting the look on her face. She was no longer a child. She was a woman, a woman aroused to passion, almost to fury.

"I am going to my husband," she said. And she took no notice of her father when he sank into the nearest chair and pressed his hand to his heart.

"I have got a blow," he said. "I have got an awful blow."

But Valentine did not heed him.

CHAPTER XXVIII

"Yes, my darling," said Mr. Paget, two hours later; his arms were round his daughter, and her head was on his shoulder. "Oh, yes, my dear one, certainly, if you wish it."

"And you'll go with me, father? Father, couldn't you come too? Couldn't we three go? Yes, that would be nice, that would be happiness."

"A good idea," said Mr. Paget, reflectively. "But really, Val, really now, don't you think Wyndham and I rather spoil you? You discover at the eleventh hour that you can't live without your husband, that as he must cross to the other side of the world, you must go there too. And now in addition I have to accompany you. Do you think you are worth all this? That any girl in the world is worth all this?"

"Perhaps not, father."

Valentine was strangely subdued and quiet.

"I suppose it would be selfish to bring you," she said; "and we shall be back in six months."

"True," said Mr. Paget in a thoughtful voice; "and even for my daughter's sake my business must not go absolutely to the dogs. Well, child, a wilful woman—you know the proverb—a wilful woman must have her way. I own I'm disappointed. I looked forward to six months all alone with you. Six months with my own child—a last six months, for of course I always guessed that when Wyndham came back you'd give yourself up to him body and soul. Oh, no, my dear, I'm not going to disappoint you. A wife fretting and mourning for her husband is the last person I should consider a desirable companion. Run upstairs now and get your maid to put your things together. I shall take you down to Southampton by an early train in the morning, and in the meantime, if you'll excuse me. Valentine, I'll go out and send a telegram to your husband."

"To tell him that I'm coming?"

"Yes, are you not pleased?"

"No, don't do that. I will meet him on board the boat. I know exactly what the scene will be. He'll be looking—no. I shan't say how he'll be looking—but I'll steal up behind him, and slip my hand through his arm, and then—and then! Father, kiss me. I love you for making me so happy."

Mr. Paget pressed his lips to his daughter's forehead. For a brief moment his eyes looked into hers. She remembered by-and-bye their queer expression. Just now, however, she was too overwrought and excited to have room for any ideas except the one supreme longing and passion which was drawing her to her husband.

"Shall we have dinner?" said Mr. Paget after another pause.

Valentine laughed rather wildly.

"Dinner? I can't eat. Had not you better go home and have something? Perhaps I did order dinner, but I can't remember. My head feels queer; I can't think properly. Go home and have something to eat, father. You can come back later on. I am going upstairs now to pack."

She left the room without a word, and Mortimer Paget heard her light step as she ran up to her bedroom. He began to talk vehemently to himself.

"Does that child, that little girl, whom I reared and fostered—that creature whom I brought into existence—think she will checkmate me now at the supreme moment. No, there are limits. I find that even my love for Valentine has a bottom, and I reach it when I see the prisoner's cell, solitary confinement, penal servitude, looming large on the horizon. Even your heart must suffer, little Valentine, to keep such a fate as that from my door. Poor little Val! Well, the best schemes, the most carefully laid plans sometimes meet with defeat. It did not enter into my calculations that Val would fall madly in love with that long-faced fellow. Pah! where's her taste? What men women will admire. Well, Valentine, you must pay the penalty, for my plans cannot be disturbed at the eleventh hour!"

Mr. Paget went softly out of the house, but he did not go, as Valentine innocently supposed, home to dinner. No, he had something far more important to attend to. Something in which he could be very largely assisted by that confidential clerk of his, Jonathan Helps.

Meanwhile, Valentine and her maid were having a busy time. Dresses were pulled out, trunks dusted and brought into the middle of the room, and hasty preparations were made for a journey.

Valentine's low spirits had changed to high ones. She was as happy as some hours ago she had been miserable. Her heart was now at rest, it had acknowledged its own need—it had given expression to the love which was fast becoming its life.

"You are surprised, Suzanne," said Mrs. Wyndham to her maid. "Yes, it is a hurried journey. I had no idea of going with Mr. Wyndham, but he—poor fellow—he can't do without me, Suzanne, so I am going. I shall join him on board the Esperance in the morning. You can fancy his surprise—his pleasure. Put in plenty of dinner dresses, Suzanne. Those white dresses that Mr. Wyndham likes—yes, that is right. Of course I shall dress every evening for dinner on board the Esperance. I wonder if many other ladies are going. Not that it matters—I shall have my husband. What are you saying, Suzanne?"

"That it is beautiful to lof," replied the maid, looking up with adoring eyes at her pretty animated young mistress.

She was both young and pretty herself, and she sympathized with Valentine, and admired her immensely for her sudden resolve.

"Yes, love is beautiful," answered Valentine gravely. Her eyes filled with sudden soft tears of happiness. "And there is something better even than love," she said, looking at Suzanne, and speaking with a sudden burst of confidence. "The highest bliss of all is to give joy to those who love you."

"And you will do that to-morrow, madame," replied Suzanne fervently. "Oh, this lof, so beautiful, so rare—you will lay it at monsieur's fee—he is goot, monsieur is, and how great is his passion for madame."

The young Swiss girl flitted gaily about, and by-and-bye the packing even for this sudden voyage was accomplished.

"You will take me with you, madame?" said Suzanne.

"No, Suzanne, there is no time to arrange that, nor shall I really want you. We may have to rough it a little, my husband and I; not that we mind, it will be like a continual picnic—quite delicious."

"But madame must be careful of her precious health."

The color flushed into Valentine's cheeks.

"My husband will take care of me," she said. "No. Suzanne, I shall not take you with me. You will stay here for the present, and my father will arrange matters for you. Now you can go downstairs and have some supper. I shall not want you again to-night."

The girl withdrew, and Valentine stood by the fire, gazing into its cheerful depths, and seeing many happy dream pictures.

"Yes, I shall certainly go with him. Even if what I dread and hope and long for is the case, I shall be with him. I can whisper it first to him. I ought to be with him>I ought to be with my husband then. Why did Suzanne speak about my health? No one will take such care of me as Gerald. Even my father cannot approach Gerald for tenderness, for sympathy when one is out of sorts. How soothing is Gerald's hand; how quieting. Once I was ill for a few hours. Only a bad headache, but it went when he made me lie very still, and when he clasped my two hands in one of his. Yes, I quite believe in Gerald. Even though I do not understand that night at the Gaiety, still I absolutely believe in my husband. He is too noble to tell a lie; he had a reason for not explaining what looked so strange that night. He had a right reason, probably a good and great one. Perhaps I'll ask him again some day. Perhaps when he knows there's a littlelittle child coming he'll tell me himself. Oh, God, kind, good, beautiful God, if you are going to give me a child of my very own, help me to be worthy of it. Help me to be worthy of the child, and of the child's father."

Mr. Paget's ring was heard at the hall door, and Valentine ran down to meet him. He had made all arrangements he told her. They would catch the . train in the morning from Waterloo, and he would call for her in a cab at a sufficiently early hour to catch it.

His words were brief, but he was quite quiet and business-like. He kissed his daughter affectionately, told her to go to bed at once, and soon after left the house.

Valentine gave directions for the morning and went back to her room. She got quickly into bed, for she was determined to be well rested for what lay before her on the following day. She laid her head on the pillow, closed her eyes, and prepared to go to sleep. Does not everybody know what happens on these occasions? Does not each individual who in his or her turn has especially desired for the best and most excellent reason a long sleep, a deep sleep, an unbroken and dreamless sleep found it recede further and further awayfound eyes more watchfulbrain more active, limbs more restless, as the precious moments fly by? How loud the watch ticks, how audible are the minutest sounds!

It was thus with Valentine Wyndham that night. No sleep came near her, and by slow degrees as the fire grew faint and the night deepened in silence and solemnity, her happy excitement, her childish joy, gave place to vague apprehensions. All kinds of nameless terrors came over her. Suppose an accident happened to the train? Suppose the Esperance sailed before its time? Above all, and this idea was agonizing, was so repellant that she absolutely pushed it from hersuppose her father was deceiving her.

She was horrified as this thought came, and came. It would come, it would not be banished. Suppose her father was deceiving her?

She went over in the silence of the night the whole scene of that evening. Her own sudden and fierce resolve, her father's opposition, his disappointmentthen his sudden yielding. The more she thought, the more apprehensive she grew; the more she pondered, the longer, the more real grew her fears. At last she could bear them no longer.

She lit a candle and looked at her watch. Three o'clock. Had ever passed a night so long and dreadful? There would not be even a ray of daylight for some time. She could not endure that hot and restless pillow. She would get up and dress.

All the time she was putting on her clothes the dread that her father was deceiving her kept strengtheningstrengthening. At last it almost reached a panic. What a fool she had been not to go to Southampton the night before. Suppose Gerald's ship sailed before she reached it or him.

Suddenly an idea came like a ray of light. Why should she wait for her father? Why should she not take an earlier train to Southampton? The relative depths of Valentine's two loves were clearly shown when she did not reject this thought. It mattered nothing at all to her at this supreme moment whether she offended her father or not. She determined to go to Southampton by the first train that left Waterloo that morning. She ran downstairs, found a time-table, saw that a train left at ., and resolved to catch it. She would take Suzanne with her, and leave a message for her father; he could follow by the . train if he liked.

She went upstairs and woke her maid.

"Suzanne, get up at once. Dress yourself, and come to me, to my room."

In an incredible short time Suzanne had obeyed this mandate.

"I am going to take you with me to Southampton. Suzanne. I mean to catch the train which leaves here at ten minutes to six. We have plenty of time, but not too much. Can you make some coffee for us both? And then either you or Masters must find a cab."

Suzanne opened her bright eyes wide.

"I will go with you, my goot madam," she said to herself. "The early hour is noting, the strangeness is noting. That olt manI hate that olt man! I will go alone with you, mine goot mistress, to find the goot husband what is so devoted. Ach! Suzanne does not like that olt man!"

Coffee was served in Valentine's bedroom. Mistress and maid partook of it together. Masters was aroused, was fortunate enough in procuring a cab, and at five o'clock, for Valentine's impatience could brook no longer delay, she and Suzanne had started together for Waterloo.

Once more her spirits were high. She had dared something for Gerald. It was already sweet to her to be brave for his sake.

Before she left she wrote a short letter to her father—a constrained little note—for her fears stood between her and him.

She and Suzanne arrived at Waterloo long before the train started.

"Oh, how impatient I am!" whispered Mrs. Wyndham to her maid. "Will time never pass? I am sure all the clocks in London must be wrong, this last night has been like three."

The longest hours, however, do come to an end, and presently Valentine and Suzanne found themselves being whirled out of London, and into the early morning of a bright clear March day.

The two occupied a compartment to themselves. Suzanne felt wide awake, talkative, and full of intense curiosity; but Valentine was strangely silent. She ceased either to laugh or to talk. She drew down her veil, and establishing herself in a corner kept looking out at the swiftly passing landscape. Once more the fear which had haunted her during the night returned. Even now, perhaps, she would not be in time!

Then she set to work chiding herself. She must be growing silly. The Esperance did not leave the dock until noon, and her train was due at Southampton soon after eight. Of course there would be lots of time. Even her father who was to follow by the later train could reach the Esperance before she sailed.

The train flew quickly through the country, the slow moments dropped into space one by one. Presently the train slackened speed—presently it reached its destination.

Then for the first time Valentine's real difficulties began. She had not an idea from which dock the Esperance was to sail. A porter placed her luggage on a fly. She and Suzanne got in, and the driver asked for directions. No, the Esperance was not known to the owner of the hackney coach.

When the porter and the cabman questioned Mrs. Wyndham she suddenly felt as if she had come up against a blank wall. There were miles of ships all around. If she could afford no clue to the whereabouts of the Esperance the noon of another day might come before she could reach the dock where it was now lying at anchor.

At last it occurred to her to give the name of her father's shipping firm. It was a great name in the city, but neither the porter nor the cabman had come under its influence. They suggested, however, that most likely the firm of Paget Brothers had an office somewhere near. They said further that if there was such an office the clerks in it could give the lady the information she wanted.

Valentine was standing by her cab, trying not to show the bewilderment and distress which had seized her, when a man who must have been listening came up, touched his hat, and said civilly:

"Pardon, madam. If you will drive or walk down to the quay, this quay quite close, there is an office, you cannot fail to see it, where they can give you the information you desire, as they are always posted up with regard to the out-going and in-coming vessels. That quay, quite near, cabby. Messrs. Gilling and Gilling's office."

He touched his hat again and vanished, being rewarded by Valentine with a look which he considered a blessing.

"Now," she said, "now, I will give you double fare, cabman, treble fare, if you will help me to get to the Esperance in time; and first of all, let us obey that good man's directions and go to Messrs. Gilling and Gilling."

The quay was close, and so was the office. In two minutes Valentine was standing, alas, by its closed doors. A sudden fierce impatience came over her, she rang the office bell loudly. Three times she rang before any one answered her summons. Then a rather dishevelled and sleepy-looking boy opened the door wide enough to poke his head out and asked her her business.

"I want to get news of the ship called the Esperance."

"Office don't open till nine."

He would have pushed the door to, but Suzanne stepping forward deftly put her foot in.

"Mine goot boy, be civil," she said. "This lady has come a long way, and she wants the tidings she asks very sore."

The office boy looked again at Valentine. She certainly was pretty; so was Suzanne. But the office really did not open till nine, and the boy could not himself give any tidings.

"You had better step in," he said. "Mr. Jones will be here at nine. No, I don't know nothing about the ship."

It was now twenty-five minutes past eight. Valentine sank down on the dusty chair which the boy pushed forward for her, and Suzanne stood impatiently by her side.

Outside, the cabman whistled a cheerful air and stamped his feet. The morning was cold; but what of that? He himself was doing a good business; he was certain of an excellent fare.

"Suzanne," said Valentine suddenly. "Do you mind going outside and waiting in the cab. I cannot bear anyone to stare at me just now."

Suzanne obeyed. She was not offended. She was too deeply interested and sympathetic.

The slow minutes passed. Nine o'clock sounded from a great church near, and then more gently from the office clock. At three minutes past nine a bilious-looking clerk came in and took his place at one of the desks. He started when he saw Valentine, opened a ledger, and pretended to be very busy.

"Can you tell me, at once, please, from which dock the Esperance sails?" asked Mrs. Wyndham.

Her voice was impressive, and sharp with pain and waiting. The clerk thought he might at least stare at her. Things were slow and dull at this hour of the morning, and she was a novelty. He could have given the information at once, but it suited him best to dawdle over it. Valentine could have stamped with her increasing impatience.

The clerk, turning the leaves of a big book slowly, at last put his finger on an entry.

"Esperance sails for Sydney th inst., noon. Albert and Victoria Docks."

"Thank you, thank you," said Valentine. "Are these docks far away?"

"Three miles off, madam."

"Thank you."

She was out of the office and in the cab almost before he had time to close his book.

"Drive to the Albert and Victoria Docks, instantly, coachman. I will give you a sovereign if you take me there in less than half an hour."

Never was horse beaten like that cabby's, and Valentine, the most tender-hearted of mortals, saw the whip raised without a pang. Now she was certain to be in time; even allowing for delay she would reach the Esperance before ten o'clock, and it did not sail until noon. Yes, there was now not the most remote doubt she was in good time. And yet, and yet—still she felt miserable. Still her heart beat with a strange overpowering sense of coming defeat and disaster. Good cabman—go faster yet, and faster. Ah, yes, how they were flying! How pleasant it was to be bumped and shaken, and jolted—to feel the ground flying under the horse's feet, for each moment brought her nearer to the Esperance and to Gerald.

At last they reached the dock. Valentine sprang out of the cab. A sailor came forward to help with her luggage. Valentine put a sovereign into the cabman's hand.

"Thank you," she said, "oh, thank you. Yes, I am in good time."

Her eyes were full of happy tears, and the cabman, a rather hardened old villain, was surprised to find a lump rising in his throat.

"Which ship, lady?" asked the sailor, touching his cap.

"The Esperance, one of Paget Brothers' trading vessels. I want to go on board at once; show it to me. Suzanne, you can follow with the luggage. Show me the Esperance, good man, my husband is waiting for me."

"You don't mean the Experiance, bound for Sydney?" asked the man. "One of Paget Brothers' big ships?"

"Yes, yes; do you know her? Point her out to me."

"Ay, I know her. I was helping to lade her till twelve last night."

"Just show her to me. I am in a frightful hurry. She is here—this is the right dock."

"Ay, the Albert and Victoria. The Experiance sailing for Sydney, noon, on the th."

"Well, where is she? I will go and look for her by myself."

"You can't, lady, she's gone."

"What—what do you mean? It isn't twelve o'clock. Suzanne, it isn't twelve o'clock."

"No, lady."

The old sailor looked compassionate enough.

"Poor young thing," he soliloquized under his breath, "some one has gone and done her. The Experiance was to sail at noon," he continued, "and she's a bunny tidy ship, too. I was lading her up till midnight; for last night there came an order, and the captain—Captain Jellyby's is his name—he was all flustered and in a taking, and he said we was to finish and lade up, and she was to go out of port sharp at eight this morning. She did, too, sharp to the minute. I seen her weigh anchor. That's her, lady—look out there—level with the horizon—she's a fast going ship and she's making good way. Let me hold you up, lady—now, can you see her now? That's the Experiance."

CHAPTER XXIX

The Esperance was a well-made boat; she was about four thousand tons, with improved engines which went at great speed. She was a trading ship, one of the largest and most important of those belonging to Paget Brothers, but she sometimes took out emigrants, and had room for a few saloon passengers; old travellers, who knew what comfort was, sometimes preferred to go in such ships as the Esperance to the more conventional lines of steamers. There was less crowding, less fuss; there was also more room and more comfort. The meals were good and abundant, and the few passengers, provided they were in any sense of the word congenial spirits, became quickly friends.

Gerald, as one of the members of the firm, was of course accommodated with the very best the Esperance could offer. He had a large state room, well furnished, to himself; he was treated with every possible respect, and even consulted with regard to trivial matters. Only, however, with regard to very trivial matters.

When he arrived at Southampton on the evening of the th, he went at once on board the Esperance.

"We shall sail at noon to-morrow," he said to the captain.

Captain Jellyby was a pleasant old salt, with a genial, open, sunburnt face, and those bright peculiar blue eyes which men who spend most of their lives on the sea often have, as though the reflection of some of its blue had got into them.

"At noon to-morrow," replied the captain. "Yes, and that is somewhat late; but we shan't have finished coaling before."

"But we stop at Plymouth surely?"

"Well, perhaps. I cannot positively say. We may be able to go straight on to Teneriffe."

Gerald did not make any further comments. He retired to his cabin and unpacked one or two things, then he went into the saloon, and taking up a book appeared to be absorbed with its contents.

In reality he was not reading. He had written a desperate letter that morning, and he was upheld even now in this moment of bitterness by a desperate hope.

Suppose Valentine suddenly found her slumbering heart awake? Suppose his words, his wild, weak and foolish words, stung it into action? Suppose the wife cried out for her husband, the awakened heart for its mate. Suppose she threw all prudence to the winds, and came to him? She could reach him in time.

He could not help thinking of this as he sat with his hand shading his eyes, pretending to read in the state saloon of the Esperance, the vessel which was to carry him away to a living death.

If Valentine came, oh yes, if Valentine came, there would be no death. There might be exile, there might be poverty, there might be dishonor, but no death. It would be all life thenlife, and the flush of a stained victory.

He owned to himself that if the temptation came he would take it. If his wife loved him enough to come to him he would tell her all. He would tell her of the cruel promise wrung from him, and ask her if he must keep it.

The hours flew by; he raised his head and looked at the clock. Nine, it was striking nine. He heard a sound on board, and his pulses quickened. It passedit was nothing. The clock struck ten, it was a beautiful starlight night. All the other passengers who had already come on board were amusing themselves on deck.

Gerald was alone in the saloon. Again there was a sound a little different from the constant cries of the sailors.

Captain Jellyby's name was shouted, and there was a rush, followed by renewed activity. Gerald rose slowly, shut his book, and went on deck. It was a dark night although the sky was clear and full of stars. A man in an overcoat and collar turned well up over his ears brushed past Wyndham, made for the gangway and disappeared.

"Good heavenshow like that man was to old Helps," soliloquized Gerald.

He stayed on deck a little longer; he thought his imagination had played him a trick, for what could bring Helps on board the Esperance. Presently the captain joined him.

CHAPTER XXX

"I am sorry, Mr. Wyndham," said Captain Jellyby, "to have to offer you on your very first night on board my good ship very broken slumbers. We shall be lading with coals all night. Are you easily disturbed by noise! But I need scarcely ask, for that noise would almost rouse the dead."

Gerald smiled.

"A broken night is nothing," he said; "at least to me. I suppose there always is a great commotion the last night before a vessel sails on a long voyage."

"Not as a ruleat least that isn't my way. We meant to break off and have a quiet time at midnight, and start operations again at six o'clock in the morning. But I've had directions from head quarters which oblige me to quicken my movements. Doocid inconvenient, too!"

"What do you mean?" said Gerald, the pulses round his heart suddenly quickening. "We sail at noon to-morrow."

"We sail at eight in the morning, my good sir, and I, for one, call it doocid inconvenient. (Yes, Cadgers, what do you want? Get all hands possible on board.) I beg your pardon, Mr. Wyndham. (Yes, Cadgers.) Back with you presently, sir."

The captain disappeared, and Wyndham went down to his cabin.

What did this sudden change mean? Who had given the order? Was that really Helps who had been on board? Well, Wyndham was in a manner master on this vessel. It was his own, part of his property; he had been told over and over again by his father-in-law that on this voyage, this pleasant voyage, he could give his own orders, and short of anything which would jeopardize the safety of the boat, the captain would humor his wishes. He would countermand an order which was putting everybody out; he did not choose to leave his native shore before the time specifiednoon on the following day. In such a short life as his even four hours were of moment. He would not lose the four hours of hope, of the possibility of hope yet left to him.

He went on deck, sought out the captain where he was standing, shouting out hoarse directions to gangs of energetic looking sailors.

"A word with you, Captain Jellyby," he said. "There is some mistake in the order which you have received. I mean that I am in a position to cancel it. I do not wish the Esperance to sail before noon to-morrow."

His voice was very distinct and penetrating, and the sailors stopped work and looked at him. Astonishment was written legibly on their faces.

"Lade away boys, work with a will," said the captain. Then he put his hand on Gerald's shoulder, turned him round, and walked a pace or two away.

"I quite understand your position, Mr. Wyndham," he said. "And in all possible matters I shall yield you due deference. But"

"Yes," said Wyndham.

"But—we sail at eight to-morrow morning, sharp."

"What do you mean? Who has given you the order?"

"I am not prepared to say. My orders are explicit. Another time, when Captain Jellyby can meet the wishes of Mr. Wyndham with a clear conscience, his orders shall also be explicit."

The captain bowed, laid his hand across his heart and turned away.

Wyndham went back to his own cabin, and was tortured all night by a desire, sane or otherwise, he could not tell which, to leave the Esperance and return to London and Valentine.

The lading of the vessel went on ceaselessly, and sharp at eight the following morning she weighed anchor and steamed away. Wyndham had lain awake all night, but at seven in the morning he fell into a doze. The doze deepened into quietness, into peaceful and refreshing slumber: the lines departed from his young face; he had not undressed, but flung himself as he was on his berth. When the Esperance was flying merrily through the water, Captain Jellyby had time to give Wyndham a thought.

"That is a nice lad," he said to himself. "He has a nice face, young too. I don't suppose he has seen five-and-twenty, but he knows what trouble means. My name is not Jack Jellyby if that young man does not know what pretty sharp trouble means. Odd, too, for he's rich and has married the chief's daughter, and what a fuss the chief made about his reception here. No expense to be spared; every comfort given, every attention shown, and his orders to be obeyed within reason. Ay, my pretty lad, there's the rub within reason. You looked keen and vexed enough last night when I had to hasten the hour for the departure of the Esperance. I wonder what the chief meant by that. Well, I'll go and have a look at young Wyndham; he may as well come with me and see the last of his native shore. As the morning is fine it will be a pretty sight."

The captain went and begged for admission to Wyndham's cabin. There was no answer, so he opened the door and poked his red smiling face round.

"Bless me, the boy's asleep," he said; and he came up and took a good look at his new passenger.

Gerald was dreaming now, and a smile played about his lips. Suddenly he opened his eyes and said:

"Yes, Valentine, yes, I'm coming!" and sprang to his feet.

The captain was standing with his legs a little apart, looking at him. The vessel gave a lurch, and Wyndham staggered.

"Are we off?" he said. "Good God, are we really off?"

"We were off an hour ago, young sir. Come up on deck and see what a pretty coast line we have just here."

Wyndham put his hand to his forehead.

"I have been cheated," he said suddenly. "Yes. I've been cheated. I can't speak about it; things weren't clear to me last night, but I had a dream, and I know now what it all means. I woke with some words on my lips. What did I say, captain?"

"You called to some fellow of the name of Valentine your brother, perhaps."

"I haven't a brother. The person to whom I called was a woman my wife. She was coming on board. She would have sailed with me if we had waited. Now it is too late."

The captain raised his shaggy brows the tenth of an inch.

"They must be sending him on this voyage on account of his health," he mentally soliloquized. "Now I see daylight. A little touched, poor fellow. Pity nice fellow. Well, the chief might have trusted me. Of course I must humor him, poor lad. Come on deck," he said aloud. "It's beastly close down here. You should have the porthole open, the sea is like glass. Come on deck and get a breath of fresh air. Isn't Valentine a rather uncommon name for a woman? Yes, of course, I heard you were married. Well, well, you'll be home again in six months. Now come on deck and look around you."

"Look here, captain," said Gerald suddenly. "I can't explain matters. I daresay you think me queer, but you're mistaken."

"They all go on that tack," muttered the captain. "Another symptom. Well, I must humor him. I don't think you queer," he said, aloud. "You're finely mistaken. You had a dream, and you called on your wife, whom you have just parted from. What more natural? Bless you. I know all about it. I was married myself."

"And you left your wife?"

"I left her, and what is worse she left me. She went up to the angels. Bless her memory, she was a young thing. I see her yet, as she bade me good-bye. Come on deck, lad."

"Yes; come on deck," said Gerald hoarsely.

All that day he was silent, sitting mostly apart and by himself.

But the captain had his eye on him. In the evening he came again to Captain Jellyby.

"You touch at Plymouth, don't you?"

"Sometimes."

"This voyage, I mean."

"No."

"I wish you to stop at Plymouth."

"Look here, my lad. 'No' is the only word I can give you. We don't touch land till we get to Teneriffe. Go and lie down and have a sleep. We shall have a calm sea to-night, and you look fagged out."

"Are you a man to be bribed?" began Wyndham.

"I am ashamed of you. I am not."

The captain turned his back on him. Wyndham caught him by his shoulder.

"Are you a man to be moved to pity?"

"Look here, my lad, I can pity to any extent; but if you think any amount of compassion will turn me from my duty, you're in the wrong box. It's my duty, clear as the sky above, to go straight on to Teneriffe, and on I shall go. You understand?"

"Yes," said Gerald, "I understand. Thank you, captain. I won't bother you further."

His voice had altered, his brow had cleared. He walked away to the further end of the deck, whistling a light air. The captain saw him stop to pay some small attention to a lady passenger.

"Bless me, if I understand the fellow!" he muttered.

CHAPTER XXXI

When a die has been castcast irrevocablyas a rule there follows a calm. It is sometimes the calm of peace, sometimes that of despair; but there is always a stillness, effort is over, words don't avail, actions are paralyzed.

Gerald Wyndham sat on deck most of that evening. There was a married lady, a certain Mrs. Harvey, on board, she was going to Australia with her husband and one little girl. She was about thirty, and very delicate. Gerald's face took her fancy, and they struck up an acquaintance.

The evening was so calm, so mild, the water so still, the sky above so clear that the passengers brought wraps and lingered long on deck. Mrs. Harvey talked all the time to Gerald. He answered her not only politely but with interest. She was an interesting woman, she could talk well, she had great sympathy, and she wanted to draw Wyndham out. In this she failed, although she imagined she succeeded. He learned much of her history, for she was very communicative, but when she joined her husband downstairs later that evening she could not tell him a single thing about their fellow-passenger.

"He has a nice face," they both remarked, and they wondered who he was.

It did not occur to them to speak of him as sad-looking. On the contrary, Mrs. Harvey spoke of his cheerful smile and of his strong appreciation of humor.

"It is delightful to meet a man who can see a joke," she said. "Most of them are so dense."

"I wonder which family of Wyndhams he belongs to," remarked the husband.

"I wonder if he is married," added the wife.

Then they both resolved that they would find out to-morrow. But they did not, for the next day Wyndham did not come on deck at all. He stayed in his own cabin, and had one or two interviews with the captain.

"You know very little about me, Captain Jellyby," he said, once.

"I know that you are married to Miss Paget," replied the captain, "and I am given to understand that she is a very charming young lady."

"I want you to keep the fact of my marriage to yourself."

The captain looked a little surprised.

"Certainly, if you wish it," he said.

"I do wish it. I am knocked over to-day, for the fact is. II have gone through some trouble, but I don't mean to inflict my troubles on you or my fellow-passengers. I hope I shall prove an acquisition rather than otherwise on board the Esperance. But what I do not want, what would be particularly repellant to me, is that the other saloon passengers should gossip about me. When they find that I don't talk about myself, or my people, or my wife, they will become curious, and ply you with questions. Will you be mum on the subject?"

"Mum as the grave," said the captain rising and stretching himself. "Lord, we'll have some fun over this. If there are a deadly curious, gossiping, wrangling, hole-picking set in this wide world, it's the saloon passengers on board a boat of this kind. I'll make up a beautiful mystery about you, my fine fellow. Won't they enjoy it! Why, it will be the saving of them."

"Make up any mystery you like," replied Wyndham, "only don't tell them the truth. That is, I mean, what you know of the truth."

"And that's nothing," muttered the captain to himself as he went away. "Bless me, he is a queer fellow. Touchedhe must be touched."

Gerald spent twenty-four hours in God only knows what deep waters of mental agony. The other passengers thought he was suffering from an attack of sea-sickness, for they were just now meeting the heavy channel sea, and the captain did not undeceive them. They passed Plymouth before Gerald again appeared on deck, and when he once more joined his fellow-passengers they were outside the Bay of Biscay.

Gerald had not suffered from any bodily discomfort, but others on board the Esperance were less fortunate, and when he once more took his place in the saloon, and went up on deck, he found that work, which all his life long seemed to fall to his share, once more waiting for him. It was the work of making other people comfortable. The Harveys' little girl was very weak and fretful. She had gone through a bad time, but when Wyndham lifted her in his arms, sat down with her in a sheltered part of the deck, and told her some funny fairy tales, his influence worked like the wand of a good magician. She smiled, told Mr. Wyndham he was a very nice man, gave him a kiss, and ran downstairs presently to eat her supper with appetite.

Little Cecily Harvey was not the only person who came under Wyndham's soothing influence. During this first evening he found himself more or less in the position of a sort of general sick-nurse. But the next day people were better, and then he appeared in another rôle. He could entertain, with stories, with music, with song. He could recite; above all things he could organize, and had a knack of showing off other people to the best advantage. Long before a week had passed, Wyndham was the most popular person on board. He was not only popular with saloon passengers, but with the emigrants. There were several on board, and he often spent some hours with them, playing with the children, and talking with the mothers, or, rather, getting the mothers to talk to him.

They were flying south now, and every day the air grew more balmy and the sea smoother. The emigrants, boys and girls, fathers and mothers, used to lie out on the deck in the sun, and a very pretty picture they made; the children rolling about laughing and playing, and the mothers, most of them were young mothers, looking on and regarding them with pride.

There was scarcely an emigrant mother on board that ship who had not confided her story, her hopes and her fears to Wyndham, before the voyage was over.

Soon that thing happened which had happened long ago at Jewsbury-on-the-Wold, which had happened in the small house in Park-lane, which had happened even with the odds against him to his wifeeverybody loved Wyndham. Hearts warmed as he came near, eyes brightened when they looked at him. He was in the position of a universal favorite. That sometimes is a dangerous position. But not in his case, for he was too unselfish to make enemies.

All this time, while his life was apparently drifting, while the hours were apparently gliding on to no definite or especial goal, to a landing at Melbourneto a journey across a new Continentwhile his days were going by to all intents and purposes like anybody else's days, he knew that between him and them lay an immeasurable gulf. He knew that he was not drifting, but going very rapidly down a hill. The fact is, Wyndham knew that the end, as far as he was concerned, was near.

His father-in-law had planned one thing, but he had planned another. He told no one of this, he never whispered this to a living creature, but his own mind was inexorably made up. He knew it when he bade his father good-bye that last Sunday; when he looked at Lilias and Marjory, and the other children, he knew it; he knew it when he kissed his wife's cheek that last morning when she slept. In his own way he could be a man of iron will. His will was as iron in this special matter. Only once had his determination been shaken, and that was when he pleaded with Valentine, and when he hoped against hope that she would listen to his prayer. The last lingering sparks of that hope died away when the captain refused to touch at Plymouth. After that moment his own fixed will never wavered.

His father-in-law had asked him for half a death; he should have a whole one. That was all. Many another man had done what he meant to do before. Still it was the End—the great End. No one could go beyond it.

He made his plans very carefully; he knew to effect his object he must be extremely careful. He would die, but it must never be supposed, never breathed by mortal soul that he had passed out of this world except by accident. He knew perfectly what the captain thought of him during the first couple of days of his residence on board the Esperance.

"Captain Jellyby is positive that I am touched in the head," thought Wyndham. "I must undo that suspicion."

He took pains, and he succeeded admirably. Wyndham was not only a favorite on board, but he was cheerful, he was gay. People remarked not on his high but on his good spirits.

"Such a merry, light-hearted fellow," they said of him.

Wyndham overheard these remarks now and then. The captain openly delighted in him.

"The ship will never be lucky again when you leave her," he said. "You're worth a free passage to any captain. Why you keep us all in good humor. Passengers, emigrants, sailors and all. Here, come along. I thought you rather a gloomy young chap when first I set eyes on you; but now—ah, well, you were homesick. Quite accountable. Here, I have a request from the second mate, and one or two more of the jack tars down there. They want you to sing them a song after supper. They say it isn't fair that we should have you to ourselves in the saloon."

Gerald laughed, said he would be happy to oblige the sailors, and walked away.

"As jolly a chap as ever I laid eyes on," muttered the captain. "I liked him from the first, but I was mistaken in him. I thought him gloomy. Not a bit. I wonder his wife could bear to let him out of her sight. I wouldn't if I were a lass. There, hark to him now! Bless me, we are having a pleasant voyage this time."

So they were. No one was ill; the amount of rough weather was decidedly below the average, and cheerfulness and contentment reigned on board.

The ship touched at Teneriffe, but only for a few hours, and then sped on her way to the Cape. It was now getting very hot, and an awning was spread over the deck. Under this the saloon passengers sat, and smoked and read. No one suspected, no one had the faintest shadow of a suspicion that black care lurked anywhere on board that happy ship, least of all in the breast of the merriest of its crew. Gerald Wyndham.

The Esperance reached the Cape in safety, there some of the passengers, Gerald amongst them, landed, for the captain intended to lie at anchor for twenty-four hours. Then again they were away, and now they were told they must expect colder weather for they were entering the Southern Ocean, and were approaching high latitudes of polar cold. They would have to go through the rough sea of the "Roaring Forties," and then again they would emerge into tropical sunshine.

Soon after they left the Cape, little Cecily Harvey fell ill. She caught a chill and was feverish, and the doctor and her mother forbade her to go on deck. She was only eight years old, a pretty, winsome child. Gerald felt a special tenderness for her, for she reminded him of his own little sister Joan. During this illness she often lay for hours in his arms, with her little feverish cheek pressed against his, and her tiny hot hand comforted by his firm cool clasp.

"Mr. Wyndham," she said on one of these occasions. "I wish you wouldn't do it."

"Do what, Cecily?"

"Run up the rigging as you do. I heard one of the sailors talking to Mrs. Meyrich the other day, and he said you were too daring, and some day you'd have a slip, and be overboard, if you did not look sharp."

"Oh, I'll take care of myself, Cecily. At one time I thought of being a sailor, and I was always climbing, always climbing at home. There isn't the least fear. I'm not rash. I'm a very careful fellow."

"Are you? I'm glad of that. Had you tall trees at your home?"

Gerald gave the little hand a squeeze.

"They were like other trees," he said. "Don't let us talk of them."

"Mustn't we? I'm sorry. I wanted to hear all about your home."

"I haven't a home, Cecily. Once I had one, but you can understand that it is painful to speak of what one has lost."

"I'm very sorry for you, dear Mr. Wyndham. Did you lose a little sister, too? Is that why you squeeze me so tight?"

"I have lost many little sisters; we won't talk of them, either. What is the matter, Cecily? Do you feel faint?"

"No, but I hate this rough, choppy sea. I want it to be smooth again as it used to be. Then I can go on deck, and lie under the awning, and you can sit near me, and tell me stories. Will you?"

Gerald did not answer.

"Will you, Mr. Wyndham?"

"I can lie to everyone else but not to the child," muttered Gerald.

He roused himself, and sought to divert her attention.

"We are in the 'Roaring Forties' now," he said. "Isn't that a funny name? The sea is always very choppy and rough here, but it won't last long. You will soon be in pleasant weather and smooth seas again."

Cecily was not satisfied, and Gerald presently left her and went on deck.

The weather was not pleasant just now, it was cold and squally, always veering about and causing a choppy and disagreeable motion with the ship. Some of the ladies took again to their beds, and went through another spell of sea-sickness; the more fortunate ones sat and chatted in the great saloon—not one of them ventured on deck. Gerald, who was not in the least indisposed in body, found plenty to do in his rôle of general cheerer and comforter. When he was not nursing little Cecily he spent some time with the emigrants, amongst whom he was a great favorite.

On this particular day a round-faced young woman of five and twenty, a certain Mrs. Notley, came up to him the moment he appeared on the lower deck.

"They do say it, sir, and I thought I'd speak to you, so that you wouldn't mind. They do say you're over rash in helping the sailors—over rash, and none so sure-footed as you think yourself."

"Folly," said Gerald, laughing good-humoredly. "So I can't run up a rope or tighten a rigging without people imagining that I am putting my precious life in jeopardy. Don't you listen to any foolish tales, Mrs. Notley. I'm a great deal too fond of myself to run any risks. I shan't slip, if that's what you mean—for that matter I have always been climbing, since I was a little chap no bigger than that urchin of yours there."

"Ay, sir, that's all very well, but it's different for all that on board ship; there may come a lurch when you least look for it, and then the surest-footed and the surest-handed is sometimes outwitted. You'll excuse my mentioning of it, sir, but you're a bonny young gentleman, and you has the goodwill of everyone on board."

"Thank you, Mrs. Notley, I like to hear you say so. It is pleasant to be liked."

"Ah, sure you are that, and no mistake, and you'll forgive me mentioning it, sir, but you'll be careful, won't you? You ain't married for sure, for your face is too lightsome for that of a married man. But maybe you has a mother and a sweetheart, and you might think of them, sir, and not be over daring."

Wyndham's face grew suddenly white.

"As it happens I have neither a mother nor sweetheart," he said. Then he turned away somewhat abruptly, and Mrs. Notley feared she had offended him.

The sailors prophesied "dirty weather;" they expected it, for this was the roughest part of the voyage. Gerald was very fond of talking to the sailors and getting their opinions. He strolled over to where a group of them were standing now, and they pointed to some ugly looking clouds, and told him that the storm would be on them by night.

Nothing very bad, or to be alarmed at, they said, still a rough and nasty sea, with a bit of a gale blowing. The women and children wouldn't like it, poor things, and it would be a dark night too, no moon.

Gerald asked a few more questions.

"I have a great anxiety to see a storm," he said. "If it gets really stormy, I'll come up; I can shelter beside the man at the wheel."

"Better not, sir," one or two said. "The vessel is sure to lurch over a good bit, and it takes more sea-weather legs than yours to keep their footing at such a time."

"All the same," remarked a burly-looking sailor, who was to take his place at the wheel for some hours that night, and thought Gerald's company would be a decided acquisition, "I could put the gent into a corner where he'd be safe enough round here, and it's something to see a gale in these parts—something to live for—not that there'll be much to-night, only a bit of a dirty sea; but still—"

"Expect me, Loggan, if it does come," said Wyndham. He laughed and turned away. He walked slowly along the upper deck. Captain Jellyby came up and had a word with him.

"Yes, we're in for a dirty night," he remarked.

Then Wyndham went downstairs. He chatted for a little with the ladies in the saloon. Then he went into his own cabin. He shut the door. The time had arrived—the hour had come.

He felt wonderfully calm and quiet; he was not excited, nor did his conscience smite him with a sense of any special wrong-doing. Right or wrong he was going to do something on which no blessing could be asked, over which no prayer could be uttered. He had been brought up in a house where prayers had been many; he had whispered his own baby prayers to his mother when he was a little child. Well, well, he would not think of these things now. The hour was come, the moment for action was ripe. There was a little daylight, and during that time he meant to occupy himself with one last task; he would write a letter to his wife, a cheerful, bright everyday letter, to the wife for whose sake he was about to rush unbidden into the arms of death. He had a part to act, and this letter was in the programme. To make all things safe and above suspicion he must write it, and leave it carelessly on his table, so that the next ship they touched should convey it to her.

He took out a sheet of foreign notepaper, and wrote steadily. His hand did not shake, he covered the whole sheet of paper; his words were bright, contented; no shadow of gloom touched them. They were full of anticipation, of pleasure in the moment—of pleasure in the coming reunion.

The writing of this letter was the very hardest task of the man's whole life. When it was over great drops of sweat stood on his forehead. He read it steadily, from beginning to end, however, and his only fear was that it was too bright, and that she might see through it, as in a mirror, the anguish beneath.

The letter was written, and now Wyndham had nothing to do. He had but to sit with his hands before him, and wait for the gathering darkness and the ever-increasing gale.

He sat for nearly an hour in his own cabin, he was past any consecutive thought now; still, so great was the constraint he was able to put over himself that outwardly he was quite calm. Presently he went into the saloon. Cecily Harvey alone was there, all the ladies having gone in to dinner. She sprang up with a cry of delight when she saw Gerald.

"Mr. Wyndham, have you come to stay with me? Why aren't you at dinner? How white you look."

"I am not hungry, Cecily. I thought you would be alone, and I came out to see you. I wanted you to give me a kiss."

"Of course I will—of course I will," said the affectionate child, throwing her arms around his neck.

"You remind me of one of the little sisters I have lost," he said hurriedly. "Thank you, Cecily, thank you. Be a good child, always. I would say 'God bless you' if I dared."

"Why don't you dare? You are a good man, a very good man, the best I know."

"Hush, Cecily, you don't know what you are talking about. Give me another kiss. Thank you sweet little girl."

He went back again to his own cabin. The longing for compassion at this crucial moment had made him run a risk in talking so to Cecily. He blamed himself, but scarcely regretted the act.

It was certainly going to be a dirty night, and already the sailors were busy overhead. The good ship creaked and strained as she to fought her way through the waters. The ladies loudly expressed their uneasiness, and the gentleman-passengers fought down some qualms which they considered unmanly.

Wyndham rose from his seat in the dark, pressed his lips to the letter he had written to his wife, suddenly he started, reeled a step and fell back.

There is no accounting for what happened—but happen it did.

Valentine herself stood beside him, stretched out her arms to him, uttered a brief cry, and then vanished.

He felt like a madman; he pressed his hands to his head and rushed on deck.

"Stand there, Mr. Wyndham, there," said the sailor Loggan. "You'll be safe enough. Oh, yes, more than one wave will wash us. Shall I lash you to the wheel, sir? Maybe it would be safer."

"No, no, thank you."

The voice was quite quiet and calm again.

Certainly the night was a rough one, but between and under the loud voice of the storm, Loggan and his companion exchanged some cheerful phrases.

"No, sir, I ain't never afeared."

"What if you were to go to the bottom?"

"The will of the good God be done, sir. I'd go a-doing of my duty."

"You're an honest fellow, Loggan; shake hands with me."

"That I will, Mr. Wyndham. What are you doing with that rope, sir? It's cold, it's slippery—oh, the knot has got loose, I'll call a man to tighten it, sir; let me—let me. You'll be over, sir, if you don't look out; we're going to lunge this way. Take care, sir—take care—for God's sake, take care!"

Wyndham took care.

CHAPTER XXXII

The summer came early that year. The rectory was a charming place in the summer, and on this particular bright day in June one of the numerous school-feasts was in course of preparation, and all the young Wyndhams were working with a will and energy which could scarcely be surpassed. The feast was in full progress; the village children consumed tea and buns, as only village children can. Augusta was refusing to help the babies to any more; Joan and Betty were half-crying because she snatched the rich currant buns out of their hands; Marjory was leading the most obstreporous members of her flock away to the other end of the long meadow, where they could play orange and lemons, nuts in May, and other festive games; and Lilias, as she helped to pack away the remnants of the feast, was answering some questions of Carr's.

"We ought to have heard by now," she was saying. "My father is a little uneasy, but I am not—at least, of course, I am anxious for Valentine. The suspense must be very trying for her!"

"When did your brother's ship sail?"

"On the th of March."

"And this is the th of June. The Esperance must have been reported at Lloyd's long ago."

"How stupid of me never to think of that," said Lilias, her face brightening. "But would they not put the arrivals in the papers? I have certainly looked and never seen it."

"You have probably overlooked it. I will write and inquire for you. The Esperance, even allowing for delays, has probably reached its destination some weeks ago. On the other hand it would be scarcely possible for you to have had a letter from your brother. Yes, you are right not to be anxious; I will go and have a chat with your father presently. Is Mrs. Wyndham well?"

"I think so—fairly well. She is coming to stay with us next week."

Carr strolled away.

"What a nice comfortable young man he is turning into," said Marjory, who came up at that moment. "Ah, yes, your face is brighter already for having had an interview with him. Whisper no secrets to me. I know—I know."

Lilias' clear brown skin was transfused with color.

"Don't be silly, Marjory," she said. "I don't mind owning that Mr. Carr is a comfortable person to talk to. He has just been removing my fears about Gerald."

"Oh, I thought you had no fears."

"Well, father's fears, then. He has been saying things to me which will remove my father's fears completely."

"That is right—Heaven be praised. You and the rector are nothing but a pair of old croaks lately. Hey-ho! I am perfectly weary of your long faces and your apprehensions. Thank goodness. Val is coming; she'll wake us up a little."

Lilias opened her dark eyes.

"I did not know you cared so much for Valentine," she said.

"I admired her very much the last time I saw her. That was a month ago—she seemed so spirited and courageous. I used to think her something of a doll, but she's a woman now, and a fine one. Perhaps it's the thought of the baby coming."

"Or perhaps," said Lilias, "she has found out at last what our Gerald is."

"Both, most likely," said Marjory. "Anyhow, she's changed; and the funniest part is that that old man—"

"What old man, Marjory?"

"Don't interrupt me—her father. I always call him that old man—well, I think he's afraid of her. She doesn't pet him the way she used, but she's very gentle with him. Oh, she's a good bit altered; there's something in her now."

"I suppose there was always something in her," said Lilias. "For Gerald"—her lips trembled—"gave up so much for her."

"No more than any man gives up for any woman," said Marjory. "A man shall leave his father and mother. Oh, yes, poor old Lil, I know how you felt it. You always made an idol of Gerald. I suppose you'll marry some day; you are so pretty—and h'm—h'm—there's somebody waiting for somebody—there, I don't want to tease, only when you do marry, my pretty sister, I wonder if he'll come inside Gerald in your heart."

"I won't marry until I love some one even better than my only brother," replied Lilias in a grave voice. "That time has not come yet," she added, and then she turned away.

The games went on as fast as ever; Marjory romped with the merriest. Lilias was graver than her sister, not so fond of pastimes, perhaps not quite so generally popular. She went into the house, sat down by the organ in the hall and began to play. She had almost as much talent as Gerald; her fingers wandered over the keys, she was in a dreamy mood, and her thoughts were carrying her back to a bygone sceneto Gerald's face on that Sunday night. She heard again the rich tones of his voice, and heard his words:

"Till in the ocean of Thy love
We loose ourselves in Heaven above."

"Oh, Gerald," she said with a kind of sob, "things have been hard for me since you went away. It was not your marriage alone, I had prepared myself for that; but it was moreit was more. The Church of Godyou gave that up. Yes, yes. There has been a shut door between us. Gerald, since you and Valentine first met; and where are you nowwhere are you now?"

"Lilias," said little Joan running in breathlessly, "father wants you in his study, quickly. I don't think he's quite well. He has just had a letter, and he looks so queer."

"I'll go to him at once," said Lilias.

She could be apprehensive enough, but in real danger, in times of real anxiety, her head could be cool and her steps firm.

"Yes, father," she said, motioning the frightened little Joan away.

She shut the library door behind her.

"Yes, father. What is it? Jo says that you have got a letter, and that you want me."

"Oh, I don't suppose it's anything," said the rector. "That is, I don't mean to be uneasy. Here's the letter. Lilias. You ought to read it, perhaps. It's from Paget. He is evidently nervous himself, but I don't suppose there is any need. Read it, and tell me what you think."

The rector thrust a sheet of paper into his daughter's hand. Then went over to one of his book shelves and pretended to be busy rummaging up some folios. Lilias read as follows:

My Dear Sir,I write on a subject of some little anxiety. I did not wish to trouble you before it was necessary, but now I confess that weI refer to my house of businesshave cause to feel uneasiness with regard to the fate of the Esperance. She is quite a month overdue at Sydney; even allowing for all possible delays, she is at least that time overdue. The last tidings of her were from the Cape, and it is feared from their date that she must have encountered rough weather in the Southern Ocean. Nothing is known, however, and every hour we look for a cable announcing her arrival at Melbourne if not at Sydney. It is possible she may have been injured, which will account for the delay, but I scarcely apprehend anything worse. I ought scarcely to say that I am anxious; up to the present there is no real cause to apprehend anything worse than an accident to the vessel. Vessels are often a month behind their time, and all is satisfactorily explained at the end. I am now troubling you with regard to another matter. I do not want my daughter and your son's wife to be needlessly alarmed. It is most important that her mind should be kept free from apprehension until after the birth of their child. You kindly asked her to go to see you. Can you have her at the rectory at once? And will you send Lilias to fetch her? I know you and yours will keep all fears from her, and, poor child, she reads my face like a book.

Yours faithfully,

"Mortimer Paget."

"Well, Lilias," said the rector. "Well? He's a little over nervous, isn't he, eh? Vessels are often a month overdue. Eh, Lilias? But of course they are. Somehow I'm not nervous since I got that letter. I was before, but not now."

He rubbed his hands together as he spoke.

"It's summer now, and we'll have Gerald back before the next snow comes. I told the boy so when he bid me good-bye; he was a bit upset that night after you girls went to bed. Poor fellow, I had quite to cheer him; he's a very affectionate lad. No, I'm not nervous, and I wonder at Paget. But what do you think, Lilias?"

Lilias folded up the letter, and put it back in her old father's hand. Then she stole her arm round his neck, and kissed him.

"We will be brave," she said. "If we have fears we won't speak of them; we have got to think of Valentine now, not of ourselves."

The rector almost shook Lilias' hand from his neck.

"Fears," he said, in a light and cheerful voice, a voice which was belied by his tremulous hands, and by his almost petulant movement. "Fears! my dear girl, they really don't exist. At this moment, were we clairvoyant, we should see Gerald either rising leisurely from a good night's rest, or sitting down to his breakfast in one of those luxurious houses one reads of in Froude's 'Oceana.' Vessels like the Esperance don't go to the bottom. Now, Lil, at what hour will you go to fetch Valentine? You will go up to town to-morrow, of course."

"By the first train," replied Lilias. Her lips quivered. She turned away; there was nothing more to be said. Her father's manner did not in the least deceive her.

"Dear old man!" she said to herself. "If he can be brave, so will I. But oh, Gerald, does any heart ache more for you than the heart of your sister Lilias?"

CHAPTER XXXIII

Valentine had got a blow. The first real great blow which had ever been dealt to her. It had a most curious effect. Instead of stunning or rendering her weak and incapable, it suddenly changed her from a child into a practical and clever and wide-awake woman. The very quality of her voice changed. It became full, and inspired respect the moment she spoke. She was quite aware that her father had deceived her, that he did not mean her to accompany Gerald to Sydney.

She said nothing about this knowledgenot even that evening when she got home and found her father looking ten years older, but standing on the step of her own little home waiting for her.

"I was too late," she said, quietly. "The Esperance sailed four hours before its time. I must do without Gerald for six months; in six months he will be home."

"In six months," echoed Mr. Paget, following her upstairs to the drawing-room. "Kiss me, my darling," he said. "Valentine, you will come back to your own home to-morrow."

Valentine raised her cheek to meet her father's lips.

"I think I would rather remain here," she said. "This, after all, is my only real home; you don't mind my keeping the house, do you, father?"

"No, my dear, if you wish it. Only I thought" His last words came out almost tremulously.

"Sometimes we are mistaken in our thoughts," responded Valentine. "I should like best to stay on in my husband's house. Six months will not be long passing; andfather. I have some news for you. In Julyif I live until JulyGod is going to give me a childGerald's child and mine. I should like it to be born here."

"Thank God," exclaimed Mr. Paget. "I am very glad of this, Valentine," he said. "Thisthisis an inestimable mercy. I hope your child will be a son. My dear daughter, this news lifts a great weight off my mind."

He looked what he felt, delighted.

"Of course you must live wherever you like best," he said. "Julythis is Marchthe child's father will be" but he did not finish this sentence.

He went away soon afterwards. Ten years had been added to his life in that one single day.

He knew, one glance into Valentine's eyes told him, that she no longer believed in him. What was any success with the heart of his darling turned aside?

He walked home feeling tottering and feeble; he had had a blow, but also a strong consolation—his daughter's child—his grandson. Of course the child should be a boy. There was something to live for in such news as this. A boy to step into his shoes by-and-by—to keep up the credit of the old house; a boy who should have no shame on him, and no dark history. Yes, yes, this was very good news, and unlooked for; he had much to live for yet.

After this Mr. Paget followed his daughter about like a shadow. Every day her mind and her powers were developing in fresh directions. She had certainly lost some of the charm of her childish ways, but her gain had been greater than her loss. Her face had always been spirituelle, the expression sprightly, the eyes under their arched brows full of light. People had spoken of the girlish face as beautiful, but now that it belonged to a grave and patient, in some respects a suffering woman, they found that it possessed more than ordinary loveliness. The soul had come back again into Valentine's eyes. She knew two things. She was loved—her husband told her that no woman had ever been loved so well before. She was also to become a mother. She considered herself, notwithstanding her crosses, blessed among women, and she resolved to live worthily.

Patience and faith both were hers, and whenever she felt inclined to rebel, to fret, to fume, she thought of the day when she should show her baby to her husband, and tell him face to face that all her heart, all her best affections were divided between him and their child.

She kept to her resolution of living on in the little house in Park-Lane. She led a busy life, interesting herself a good deal in the anxieties and cares of others. When a woman takes up that rôle she always finds abundance to do, for there are few pairs of shoulders that have not a burden to carry. She also wrote by every mail to her husband. She had already received one letter from him, posted at Teneriffe. This letter was affectionate—cheerful. Valentine read it over and over. It was a very nice letter, but its words did not reach down into her heart as that other letter of Gerald's, written before he sailed, had done. She was puzzled by it. Still she owned to herself that it was just the letter she ought to receive, just the pleasant happy words of a man who was leading a busy and useful life; who was going away for a definite object, and hoped soon to return to his wife and his home.

All went well with Valentine until a certain day. She rose as usual on the morning of that day, went down to breakfast, opened one or two letters, attended to a couple of domestic matters, and went slowly back to the drawing-room. She liked to dust and tidy her little drawing-room herself. She had put it in order this morning, had arranged fresh flowers in the vases, and was finally giving one or two fresh touches to Gerald's violin, which she always kept near her own piano, when she was startled by the consciousness that she was not alone.

She raised her head, turned quickly, a cold air seemed to blow on her face.

"Valentine!" said her husbands voice, in a tone of unspeakable agony.

She fancied she even saw his shadowy outline. She stretched out her arms to himhe faded away.

That afternoon Mrs. Wyndham paid her father a visit in the City. She was shown into his private room by Helps, who eyed her from head to foot with great anxiety.

Mr. Paget looked into her face and grew perceptibly paler. He was certainly nervous in these daysnervous, and very much aged in appearance.

"Is anything wrong, Valentine?" he could not help saying to his daughter. It was the last sentence he wished to pass his lipshe bit them with vexation after the words had escaped them.

"Sit down, my dear; have you come to take me for a drive, likelikeold times?"

"I have not, father. I have come to know when you expect to hear tidings of the arrival of the Esperance at Sydney."

"Not yet, Valentine. Impossible so soon. In any case we shall have a cable from Melbourne firstthe vessel will touch there."

"When are you likely to hear from Melbourne?"

"Not for some days yet."

"But you know the probable time. Can you not ascertain it? Will you hear in ten days? In a week? In three days?"

"You are persistent, Valentine."

Mr. Paget raised his eyes and looked at her from head to foot.

"I will ascertain," he said in an almost cold voice, as he sounded an electric bell by his side.

Helps answered the summons.

"Helps, when is the Esperance due at Melbourne?"

Again Helps glanced quickly at Mrs. Wyndham; he was standing rather behind her, but could catch a glimpse of her face.

"By the end of May," he said, speaking slowly. His quick eyes sought his chief's; they took their cue. "Not sooner," he continued. "Possibly by the end of May."

"Thank you," said Valentine.

The man withdrew.

"I have nearly a month to wait," she said, rising and looking at her father. "I did not know that the voyage would be such a lengthy one. When you do hear the news will be bad, father; yes, the news will be bad. I have nothing to say about it, no explanation to offer, only I know."

Before Mr. Paget could make a single reply, Valentine had left him. He was decidedly alarmed about her.

"Can she be going out of her mind?" he soliloquized. "Women sometimes do before the birth of their children. What did she mean? It is impossible for her to know anything. Pshaw! What is there to know? I verily believe I am cultivating that abomination of the agenerves!"

Whatever Valentine did mean, she met her father that evening as if nothing had happened. She was bright, even cheerful; she played and sang for him. He concluded that she was not out of her mind, that she had simply had a fit of the dismals, and dismissed the matter.

The month passed by, slowly for Valentine—very slowly, also, for her father. It passed into space, and there was no news of the Esperance. More days went by, no news, no tidings of any sort. Valentine thought the vessel was a fortnight overdue. Her father knew that it was at least a month behind its time. When he wrote his letter to the rector of Jewsbury-on-the-Wold he felt even more anxious than his words seemed to admit.

The day after the receipt of this letter Lilias came to town and took Valentine home with her. The next morning Mr. Paget went as usual to his office. His first inquiry was for news of the Esperance. The invariable answer awaited him.

"No tidings as yet."

He went into the snug inner room where he lunched, where Valentine's picture hung, and where he had made terms with Gerald Wyndham. He sank down into an easy-chair, and covered his face with his hands.

"Would to God this suspense were at an end," he said.

The words had scarcely passed his lips when Helps knocked for admission at the inner door, he opened it, caught a glimpse of his servant's face, and fell back.

"You heard," he said. "Come in and tell me quick. The Esperance is lost, and every soul on board—"

"Hush, sir," said Helps. "There's no news of the Esperance. Command yourself, sir. It isn't that—it's the other thing. The young gentleman from India, he's outside—he wants to see you."

"Good God, Helps. Positively I'm faint. Shut the door for a moment; he has come, then. You are sure?"

"This is his card, sir. Mr. George Carmichael."

"Give me a moment's time, Helps. So he has come. It would have been all right but for this confounded uncertainty with regard to the Esperance. But it is all right, of course. Plans such as mine don't fail, they are too carefully made. All the same, I am shaken, Helps. Helps, I am growing into an old man."

"You do look queer, Mr. Paget; have a little brandy, sir; you'd better."

"Thank you; a little, then. Open that cupboard, you will find the flask. Brandy steadies the nerves. Now I am better. Helps, it was in this room I made terms with young Wyndham."

"God forgive you, sir, it was."

"Why do you say that? You did not disapprove at the time."

"I didn't know Mr. Wyndham, sir; had I known, I wouldn't have allowed breathing man to harm a hair of his head."

"How would you have prevented it?"

"How?"

The old clerk's face took an ugly look.

"Split on you, and gone to prison, of course," he said. "Now, shall I send Mr. George Carmichael in? It was for his sake you did it. My God, what a sin you sinned! I see Mr. Wyndham's face every night of my life. Good God, why should men like him be hurled out of the world because of sinners like you and me?"

"He's not hurled out of the world," exclaimed Mr. Paget.

He rose and swore a great oath. Then he said in a quieter voice:

"Ask Mr. Carmichael to step into my office."

"Into this room, sir?"

"Into this room. Go, fool."

Certainly Mr. Paget had some admirable qualities. By the time a pale-faced, slight, languid-looking man made his appearance, he was perfectly calm and self-possessed. He spoke in a courteous tone to his visitor, and bade him be seated.

They exchanged a few common-places. Then Mr. George Carmichael, who showed far more uneasiness than his host, explained the motive of his visit.

"You knew my father," he said. "Owing to a strange circumstance, which perhaps you are aware of, but which scarcely concerns the object of this call, certain papers of importance did not come into my hands until I was of age. These are the papers."

He placed two yellow documents on the table.

"I find by these that I am entitled to money which you hold in trust."

"You are," said Mr. Paget, with a kindly smile.

"I am puzzled to know why I was never made aware of the fact. I was brought up as a poor man. I had no expectations. I have not been educated to meet the position which in reality awaited me. Somebody has done me a wrong."

"I assure you not me, Mr. Carmichael. Perhaps, however, I can throw some light on the subject. If you will do me the favor of dining with me some evening we can talk the matter over at our leisure."

"Thank you, I have very little leisure."

The stranger was wonderfully restless.

"After a struggle I have succeeded in obtaining a good post in Calcutta. I hurried over to see you. I must hurry back to my work. Oh, yes, thanks, I like India. The main point is, when can you hand me over my money. With interest it amounts to"

"Including interest it amounts to eighty thousand pounds, Mr. Carmichael. Allow me to congratulate you, sir, as a man of fortune. There is no need to hurry back to that beggarly clerkship."

"It's not a clerkship, Mr. Paget, nor beggarly. I'm a partner in a rising concern. The other man's name is Parr; he has a wife and children, and I wouldn't desert him for the world. Eighty thousand pounds! By Jove, won't Parr open his eyes."

Mr. George Carmichael was now so excited that his shyness vanished.

"When can I have my money, sir?"

"In a month's time."

"Not until then? I wanted to go back to India next week."

"It can be sent after you."

A slow suspicious smile crept round the young man's lips; he looked more well-bred than he was.

"None of that," he said. "I don't stir until I get the cheque. I say, can't you give it me at once? It's mine."

"Not a day sooner than a month. I must take that time to realize so large a sum. You shall have it this day month."

"Beastly inconvenient. Parr will be in no end of a taking. I suppose there's no help for it, however."

"None."

"This is the th of June. Now you're not playing me a trick, are you? You'll pay me over that money all square on the th of July."

Mr. Paget had an imposing presence. He rose now, slowly, stood on the hearthrug, under his daughter's picture, and looked down at his guest.

"I am sorry for you," he said. "Your education has certainly been imperfect. Your father was a gentleman, and my friend. You, I regret to say, are not a gentleman. I don't repeat my invitation to dine at my house. With regard to the money it shall be in your hands on the th July. I am rather pressed for time this morning, Mr. Carmichael, and must ask you to leave me. Stay, however, a moment. You are, of course, prepared to give me all proofs of identity?"

"What do you mean, sir?"

"What I say. The certificate of the marriage of your parents and certificate of the proof that you are the person you represent yourself to be must be forthcoming. I must also have letters from your friends in India. No doubt, of courseno doubt who you are, but these things are necessary."

Notwithstanding that he was the owner of eighty thousand pounds, Mr. George Carmichael left the august presence of the head of Paget Brothers feeling somewhat crestfallen.

He had scarcely done so before Helps rushed in.

"A cable, sir! Praise the Lord, a cable at last!"

He thrust the sheet of paper into his employer's hands. It came from Melbourne, and bore the date of the day before.

"Esperance arrived safely. Delay caused by broken machinery. Accident of a painful nature on board. Full particulars by mail.

"Jellyby."

CHAPTER XXXIV

Mr. Paget was most careful that the full contents of the cable did not go to his daughter at Jewsbury-on-the-Wold. He read it three or four times, then he took up a telegraph form and wired to her as follows:

"Esperance arrived safely. Delay caused by injury to machinery."
This telegram caused intense rejoicing at the rectory, and Mr. Paget had his gloomy part to himself. He conned that part over and over.

A serious accident. To whom? About whom? What a fool that Jellyby was not to have given him more particulars. Why did that part of the cablegram fill him with consternation? Why should he feel so certain that the accident in question referred to his son-in-law? Well, he must wait over a month for news, and during that month he must collect together eighty thousand pounds. Surely he had enough to think of. Why should his thoughts revert to Wyndham with an ever-increasing dread?

"Wyndham is safe enough," he said. "Jolly enough, too, I make no doubt. His money waits for him at Ballarat. Of course bad news will come, but I shall see through it. Oh, yes, I shall see through it fast enough."

Days of suspense are hard dayslong and weary days. As these days crept one by one away Mr. Paget became by no means an easy person to live with. His temper grew morose, he was irritable, manifestly ill at ease, and he would often for hours scarcely utter a word.

The th of July passed. Mr. Carmichael again called for his money. A part was paid to him, the balance the head of the great shipping firm assured the young man could not possibly be forthcoming for another month or six weeks.

"I am sorry," Mr. Paget said, "extremely sorry not to be able to fulfil my word to the letter. But I must have time to realize such a large sum, and I greatly fear I must claim it."

Mr. Carmichael had a cheque in his hand for ten thousand pounds. He could scarcely feel discontented at such a moment, and took his departure grumbling but elated.

"Helps," said Mr. Paget, "I have taken that ten thousand pounds out of the business, and it can ill afford to lose it. If news does not come soon we are undone, and all our plotting and planning won't save the old place nor the honor of the old house."

"No fear," muttered Helps. "The news will come. I have bad dreams at night. The house will be saved. Don't you fret, Mr. Paget."

He went out of the room looking as morose and ugly as possible, and Mortimer Paget hurled no blessings after him.

The next day was fraught with tidings. A thick packet lay on the chief's desk, bearing the imprint of the Esperance on it. By the side of the packet was a telegram. He opened the telegram first:

"Jewsbury-on-the-Wold, a.m.
"Valentine had a son this morning. Both doing well."
The tears absolutely sprang to Mr. Paget's eyes. His hands trembled; he looked round furtively; there was no one by. Then he raised the telegram to his lips and kissed it. Valentine had a son—he had a grandson. Another head of the old house had arisen on the horizon.

He rang his electric bell; he was so excited that he could not keep these tidings to himself.

"I have sent for you to receive your congratulations. Helps," he said; "and—and here's a cheque for ten pounds. You must go home early and have a good supper—champagne and all that sort of thing. Not a word, Helps, my good fellow, you deserve it. You quite deserve it!"

"May I ask what for, Mr. Paget? Forgive me, sir. I see that the packet from the Esperance has come."

"So it has. It can wait. Take your money, Helps, and drink my grandson's health. He arrived this morning, bless him—my daughter had a son this morning."

"Indeed, sir. It's a pity the father isn't there. It would have been pretty to have seen Mr. Wyndham as a father. Yes, sir. I'm glad your young lady is doing well. Babes come with trouble, and it seems to me they mostly go with trouble. All the same, we make a fuss of them—and the world's too full as it is."

"This child supplies a long felt need," replied the baby's grandfather, frowning. "He is the future head of the house."

"Poor innocent. Yes, sir, I congratulate you as in duty bound. You'll soon read that packet, won't you, sir. It seems a sort of a coincidence like, getting news of the father and the babe in one breath."

"I'll read the packet presently," said Mr. Paget. "Go away now, Helps; don't disturb me."

Left alone, the pleased man spread out the pink sheet of paper in such a position that his eye could constantly rest on it. Then he broke the seal of Captain Jellyby's yarn, and began to read.

CHAPTER XXXV

Esperance, April .
"My Dear Sir,

"I begin a letter to you under peculiarly afflicting circumstances. Your son-in-law, the favorite of every one on board, one of the nicest young gentlemen I have had the luck to meet, fell overboard last night, between nine and ten o'clock, when a very heavy sea was running. He was standing at the wheel, talking to a sailor of the name of Loggan. Loggan said he was very cheerful and keen to watch the storm. He was helping to tighten up a bit of rope when the boat gave a lurch. Loggan shouted to him to take care, but he was taken off his feet, and the next moment was in the water. We put out the boats and did all in our power, but in addition to the storm the night was very dark, and we never saw nor heard anything more of the unfortunate young gentleman. The night was so rough he must have gone to the bottom almost directly. I cannot express to you, sir, what a gloom this has cast upon all on board. As I said already, your son-in-law was beloved by passengers and sailors alike. His death was due to the most ordinary accident.

"Well, sir, regrets are useless, but if regrets would bring Mr. Wyndham back, he would be safe and well now; he was one of the most taking young men I ever came across, and also one of the best. Please give my respectful condolences to his poor young widow"

Here there was a break in the narrative. It was taken up some days later.

"I had scarcely written the last when an awful thing happened. There was a fearful crash on board, and in short, sir, our funnel was blown down. I can scarcely go into particulars now, but for many days we lay at the mercy of the waves, and I never thought to see land any more. It speaks well for the worthiness of the Esperance that she weathered such a gale. But for many days and nights the destruction to your property, for the water poured in in all parts, and the miserable state of the passengers, baffles description. The ship was in such a condition that we could not use steam, and when the storm abated had to drift as best we could. For our main masts were also broken, and we could put on scarcely any sail. Our provisions were also becoming short.

"A week ago, by the mercy of God, we came within hail of the steamer Salamanca, which towed us into port, and the Esperance has been put into dock at Melbourne for repairs.

"Under these appalling circumstances, Mr. Wyndham's loss has not been forgotten, but to a certain extent cast on one side. Perhaps I ought to say here; sir, that when your son-in-law commenced his voyage to Sydney under my auspices, he appeared to be in such a state of agitation, and in such distress of mind, that I feared for his brain, and wondered if you had sent him on this voyage by a doctor's orders. He made also a request to me which seemed to confirm this view. He begged me not to let out to anyone on board the smallest particulars (I really did not know any) of his history. In especial he did not wish his wife spoken of. He looked strange when he made these requests, and even now I can see the despair in his eyes when I refused—you will remember, sir, by your express desire—to touch at Plymouth. I may as well say frankly, that had Mr. Wyndham continued as depressed as he was the first few days of the voyage, I should have scarcely considered his untimely end altogether due to accident. But I am happy to be able to reassure your mind on that point. That he felt the separation from his wife terribly at first there is no doubt, but there is also no doubt that he got over this feeling, that he was healthily happy, and altogether the brightest fellow on board. In short, sir, he was the life of the ship; even now we are never done lamenting him. Untimely as his fate was, no one could have been more ready to rush suddenly into the presence of his Maker. I enclose with this a formal certificate of Mr. Wyndham's death, with the latitude and longitude of the exact spot where he must have gone down accurately described. This certificate is duly attested by the Consul here, and I delayed one day in writing to you in order that it should go.

"I remain, sir.
"Yours respectfully,
"Harry Jellyby."

"P.S.—I forgot to mention that two of our boats have been absolutely lost; but I will send you a full list of casualties by next mail."

Helps had never felt more restless than he did that morning; he could not attend to his ordinary avocations. Truth to tell, Helps' position in the house of Paget Brothers had always been more or less a dubious one. It was patent to all that he was confided in to a remarkable degree by the head of the house. It was also observed that he had no special or defined post. In short that he did a little of everybody's work, and seemed to have nothing absolutely depending on himself.

All the same, when Helps was away the whole establishment felt a loss. If the old clerk was useful for no other purpose, he was at least valuable as a scape-goat. He could bear blame which belonged to others. It was convenient to make excuses, and to shift uncomfortable omissions of all sorts from one's own shoulders.

"Oh, I thought Helps would have seen to that."

Helps saw to a great deal, and was perfectly indifferent to these inuendoes. Of one thing he was certain, that they would never reach the chief's ears.

On this particular morning Helps would assist no one; he had ten pounds in his pocket, and he knew that the future owner of the great business lay in his cradle at Jewsbury-on-the-Wold. Little cared he for that.

"What news of Mr. Wyndham?" This was his thought of thoughts. "What secret lies hidden within that sealed packet? What is my master doing now? When will he ring for me? How soon shall I know the best and the worst? Oh, God, why did I let that young man go? Why didn't I split? What's prison, after all? My God, what is prison compared to a heart on fire!"

Helps pottered about. He was a very wizened grey little fellow. The clerks found him decidedly in the way. They muttered to one another about him, and Mr. Manners, one of the juniors, requested him in a very cutting voice to shut the door and go away.

Helps obeyed the command to the very letter. By this time his state of mind might have been described as on the rack. For two hours Mr. Paget had been reading that letter. Impossible; no letter would take that time to read. Why had he not rung? Surely he must know what Helps was enduring. Surely at this crisis of his fate—at this crisis of both their fates—he must want to see his faithful servant. Why then did he not ring?

At last in despair Helps knocked at the door of the outer office. There was no answer. He turned the handle, pushed the door ajar and went in. The room was empty. Mr. Paget's pile of ordinary business letters lay unopened on his desk. Helps went up to the door of the inner room, and pressed his ear against the keyhole. There was not a stir within. He knocked against a chair, and threw down a book on purpose. If anything living would bring Mr. Paget out it was the idea of anyone entering, or disarranging matters in his office. Helps disarranged matters wildly; he threw down several books, he upset more than one chair; still the master did not appear. At last he knocked at the door of the inner room. There was no response. Then he knocked again, louder. Then he hammered with his fists. Then he shook the door. No response. The inner room might as well have been a grave. He rushed away at last for tools to break open the door. He was terribly frightened, but even now he had sufficient presence of mind not to bring a third person to share his master's secret. He came back with a pick-lock, a hammer and one or two other implements. He locked the door of the outer office, and then he set boldly to work. He did not care what din he made; he was past all thought of that now. The clerks outside got into a frantic state of excitement; but that fact, had he known it, would have made no difference to Helps.

At last his efforts were crowned with success. The heavy door yielded, and flew open with a bang. Helps fell forward into the room himself. He jumped up hastily. A quiet, orderly, snug room! The picture of a fair and lovely girl looking down from the wall! a man with grey hair stretched on the hearthrug under the picture! a man with no life, nor motion, nor movement. Helps flew to his master. Was he dead? No, the eyes were wide open; they looked at Helps, and one of the hands was stretched out, and clutched at Helps' arm, and pulled it wildly aside.

"What is it, my dear master?" said the man, for there was that in the face which would have melted any heart to pity.

"Don't! Stand out of my light," said Mr. Paget. "Hold mesteady melet me get up. He's therethere by the window!"

"Who, my dear sir? Who?"

"The man I've murdered! He's there. Between me and the light. It's done. He's standing between me and the light. Tell him to move away. I have murdered him! I know that. Between me and the lightthe light! Tell him to move awaytell himtell him!"

Mortimer Paget gave a great shriek, and covered his terrified eyes with his trembling hands!

CHAPTER XXXVI

"What is the matter, Lilias? I did not do anything wrong."

The speaker was Augusta Wyndham.

Three years have passed away since she last appeared in this story; she is grown up now, somewhat lanky still, with rather fierce dark eyes, and a somewhat thin pronounced face. She is the kind of girl who at eighteen is still all angles, but there are possibilities for her, and at five and twenty, if time deals kindly with her, and circumstances are not too disastrous, she might be rounded, softened, she might have developed into a handsome woman.

"What is it, Lilias?" she said now. "Why do you look at me like that?"

"It is the same old story, Gussie," replied Lilias, whose brown cheeks were paler, and her sweet eyes larger than of old; "you are always wanting in thought. It was thoughtless of you to make Valentine walk home, and with little Gerry, too. She will come in fagged and have a headache. I relied on your seeing to her, Gussie; when I asked you to take the pony chaise I thought of her more than you, and now you've come back in it all alone, without even fetching baby."

"Well, Lilias." Augusta paused, drew herself up, leant against the nearest paling, crossed her legs, and in a provokingly petulant voice began to speak.

"With how much more of all that is careless and all that is odious are you going to charge me?" she said. "Oh, of course, 'Gussie never can think.' Now I'll tell you what this objectionable young woman Augusta did, and then you can judge for yourself. I drove to Netley Farm, and got the butter and the eggs, and then I went on to see old James Holt, the gardener, for I thought he might have those bulbs we wanted ready. Then I drew up at the turnstile, and waited for that precious Mrs. Val of yours."

"Don't," said Lilias. "Remember whose"

"As if I ever forgetbut hehe had others beside herhe never had any Augusta except me," two great tears gathered in the great brown eyes; they were dashed hastily aside, and the speaker went on.

"There's twice too much made of her, and that's a fact. You live for her, you're her slave, Lilias. It's perfectly ridiculousit's absurd. You have sunk your whole life into hers, and since Marjory's wedding things have been worse. You simply have no life but in her. He wouldn't wish it; he hated anyone to be unselfish except himself. Well, then—oh, then, I won't vex the dear old thing. Have you forgiven me, Lil? I know I'm such a chatter-pate. I hope you have forgiven me."

"Of course I have, Gussie. I'm not angry with you, there's nothing to be angry about. You are a faulty creature, I admit, but I also declare you to be one of the greatest comforts of my life."

"Well, that's all right—that's as it should be. Now for my narrative. I waited by the turnpike. Valentine and baby were to meet me there. No sign of them. I waited a long time. Then I tied Bob to the gate, and started on discovery bent. You know it is a pretty lane beyond the turnpike, the hedges hid me. I walked along, whistling and shaking my whip. Presently I was assailed by the tuneful duet of two voices. I climbed the hedge and peeped over. I looked into a field. What did I see? Now, Lilias the wise, guess what I saw?"

"Valentine and our little Gerald," responded Lilias. "She was talking to him; she has a sweet voice, and surely there never was a dearer little pipe than wee Gerry's. They must have looked pretty sitting on the grass."

"They looked very pretty—but your picture is not quite correct. For instance, baby was sound asleep."

"Oh, then, she had him in her arms, and was cooing to him. A lovelier scene than ever, Augusta."

"A very lovely scene, Lilias; only, one woman's voice would not make a duet."

Something in Augusta's eyes caused Lilias to droop her own. She turned aside to pick a spray of briony.

"Tell me what you saw," she said abruptly.

"I saw Valentine and Adrian Carr. They were sitting close together, and baby was asleep on his breast, not on hers, and he was comforting her, for when I peeped over I saw him touch her hand, and then I saw her raise her handkerchief and wipe away some tears. Crocodile's tears, I call them. Now, Lilias, out of my way. I mean to vault over this gate."

"What for, dear?"

"To relieve my feelings. Now I'm better. Won't you have a try?"

"No, thank you, I don't vault gates."

"Aren't you going to show anything? Good gracious, I should simply explode if I had to keep in things the way you do. Now, what's the matter? You look white all the same; whiter than you did ten minutes ago. Oh, if it was me, I couldn't keep still. I should roar like a wounded lion."

"But I am not a wounded lion, Augusta, dear."

Lilias laid her hand on her sister's shoulder.

"I am older than you," she continued, "and perhaps quieter. Life has made me quieter. We won't say anything about what you saw, Augusta. Perhaps none of us have such a burden to bear as Valentine."

"Now, Lilias, what stuff you talk. Oh, she's a humbug, and I hate her. There, I will say it, just for once. She took Gerald away, and now she wants to take Adrian from you. Oh, I know you're an angelyou'd bear anything, but I'm not quite a fool."

"They are coming; you must hush," said Lilias, putting her hand across her young sister's lips.

Augusta cast two wrathful eyes behind her, lightly vaulted back over the gate, and vanished from view round the first corner. Lilias opened the gate, and went slowly to meet the group who were coming down the dusty country road.

Valentine was in black, but not in widow's weeds. She had a shady hat over her clustering bright hair, and round this hat, the baby, little Gerry, had stuck quantities of leaves and grasses and what wild flowers his baby fingers could clutch. With one hand she was holding up her long dress; her other held a basket of primroses, and her face, bright now with color in the cheeks, laughter on the lips, and the fire of affection in the eyes, was raised to where her sturdy little son sat on Carr's broad shoulder.

The child was a handsome little fellow, cast in a far more masculine mould than his father, to whom he bore scarcely any resemblance.

As Lilias, in her dark grey dress, approached, she looked altogether a more sorrowful and grief-touched figure than the graceful, almost childish young widow who came to meet her.

So Carr thought, as with a softened light in his eyes he glanced at Lilias.

"A certain part of her heart was broken three years ago," he inwardly commented. "Can Iis it in my powerwill it ever be in my power to comfort her?"

But Lilias, knowing nothing of these feelings, only noted the happy-looking picture.

"Here we are!" said Carr, catching the boy from his shoulder and letting him jump to the ground. "Run to your auntie now, little man."

Off waddled the small fat legs. Lilias stooped and received the somewhat dusty embrace of two rounded arms, while cherub lips were pressed on hers.

"You do comfort me, little Gerry," she gasped under her breath.

Then she rose, almost staggering under his weight.

"Let me carry him for you," said Carr, coming up to her.

"No, thank you, I like to have him," she said; and she turned and walked by Valentine's side.

"Are you tired, Val? I did not mean you to walk home. I sent Augusta with Bob and the basket chaise. I thought you knew they were to meet you at the turnpike."

"I'm afraid I forgot," answered Valentine. "I met Mr. Carr, and we came to a delicious field, full of primroses, and baby wanted to pick lots, didn't you, treasure? We sat and had a rest; I am not very tired, and Mr. Carr carried this big boy all the way home. Hey-ho," she continued, throwing off her hat, and showing a head as full of clustering richly-colored hair as of old, "what a lovely day it is, it makes me feel young. Come along, baby, we'll race together to the house. It's time for you to go to sleep, little master. Now, thenbaby first, mother afterone, two, three and away!"

The child shouted with glee, the mother raced after him, they disappeared through the rose-covered porch of the old rectory. Lilias raised two eyes full of pain to Carr's.

"Is she beginning to forget?" she asked.

"No; why should you say so? She will never forget."

"She looked so young just now—so like a child. Poor Val! She was only twenty-two her last birthday. Mr. Carr. I don't want her to forget."

"In one sense rest assured she never will—in another—would you wish her to endure a life-long pain?"

"I would—I would. It was done for her—she must never forget."

"You always allow me to say plain words, don't you?" said Carr. "May I say some now?"

"Say anything you please, only don't teach her to forget."

"What do you mean?"

The man's eyes blazed. Lilias colored all over her face.

"I mean nothing," she said hurriedly. "Come into the flower-garden. We shall have a great show of roses this year. Come and look at the buds. You were going to say something to me," she added presently.

"Yes. I was going to prepare you for what may come by-and-bye. It is possible that in the future—remember. I don't know anything—but it is possible that in the future your young sister-in-law may once more be happy. I don't know how—I am not going to prognosticate anything, but I think as a rule one may safely infer that the very bitterest grief, the most poignant sorrows which come before twenty are not abiding. Mrs. Wyndham has her child. It would not do for the child to associate only sorrow with the mother's face. Some time in the future she will be happy again. It is my opinion that your brother would be glad of this."

"Hush; you don't know. My brother—my only brother! I at least can never be the Lilias of old."

"I believe you," said Carr much moved by her tone. "You, too, are very young; but in your heart, Miss Wyndham, in your heart, you were an older woman, a woman more acquainted with the grave side of life, than that poor young thing was when the blow fell."

Lilias did not answer for a moment or two.

"I am glad Marjory is out of it all," she said then. "You know what a long nervous illness she had at the time. Dear old Marjory, she was such a tempestuous darling."

"But she is happy now."

"Oh, yes, she has her husband. Philip is very good, he suits Marjory. Yes, she is quite happy now, and I am not miserableyou mustn't think it. I know in whom I have believed."

Her eyes were raised to the sky overhead.

"I know He won't fail me. Some day Gerald and I shall meet."

"Some day, assuredly," answered Carr.

"And in the meantime, I am not unhappy, only I don't intend ever to forget. Nor shall she."

"One question," said Carr. "Have you heard news lately of Mrs. Wyndham's father?"

"I believe he has recovered. He never comes here. I must own I have a great antipathy to Valentine's father. I don't want to hear of him nor to think of him."

"I can understand that. Still, if it will not trouble you greatly I should like to ask you a question or two with regard to him. He was very ill, at theat the time, wasn't he?"

"He was very ill, mentally, he was quite off his head for several months."

"Don't you think that was rather strange?"

"I never thought much about it, as far as he was concerned. Of course he must have had a dreadful shock."

"But not such a shock as you had. Not a shock to be named with what that poor girl, his daughter, went through. Your brother was not his own son, andand"

"I never thought about it, Mr. Carr. I heard that he was ill, and that the illness was mental. He has been quite well again for some time."

"I assure you you're mistaken. I met him a fortnight ago in town. I never saw a man so completely altered in the whole course of my life."

"Please don't tell me about him. It never was, nor could be, an interesting subject. Ah, there is my dear father calling me. I must run to him."

The rector was seen approaching. His figure was slightly more bent, and his hair whiter than of old. Lilias linked her hand within his arm, and Carr turned away.

"I can never have it out with her," he said to himself. "I never seem to have the courage when I'm with her. And besides, I don't believe she'd leave her father. But if she did—if I ever could hope to win her for my wife, then I might venture to whisper to her some of my suspicions. How little she guesses what my thoughts are. Can I act in any way without consulting her? I have a good mind to try."

CHAPTER XXXVII

The house of Paget Brothers was never more flourishing than during the spring and summer of . It was three years since the death of its junior partner, Gerald Wyndham, and three years since Mortimer Paget had paid away in full the trust money of eighty thousand pounds which he owed to George Carmichael, of the firm of Carmichael. Parr and Co., Calcutta. Although none of the parties concerned quite intended it, certain portions of the story of this trust got abroad, and became the subject of a nine days' gossip in the City and elsewhere. It had never even been whispered that Paget Brothers were in difficulties. Still such a sum would not be easy to find even in the wealthiest concern. Then the fact also trickled out that Wyndham's life had been insured, heavily insured, in three or four different offices. His death must have come in handily, people said, and they said no more—just then.

The fact was, that had one been even inclined to suspect foul play, Mr. Paget's dangerous illness at the time would have prevented their doing so. Surely no man ever before grieved so bitterly for a dead son-in-law as did this man. The blow had felled him with a stroke. For many months his mind gave way utterly. The words spoken in delirium are seldom considered valuable. What Mr. Paget did or said during the dark summer which followed Wyndham's death never got known. In the autumn he was better; that winter he went abroad, and the following spring he once more was seen in the City.

He looked very old, people said, but he was as shrewd and careful a business man as ever.

"I have to put things in order for my grandson," he would say.

Nobody ever saw him smile just then, but a light used to come into his sunken dark eyes when the child's name was mentioned.

Valentine and the boy spent most of their time in the old house in Park-Lane. She was very gentle with her father, but the relations they had once borne to each other were completely altered. He now rather shrank from her society. She had to seek him, not he her. He was manifestly ill at ease when in her presence. It was almost impossible to get him to come to see her in her own house. When he did so he was attacked by a curious nervousness. He could seldom sit still; he often started and looked behind him. Once or twice he perceptibly changed color, and on all occasions he gave a sigh of relief when he said good-bye.

The child visited his grandfather oftener than the mother did. With the child Mortimer Paget was absolutely at home and happy.

The third summer after Wyndham's death passed away. Valentine spent most of the time at Jewsbury-on-the-Wold. Mr. Paget went abroad, as he always did, during August and September. In October he was once more in town. Valentine came back to London, and their small world settled down for its usual winter routine.

On all sides there were talks of this special winter proving a hard one, the cold commenced early and lasted long. In all the poorer quarters of the great city there were signs of distress. Want is a haggard dame. Once known her face is dreaded. As the days grew short, the darkness deepened, and the fogs became frequent, she was often seen stalking about the streets. Poorly clad children, shivering women, despairing defiant-looking men all trembled and fled before her. The cold was intense, work became slack, and then, to increase all other evils, the great cruel monster, Strike, put down his iron heel. Want is his invariable handmaid. Between them they did much havoc.

It was on a certain short November day of this special winter that Mortimer Paget arrived early at his office. He drove there in his comfortable brougham, and stepped out into the winter cold and fog, wrapped up in his rich furs. As he did so a woman with two small children came hastily up, cast a furtive glance to right and left, saw no policeman near, and begged in a high piteous whining voice for alms.

Mr. Paget had never been known to give alms indiscriminately. He was not an uncharitable man, but he hated beggars. He took not the least notice of the woman, although she pushed one of the hungry children forward who raised two piteous blue eyes to the hard man's face.

"Even a couple of pence!" she implored. "The father's on strike, and they've had nothing to eat since yesterday morning."

"I don't give indiscriminate charity," said Mr. Paget. "If your case is genuine, you had better apply at the nearest office of the Charity Organization."

He was pushing open the outer office door when something arrested his attention.

A man came hurriedly up from a side street, touched the woman on the shoulder, lifted one of the hungry children into his arms, and the whole party hurried away. The man was painfully thin, very shabbily dressed, in a long frock coat, which was buttoned tight. He had a beard and moustache, and a soft slouch hat was pushed well forward over his eyes.

The woman's face lit up when she saw him. Both the children smiled, and the whole group moved rapidly away.

The effect of this shabby man's presence on those three helpless and starving creatures was as if the sun had come out. Mr. Paget staggered to his office, walked through the outer rooms as if he were dazed, sought his sanctum, and sat down shaking in every limb.

Since his strange illness of three years ago, Helps had been more like a servant and nurse to him than an ordinary clerk. It was his custom to attend his master on his first arrival, to see to his creature comforts, to watch his moods.

Helps came in as usual this morning. Mr. Paget had removed his hat, and was gazing in a dull vacant way straight before him.

"You are not yourself this morning, sir," said the clerk.

He pushed a footstool under the old man's feet, removed the fur-lined overcoat and took it away. Then standing in front of him he again said:

"Sir, you are not yourself to-day."

"The old thing, Helps," said Mr. Paget. He shook himself free of some kind of trance with an effort. "The doctors said I should be quite well again, as well as ever. They are mistaken, I shall never be quite well. I saw him in the street just now, Helps."

"Indeed, sir?"

It was Helps' rôle as much as possible to humor his patient.

"Yes, I saw him just now—he takes many guises; he was in a new one to-day—a starved clerk out of employment. That was his guise to-day. I should not have recognized him but for his hand. Perhaps you remember Wyndham's hand, Helps? Very slender, long and tapered—the hand of a musician. He took a ragged child in his arms, and his hand—there was nothing weak about it—clasped another child who was also starved and hungry. Undoubtedly it was Wyndham—Wyndham in a new guise—he will never leave me alone."

"If I were you, Mr. Paget," said Helps after a pause. "I'd open the letters that are waiting for replies. You know what the doctor said, that when the fancy came you mustn't dwell on it. You must be sure and certain not to let it take a hold on you, sir. Now you know, just as well as I do, that you didn't see poor Mr. Wyndham—may Heaven preserve his soul! Is it likely now, sir, that a spirit like Mr. Wyndham's, happy above the sky with the angels, would come down on earth to trouble and haunt you? Is it likely now, sir? If I were you I'd cast the fancy from me!"

Mr. Paget raised his hand to sweep back the white hair from his hollow, lined face.

"You believe in heaven then, Helps?"

"I do for some folks, sir. I believe in it for Mr. Gerald Wyndham."

"Fudge; you thought too well of the fellow. Do you believe in heaven for suicides?"

"Sir—no, sir—his death came by accident."

"It did not; he couldn't go through with the sacrifice, so he ended his life, and he haunts me, curse him!"

"Mr. Paget, I hope God will forgive you."

"He won't, so you needn't waste your hopes. A man has cast his blood upon my soul. Nothing can wash the blood away. Helps, I'm the most miserable being on earth. I walk through hell fire every day."

"Have your quieting mixture, sir; you know the doctor said you must not excite yourself. There, now you are better. Shall I help you to open your letters, sir?"

"Yes, Helps, do; you're a good soul, Helps. Don't leave me this morning; he'll come in at the door if you do."

There came a tap at the outer office. Some one wanted to speak to the chief. A great name was announced.

In a moment Mr. Paget, from being the limp, abject wretch whom Helps had daily to comfort and sustain, became erect and rigid. From head to foot he clothed himself as in a mask. Erect as in his younger days he walked into the outer room, and for two hours discussed a matter which involved the loss or gain of thousands.

When his visitor left him he did so with the inward remark:

"Certainly Paget's intellect and nerve may be considered colossal."

CHAPTER XXXVIII

Esther Helps still took charge of her father's house in Acacia Villas. She was still Esther Helps. Perhaps a more beautiful Esther than of old; a little steadier, too, a little graveraltogether a better girl.

For some unaccountable reason, after that night at the theatre when Wyndham had sat by her side and taken her back from destruction to her father's arms, she had almost ceased to flirt. She said nothing now about marrying a gentleman some day, and as the men who were not gentlemen found she would have nothing to do with them, it began to be an almost understood thing among her friends that Esther, lovely as she was, would not marry. This resolve on her part, for it amounted to an unspoken resolve, was followed by other changes. She turned her attention to her hitherto sadly neglected mind. She read poetry with Cherry, and history and literature generally by herself. Then she tried to improve her mode of speech, and studied works on etiquette, and for a short time became frightfully stilted and artificial. This phase, however, did hot last long. The girl had really a warm and affectionate heart, and that heart all of a sudden had been set on fire. The flame never went out. It was a holy flame, and it raised and purified her whole nature.

She loved Wyndham as she might have loved Christ had He been on earth. Wyndham seemed to her to be the embodiment of all nobility. He had saved her, none knew better than she did from how much. It was the least she could do to make her whole life worthy of her savior. She guessed by instinct that he liked refinement, and gentle speech, and womanly ways. So it became her aim in life to seek after those things, and as far as possible to acquire them.

Then the news of his death reached her. Only Cherry knew how night after night Esther cried herself to sleep. Only Cherry guessed why Esther's cheeks were so sunken and her eyes so heavy. Her violent grief, however, soon found consolation. Gerald had always been only a star to be gazed at from a distance; he was still that. When she thought of heaven she pictured seeing him there first of all. She thought that when the time came for her to go there he might stand somewhere near the gates and smile to see how she, too, had conquered, and was worthy.

Now she turned her attention to works of charity, to a life of religion. It was all done for the sake of an idol, but the result had turned this flippant, worldly, vain creature into a sweet woman, strong in the singleness of her aim.

Esther cared nothing at all about dress now. She would have joined a Deaconess' Institution but she did not care to leave her father. She did a great deal of work, however, amongst the poor, and at the beginning of this severe winter she joined a band of working sisters in East London as an associate. She usually went away to her work immediately after breakfast, returning often not until late at night, but as she wore the uniform of the association, beautiful as she was she could venture into the lowest quarters, and almost come home at any hour without rendering herself liable to insult.

One night as Cherry was preparing supper she was surprised to hear Esther's step in the passage two or three hours before her usual time of returning. Cherry was still the same strange mixture of poet and cook that she had ever been. With the "Lays of Ancient Rome" in one hand and her frying-pan held aloft in the other, she rushed out to know what was the matter.

"Why, Essie," she exclaimed, catching sight of her cousin's face. "You're ill, Essie; come in and sit down by the fire. I do hope to goodness you haven't gone and caught nothing."

"I have caught nothing," said Esther. "I am not ill."

She untied her bonnet strings and loosened her long straight cloak.

"Is father in, Cherry? I want to see him the minute he returns."

"You'll have to wait then," said Cherry, turning away in a half offended manner. If Esther did not choose to confide in her she was not going to force confidence.

She resumed her cooking with vigor, reading aloud portions from the volume on her knees as she did so.

"The Lady Jane was tall and slim;
The Lady Jane was fair"
"Essie, I wish you wouldn't fidget so. Whatever is the matter?"

"I want my father," repeated Esther.

"Well, he's not in. Uncle's never back till an hour after this. I tell him he's more and more of a nurse and less and less of a clerk every day of his life; he don't like it, but it's true. That old Mr. Paget is past bearing."

Esther rose with a sigh, folded her cloak, laid it on a chair, placed her bonnet on top of it, and going over to the fireplace gazed into the flames.

Cherry's cooking frizzled and bubbled in the pan, Cherry's own head was bent over her book.

"This is the rarest fun," she exclaimed suddenly. "Didn't Lady Jane pay Sir Thomas out? Lord, it were prime. You never will read the 'Ingoldsby Legends,' Esther. Now I call them about the best things going. How white you do look. Well, it's a good thing you are in time for a bit of supper. I have fried eggs and tomatoes to-night, browned up a new way. Why don't you take your cloak and bonnet upstairs, Essie, and sit down easy like? It fidgets one to see you shifting from one foot to another all the time."

"I'm going out again in a minute," said Esther. "I came in early because I wanted my father. Oh, there's his latch-key in the door at last. Don't you come, Cherry. I want to speak to him by myself."

Cherry's hot face grew a little redder.

"I like that," she said to herself. "It's drudge, drudge with medrudge, drudge from morning till night; and now she won't even tell me her secrets. I never has no livening up. I liked her better when she was flighty and flirty, that I dida deal better. We'll, I'll see what comes of that poor Sir Thomas."

Meanwhile Esther, with one hand on her father's shoulder, was talking to him earnestly.

"I want you to come back with me, fatherback this very minute."

"Where to, child?"

"To Commercial Road. There's to be a big meeting of the unemployed, and the Sisters and I, we was to give supper to some of the women and children. The meeting will be in the room below, and the supper above. I want you to come. Some gentlemen are going to speak to them; it won't be riotous."

Helps drew a deep sigh. It was a damp drizzling night, and he was tired.

"Can't you let me be this time, Essie?" he said.

"No, father, no, you must come to-night."

"But I can't do nothing for the poor fellows. I pity them, of course, but what can I do?"

"Nothing, only come to the meeting."

"But what for, Essie?"

"To please me, if for no other reason."

"Oh, if you put it in that way."

"Yes, I put it that way. You needn't take off your great coat. I'll have my cloak and bonnet on again in a jiffy."

"What, child, am I to have no supper?"

Poor Helps found the smell from the kitchen very appetising.

"Afterwards, when you come back. Everything good when you come back. Now, do come. It is so important."

She almost dragged him away. Cherry heard the house door bang after the two.

"Well, I'm done," she exclaimed! "See if I'll cook for nobody another time."

Esther and her father found an omnibus at the corner of their street. In a little over half-an-hour they were in Commercial Road; a few minutes later they found themselves in the large barn-like building which was devoted to this particular mission.

The ground floor consisted of one huge room, which was already packed with hungry-looking men and half-grown boys.

"Stand near the door," said Esther, giving her father explicit directions. "Don't stay where the light will fall on your face. Stand where you can look but can't be seen."

"You don't want me to be a spy, child. What is the meaning of all this?"

"You can put any meaning you like on it. Only do what I tell you. I want you to watch the men as they come in and out of the room. Watch them all; don't let one escape you. Stay until the meeting is over. Then tell me afterwards if there is any one here whom you know."

"What is the girl up to?" muttered Helps.

But Esther had already slipped upstairs. He heard sounds overhead, and women and children going up the stairs in groups; he saw more than one bright-looking Sister rushing about, busy, eager, and hopeful. Then the sounds within the large lower room showed him that the meeting had begun, and he turned his attention to the task set him by his daughter.

Certainly Esther was a queer girl, a dear, beautiful girl, but queer all the same. In what a ridiculous position she had placed him in; a tired elderly clerk. He was hungry, and he wanted his supper; he was weary, and he sighed for his pipe and his easy-chair. What had he in common with the men who filled this room. Some of them, undoubtedly, were greatly to be pitied, but many of them only came for the sake of making a fuss and getting noticed. Anyhow, he could not help them, and what did Esther mean by getting him to stand in this draughty doorway on the chance of seeing an old acquaintance; he was not so much interested in old acquaintances as she imagined.

The room was now packed, and the gentleman who occupied the platform, a very earnest, energetic, thoughtful speaker, had evidently gained full attention. Helps almost forgot Esther in the interest with which he listened. One or two men offered to make way for him to go further into the room; but this he declined. He did not suppose any friend of Esther's would appear; still he must be true to the girl, and keep the draughty post she had assigned him.

At the close of the first address, just when a vociferous clapping was at its height, Helps observed a tall very thin man elbowing his way through the crowd. This crowd of working men and boys would not as a rule be prepared to show either forbearance or politeness. But the stranger with a word whispered here, or a nod directed there, seemed to find "open sesame" wherever he turned. Soon he had piloted his way through this great crowd of human beings almost to the platform. Finally he arrested his progress near a pillar against which he leaned with his arms folded. He was more poorly dressed than most of the men present, but he had one peculiarity which rendered him distinguishable; he persistently kept his soft felt hat on, and well pushed forward over his eyes.

Helps noticed him, he could scarcely himself tell why. The man was poor, thin. Helps could not get a glimpse of his face, but there was something in his bearing which was at once familiar and bespoke the gentleman.

"Poor chap, he has seen better days," muttered Helps. "Somehow, he don't seem altogether strange, either."

Then he turned his attention once more to watch for the acquaintance whom Esther did not want him to miss.

The meeting came to an end and the men began to stream out. Helps kept his post. Suddenly he felt a light hand touch his arm; he turned; his daughter, her eyes gleaming with the wildest excitement, was standing by his side.

"Have you seen him, father?"

"Who, child—who? I'm precious hungry, and that's the truth, Esther."

"Never mind your hunger now—you have not let him escape—oh, don't tell me that."

"Essie, I think you have taken leave of your senses to-night. Who is it that I have not let escape?"

"A tall man in a frock coat, different from the others; he has a beard, and he wears his hat well pushed forward; his hands are white. You must have noticed him; he is certain to be here. You did not let him go?"

"I know now whom you mean," said Helps. "I saw the fellow. Yes, he is still in the room."

"You did not recognize him, father?"

"No, child. That is, I seem to know something about him. Whatever are you driving at, Esther?"

"Nothing—nothing—nothing. Go, follow the man with the frock coat. Don't let him see you. Find out where he lives, then bring me word. Go. Go. You'll miss him if you don't."

She disappeared, flying upstairs again, light as a feather.

Helps found himself impelled against his will to obey her.

"Here's a pretty state of things," he muttered. "Here am I, faint for want of food, set to follow a chap nobody knows nothing about through the slums."

It never occurred to Helps, however, not to obey the earnest dictates of his daughter.

He was to give chase. Accordingly he did so. He did so warily. Dodging sometimes into the road, sometimes behind a lamp post in case the tall man should see him. Soon he became interested in the work. The figure on in the front, which never by any chance looked back, but pursued its course undeviatingly, struck Helps once more with that strange sense of familiarity.

Where had he seen a back like that? Those steps, too, the very way the man walked gave him a queer sensation. He was as poor looking a chap as Helps had ever glanced at, and yet the steps were not unknownthe figure must have haunted the little clerk in some of his dreams.

The pursuer and pursued soon found themselves in quarters altogether new to Helps. More and more squalid grew the streets, more and more ruffianly grew the people. There never was a little man less likely to attract attention than this clerk with his humble unpretentious dress and mien. But in these streets he felt himself remarkable. A whole coat, unpatched trousers, were things to wonder at here. The men and the women, too, took to jostling him as he passed. One bold-faced girl tilted his hat well forward over his eyes, and ran away with a loud laugh.

Helps felt that even for Esther's sake he could not proceed any further. He was about to turn back when another glance at the figure before him brought such a rush of dazed wonderment, of uncanny familiarity, that all thought of his own possible danger deserted him, and he walked on, eager as Esther herself now in pursuit.

All this time they had been going in the direction of the docks. Suddenly they turned down a very badly lighted side street. There was a great brewery here, and the wall of the brewery formed for a long way one side of the street. It was so narrow as to be little better than a lane, and instead of being a crowded thoroughfare was now almost deserted. Here and there in the brewery wall were niches. Not one of these niches was empty. Each held its human beingman, woman, or child. It seemed to be with a purpose that the tall stranger came here. He slackened his pace, pushed his hat a little back, and began to perform certain small ministrations for the poor creatures who were to pass the night on the cold damp pavement.

A little girl was asleep in one of the niches; he wrapped her shawl more closely round her, tucking it in so as to protect her feet. Her hair hung in a tangled mass over her forehead. He pushed it back with a tender hand. Finally he pressed into the little thin palm two lollypops; they would give comfort to the child when she awoke.

Helps kept behind, well in the shadow; he was absolutely trembling now with suppressed excitement. He had seen by the glitter of the flaring gas the white hand of the man as he pushed back the child's elf-locks. The two went on again a few steps. The man in front stopped suddenlythey were passing another niche. It had its occupant. A girl was stretched prone on the ground—a girl whose only covering was rags. As they approached, she groaned. In an instant the stranger was bending over her.

"You are very ill, I fear. Can I help you?"

"Eh? What's that?" exclaimed the girl.

She raised her head, stretching out something which was more like a claw than a hand.

"What's that noise?" she repeated.

The noise had been made by Helps. It was an amazed terrified outcry when he heard the voice of the man who was bending over the girl. The man himself had observed nothing.

"You are very ill," he repeated. "You ought to be in a hospital."

"No, no, none of that," she said, clutching hold of his hand. "I ha' lain down to die. Let me die. I wor starving—the pain wor awful. Now I'm easy. Don't touch me—don't lift me; I'm easy—I'm a-goin' to die."

The stranger knelt a little lower.

"I won't hurt you," he said. "I will sit here by your side. Don't be frightened. I am going to raise your head—a little—a very little. Now it rests on my knee. That is better."

"Eh, you're a good man; yes, that's nice."

Her breath came in great pants. Presently she began to wander.

"Is that you, mother? Mother, I've been such a bad gel—bad every way. The Almighty's punishing me. I'm dying, and He's a sending me to hell."

"No," said the quiet voice of the man. "No; you are the one He wants. He is seeking you."

"Eh?" she said. Once more her clouded brain cleared. "Eh, how my breath does go. I'm a-going to hell!"

"No. He has sent me to find you; you are not going there."

"How do you know?"

She turned herself an inch or two in her astonishment and stared up at him.

Something in his face seemed to fill her with astonishment.

"Take off your hat," she said. "Are you Jesus Christ?"

It was at this juncture that Helps turned and fled.

He ran as he never ran before in the whole course of his life. Nobody saw him go, and nobody obstructed him in his headlong flight. Presently he got back to the Mission Hall. The place was closed and dark. He was turning away when a woman came out of the deep shelter of the doorway and touched his arm.

"Essie, is that you? My God, Essie, I've seen a ghost!"

"No, father, noa living man."

"This is awful, child. I'm shaking all over. I'd sooner be in my grave than go through such a thing again."

"Lean on me, father. We'll walk a bit, and soon find a cab-stand. We'll have a cab home. It's about time you had your supper. Don't talk a bit. Get back your poor breath."

As they were driving home a few minutes later, in a hansom, she turned suddenly.

"And you've got Mr. Wyndham's address?"

"Good heavens, Essie, don't say his name like that! I suppose it's a sign of the end that I should have seen a spirit."

"Nonsense, father, you saw no spirit. That's Mr. Gerald Wyndham in the flesh, as much as you and I are in the flesh. You saw no spirit, but a living man. I recognized him this morning, but I wasn't going to take my own word for it, so I got you to look him up. They call him Brother Jerome down here. Nobody knows anything at all about him, how he lives, nor nothing; only that he goes in and out amongst the people, and is always comforting this one or cheering that, and quieting down rows, and soothing people, andanddoing more in a day than the Sisters or I could do in a week. I've heard of him for a month past, but I only saw him to-day. He's a mystery, and people wonder about him, and no one can tell how he lives, nor where he sleeps. I know, though. He sleeps out of doors, and he starves. He shan't starve any longer."

CHAPTER XXXIX

"Esther," said Helps, late that night, after Cherry, in a very sulky humor, had gone to bed, "Esther, this is a very terrible, a very awful thing for me!"

"How so, father!"

She was kneeling by his side. Now she put her arm round his neck, and looked into his face. Her beating, throbbing, exulting heart told her that her discovery of that day was new life to her.

"I am glad," she continued, after a solemn pause; "yes. I don't mind owning I am very glad that a good man like Mr. Wyndham still lives."

"Child, you don't know what you are talking about. It is awfulawfulhis coming back. Even if he is alive he ought to have stayed away. His coming back like this is terrible. It means, it means"

"What, father?"

"Child, it must never be known: he must be warned; he must go away at once. Suppose anybody else saw him?"

"Father," said Esther.

She rose and stood over the shrinking old man.

"You have got to tell me the meaning of those queer words of yours. I guessed there was a mystery about Mr. Wyndham; now I am certain. If I don't know it before I leave the room to-night, I'll make mischief. There!"

"EssieEssieI thought you had turned into a good girl."

"I'll turn bad again. Listen. I love that man. Not as a girl loves her lovernot as a wife cares for her husband. He is married, and I should not be ashamed to tell his wife how I love him. I glory in my love; he saved me. Father, I wasn't coming home at all that night. He saved me; you can understand how I feel for him. My life wouldn't be a great deal to give up for him. There has been mischief done to him, that I am sure. Now tell me the truth; then I'll know how to act. Oh, father, you're the dearest and the kindest. Tell me the truth and you won't repent it."

"No, Essie, child, I don't suppose I shall repent. Sit there. You know too much, you may as well know all. Mr. Wyndham's life was insured."

"Yes?"

"Heavily, mark you, heavily."

"Yes." She covered her face with her hands. "Let me think. Say, father"she flung her hands into her lap"was this done on purpose?"

"Ay, child, ay; and a better man never lived. Ay, it was done on purpose."

"He was meant not to come back?"

"That's it, Essie, my dear. That's it."

"I see; yes, I see. Was the insurance money paid?"

"Every farthing of it, child. A large sum paid in full."

"If he appeared again it would have to be refunded?"

"If it could be, child."

"If it couldn't?"

"Then the story, the black story of why it was wanted, would have to come out; andandEsther, is the door locked? Come close, Essie. Your old father and my master would end our days in penal servitude."

"Now I see," said Esther.

She did not scream nor utter any loud exclamation, but began to pace softly up and down the room. Mentally she was a strong girl; her calm in this emergency proved her mettle.

After a few moments Helps began to speak; his words were wild and broken.

"Over and over I thought I'd rather," he said. "Over, and over, and overwhen I saw what it meant for him, poor young gentleman. But I can't, Essie, I can't. When it comes to the pinch I can't do it. We thought he was dead, my master and I, and my master he went off his head. And over he said, yes, over and over'Helps, a clean cell and a clean heart would be heaven to this.' But, bless you, Essie, he couldn't stand it either at the pinch. We thought Mr. Wyndham lying under the sea. Oh, poor young gentleman, he had no right to come back."

"No right? He has a wife and a child."

"A widow and orphan, you mean. No, Esther, he should have stayed away. He made a vow, and he should have stuck to it."

"He has not broken his vow, father. Oh, father, what a wicked thing you have done; you and that master to whom you have given your life. Now let me think."

"You won't send me to prison, Esther?"

"No, no. Sit down. I must think things out. Even now I don't know clearly about Mr. Wyndham; you have only treated me to half-confidences. Stay, though, I don't wish to hear more. You mustn't go to prison. Mr. Wyndham mustn't starve. I have it. Mr. Wyndham shall come here."

"Esther!"

Poor old Helps uttered a shriek, which caused Cherry to turn uneasily on her pillow.

"Keep yourself quiet, father. I'm a determined woman, and this thing shall be. Mr. Wyndham shall eat of our bread, and we will shelter him; and II, Esther Helpswill undertake to guard his secret and yours. No one living shall guess who he is."

"You forgetoh, this is an awful thing to do. You forgetthere's Cherry."

"I'll blind Cherry. If I can't, she must go. I shall bring Mr. Wyndham home to-morrow night!"

"Esther, this will kill me."

"No, it won't. On the contrary, you'll be a better and a happier man. You wouldn't have him starve, when through him you have your liberty? I'm ashamed of you."

She lit her candle and walked away.

Old Helps never went to bed that night.

CHAPTER XL

Esther did not go out next morning. Cherry was surprised at this. Helps went off at his usual hour. Cherry noticed that he ate little or no breakfast; but Esther did not stir. She sat quietly by the breakfast table. She ate well and deliberately. Her eyes were bright, her whole face was full of light and expression.

"Ain't you going down as usual to these dirty slums?" quoth Cherry. "I'm sick of them. You and your clothes both coming in so draggled like at night. I'm sick of the slums. But perhaps you mean to give them up."

"Oh, no," said Esther, waking from a reverie into which she had fallen, "but I'm not going this morning. I've something else to attend to."

"Then perhaps, Esther," said Cherry, with her round eyes sparkling, "you'd maybe think to remember your promise of getting that pink gauze dress out of your trunk; you know you promised it to me, and I've a mind to make it up with yellow bows. I'm sure to want it for something about Christmas."

"You shall have it," said Esther, in a sharp, short voice.

The abstracted look returned to her face. She gazed out of the window.

"Law, Essie, ain't you changed, and for the worse, I take it!" remarked Cherry. "I liked you a sight better when you were flighty and frivolous. Do you remember the night you went to the theatre with that Captain something or other? My word, wasn't uncle in a taking. 'Twas I found your tickets, and put uncle up to getting a seat near you. Weren't you struck all of a heap when you found him there? I never heard how you took it."

"Hush," said Esther, rising to her feet, her face growing very white. "I was mad, then, but I was saved. That's enough about it. Cherry, you know the box-room?"

"Yes," said Cherry. "It's stuffed pretty well, too. Mostly with your trunks, what you say belonged to your mother."

"So they did. Well, they must go downstairs."

"Wherever to? There isn't a corner for them in this scrap of a house."

"Corners must be found. Some of the trunks can go in our bedroomsome into father's; some into the passage, some into the drawing-room if necessary. You needn't stare, it has got to be done."

Esther stamped her foot and looked so imperious that Cherry shrank away.

"I suppose you're a bit mad again," she muttered, and she began to collect the breakfast things on a tray.

"Stop, Cherry, we may as well talk this out. I'll go upstairs now and help you with the boxes. Then we'll clean out the attic; if I had time I'd paper it, but there ain't. Then I'm going out to buy a bedstead and bedding, and a table and washhand stand. The attic is to be made into a bedroom for"

Here she paused.

"Well," said Cherry, "for whom, in the name of goodness?"

Esther gulped something down in her throat.

"There's a good man in the East of London, a very good man; he has no money, and he's starving, and he has to sleep out of doors; andandI can't stand it, Cherryand I spoke to father, and we have agreed that he shall have the attic and his food. That's it, his name is Brother Jerome; he's a sort of an angel for goodness."

"Slums again," said Cherry; "I'll have nothing to do with it."

She took up her tray and marched into the kitchen. Esther waited a minute or two, then she went to her room, put on a coarse check apron, and mounted the narrow attic stairs. She commenced pulling the trunks about; she could not lift them alone, but she intended to push them to the head of the stairs and then shove them down.

Presently a thumping step was heard, and Cherry's round face appeared.

"Disgusting job, I call it," she said; "but if I must help you, I suppose I must. I was going to learn 'Lord Tom Noddy' this morning. I thought I might wear the pink gauze with yellow bows, and recite it at Uncle Dan's Christmas party. Cousin Tom says I'm real dramatic when I'm excited, and that's a beautiful piece, so rhythmic and flowing. But then we all have to bend to you, Esther, and if I must help you I suppose I must."

"I think you had better, dear, and some day perhaps you won't be sorry. He's a good man, Brother Jerome is, he won't be no trouble. I'll clean his room for him myself once it's put in order, and he's sure to go out early in the morning. He'll breakfast upstairs, and I'll take him his breakfast, and his supper shall be ready for him here at night. We must see if that chimney will draw, Cherry, for of course he'll want his bit of fire."

After this the two girls worked with a will; they cleaned and polished the tiny window, they scrubbed the floor and brushed down the walls, and polished the little grate. Then Esther went out and made her purchases. The greater part of a five pound note was expended, and by the afternoon Gerald Wyndham's room was ready for him.

"Brother Jerome will come home with me to-night. Cherry," said Esther. "I may be late—I'm sure to be late—you needn't sit up."

"But I'd like to see him. Slums or no slums, he has given me a pair of stiff arms, and I want to find out if he's worth them."

"Oh, he's nothing to look at. Just a tall, thin, starved-looking man. He'll be shy, maybe, of coming, and you'd much better go to bed. You'll leave some supper ready in his room."

"What shall I leave?"

"Oh, a jug of beer and some cheese, and the cold meat and some bread and butter. That's all, he's accustomed to roughing it."

"My word, you call that roughing. Then the slums can't be so bad. I always thought there was an uncommon fuss made about them. Now I'll get to 'Lord Tom Noddy,' and learn off a good bit before tea time; you might hear me recite if you had a mind, Essie."

CHAPTER XLI

"Oh, yes, she's the sweetest missus in the world!"

That was the universal opinion of the servants who worked for Valentine Wyndham. They never wanted to leave her, they never grumbled about her, nor thought her gentle orders hard. The nurse, the cook, the housemaid, stayed on, the idea of change did not occur to them.

Valentine and her little son came back to the house in town at the end of October. Lilias came with them, and Adrian Carr often ran up to town and paid a visit to the two.

One day he came with a piece of news. He had got the offer of an incumbency not very far from Park-Lane. A fashionable church wanted a good preacher. Carr had long ago developed unusual powers as a pulpit orator, and the post, with a good emolument, was offered to him. He came to consult Lilias and Valentine in the matter.

"Of course you must go," said Lilias. "My father will miss you—we shall all—but that isn't the point. This is a good thing for you—a great thing—you must certainly go."

"And I can often see you," responded Carr, eagerly. "Mrs. Wyndham will let me come here, I hope, and you will often be here."

"I wish you would spend the winter with me, Lilias," said Valentine. She had interpreted aright the expression in Carr's eyes, and soon afterwards she left the room.

She went up to her own room, shut and locked the door, and then stood gazing into the fire with her hands tightly locked together. She inherited one gift from her father. She, too, could wear a mask. Now it dropped from her, and her young face looked lined and old.

"It isn't the grief of losing him," she murmured under her breath. "It's the pain—the haunting fear—that things are wrong. Have I known my father all these years not to note the change in him? He shrinks from me—he dreads me. Why? His conscience is guilty. Oh, Gerald, if I had only let you look into my heart, perhaps you would not have gone away. Oh, if only I had been in time to go on board the Esperance you would have been living now. Yes, Gerald, the terror never leaves me day and night; you are dead, but God did not mean you to die. My own Gerald—my heart would have been broken, or I should have lost my reason, if I had not confided my fears to Mr. Carr. Some people perhaps think I have forgotten—some again that I have ceased to love my husband. How little they know! Of course I am bright outwardly. But my heart is old and broken. I have had a very sad life—I am a very unhappy woman. Only for little Gerry I couldn't live. He is sweet, but I wish he were more like his father. Ah, there is nurse's knock at the door. Coming, nurse. Is baby with you?"

Mrs. Wyndham unlocked her door, and a little round, dimpled, brown-tinted child scampered in. He was followed by his nurse, a grave, nice-looking woman of about thirty. She was a widow, and had a son of her own.

"Has baby come to say good-night, Annette? Come here, sweet. Come into mother's arms."

She sat down on a low chair by the fire, and the little man climbed on her knee.

"I don't 'ike oo. I 'ove oo," he said.

"He's always saying that, ma'am," remarked the nurse. "He likes his toys—he loves his mother."

"Course I 'ove my mother."

He laid his brown curly head on her breast.

"Nurse, is anything the matter? You don't look well."

"That's it, madam. I'm not ill in body, but I'm sore fretted in mind. Now, baby, darling, don't you pull your dear ma to bits! The fact is, ma'am, and sore I am to say it, I'm afraid I must leave this precious child."

"Nurse!"

Valentine's arms dropped away from baby; baby raised his own curly head, and fixed his brown eyes on the woman, his rosy lips pouted.

"Sore I am to say it, ma'am," repeated Annette, "but there's no help. I've put off the evil day all I could, ma'am; but my mother's old, and my own boy has been ill, and she says I must go home and see after them both. Of course, madam, I'll suit your convenience as to the time of my going, and I hope you'll get some one else as will love the dear child. Come to bed, master baby, dear; your mother wants to go down to dinner."

A few days after this, as Helps was taking his comfortable breakfast, cooked to perfection by Cherry's willing hands, he raised his eyes suddenly, looked across at his daughter Esther, and made a remark.

"I'm told poor young madam is in no end of a taking."

"What young madam, father?"

"Mrs. Wyndham. The nurse is going and the child has got whooping cough. He's bad, too, poor little 'un, and frets about the nurse like anything. My master's in a way, too; he's wrapped up in that little lad. It was he told me; he said perhaps you'd know of a nurse as would suit. Esther."

"Don't stare so, Cherry," said Esther. "Anybody would think father was talking of ghosts, to see the bigness of your eyes. Well, father, yes, I'll think about a nurse. I'm sorry the child is ill."

"Don't you go and get a nurse from the slums," retorted Cherry. "You're all slums, you are. My word, I am having a time since that new lodger took possession."

Here Cherry paused to pour fresh water into the tea-pot. Esther and her father exchanged frightened glances.

"Brother Jerome, indeed!" proceeded this energetic young person. "He's a mighty uneasy sort of Brother Jerome. His good deeds don't seem to quieten him, anyway. And why does he always keep a hat stuck on his head, and never raise it when he passes me on the stairs. I know I'm broad and I'm stout, and I've no looks to boast of, but it's meant for men to raise their hats to women, and I don't see why he shouldn't. Then at night he walks the boards overhead fit to work on anybody's nerves. I don't recite half so dramatic as I did, because I can't get my sleep unbroken."

"Your tongue ain't stopped, anyway," said her uncle, almost crossly. "Esther, you'll think about the nurse for young madam."

He rose and left the room.

Esther sat still a little longer. She heard Cherry rattling the plates in the kitchen. Presently, she got up, put on her bonnet and cloak, called good-bye to her cousin, and went out. There could scarcely be a better Sister of the Poor than Esther Helps. She was near enough to them socially to understand their sorrows. She had never known starvation, but she could take in what tiny means meanttheir mode of speech was comprehensible to her, she was sufficiently unfastidious to go into their dirty rooms, to witness their uncouth, semi-savage ways without repulsion. She liked the life, it suited her, and her it. She was the kind of woman to be popular as a district visitor. She had abundance of both sympathy and tact. When her sympathies were aroused, her manners could be affectionate. In addition, she had a very lovely face. The poor of East London adore beauty; it comes so rarely near them in any case that they look upon it as an inestimable treasure. The women and children liked to watch Esther when she talked and when she smiled. The men treated her with the respect due to a regal presence.

Esther went down as usual to her mission work to-day. Sister Josephine, the head of this branch of work, greeted the handsome girl with a smile when she came in, drew her aside, and spoke to her about a particularly difficult undertaking which was soon to be commenced. This undertaking would require the utmost tact and talent; the sister asked Esther if she would be willing to become the head of the movement.

"I don't know anyone more suitable," she said in conclusion. "Only if you come, you must consent to sleep away from home. Some of our workour principal workwill take place at night."

Esther's clear ivory-tinted skin became a shade paler. She looked full at the sister with troubled but unshrinking eyes.

"You do me a great honor," she said. "But I am afraid I must decline it. At present I cannot sleep away from home. It is also possibleyes, it is quite possiblethat I may have to give up the work altogether for a time."

"Esther, are you putting your hand to the plough and looking back?"

"I don't know, Sister Josephine. Perhaps I am."

The sister laid her hand solemnly on the girl's arm.

"Esther, if you love anyone better than God, you have no right to come here," she said.

Then she turned away and walked sorrowfully down the long mission room. She was disappointed in Esther Helps, and though Esther's own heart never faltered, she felt a sharp pang pierce it.

That night she came home late.

"Has Brother Jerome come in?" she asked Cherry.

"No. How you do fash about that man! His supper's waiting for him, and I saw to his fire. Now I'm going to bed. I'm dead tired."

"Do, Cherry. I'll sit up for Brother Jerome."

"Ask him, for goodness sake, not to march the boards so frequent. He'll have my grey hairs to account for. He's picked up a cough, too, and between the creaking of the boards, and the coughing, I have nice nights lately."

"You study too much, Cherry, or you wouldn't mind such little noises. Now go to bed, dear. I'll give Brother Jerome a hint."

"Good-night, Esther. Uncle's been in bed an hour or more. I hope that brother of the slums won't keep you long."

Cherry ran upstairs, and Esther went into the bright warm little kitchen. She left the door wide open, and then she sat and waited.

The substance of Sister Josephine's words rang in her ears.

"If you love another better than God, you have no right to come here."

Did she love another better than God? No, no, impossible. A man had influenced her life, and because of his influence she had given herself up, soul and body, to God's service. How could she love the man best? He had only pointed to the higher way.

Then she heard his step outside; his latch-key in the door, and she felt herself tremble. He went straight upstairs, never glancing in the direction of the kitchen; as he went he coughed, and his cough sounded hollow. His figure, never remarkably upright, was much bent.

Esther waited a few minutes; then, her heart going pit-a-pat, she crept very softly upstairs, passed her own room and Cherry's, and knocked at Wyndham's door.

He came and opened it.

"Can I speak with you, brother?"

"Certainly. Come in, Esther?"

The attic had been converted into a wonderfully snug apartment. The bed and washing apparatus were curtained off, and the part of the room which surrounded the hearth revealed a bright fire, a little table on which a tempting cold supper was spread, and a deep easy chair.

"Sit down, brother," said Esther, "and eat. Let me help you. I can talk while you eat your supper. Are you very tired to-night? Yes, I am afraid you are dreadfully tired."

"I am always tired, Esther. That is in the condition of things."

He sank back into his chair as if he were too weary to keep out of it. Then, with a flash of the old Gerald Wyndham in his eyes and manner, he sprang up.

"I was forgetting myself. Will you sit here!"

"What do you take me for, Mr.Brother Jerome, I mean. I have come up here to see you eat, to see you rest, and tototalk to you."

"Esther, I have no words to thank you. You are, yes, you are the noblest woman I know."

She flushed all over; her eyes shone.

"And isn't that thanks for ever and ever?" she said in a voice in which passion trembled.

Wyndham did not notice. He had taken off his hat, and Cherry's good supper stood by his side. He ate a little, then put down his knife and fork.

"Ain't you hungry, sir?"

"No. At first, when I came here, I was so starved that I never could eat enough. Now I am the other way, not hungry at all."

"And, sir, you have got a cough."

"Yes, I had a very bad wetting last week, and a cough is the result. Strange. I had no cough when I slept out of doors."

"Mr. Wynd—Brother Jerome, I mean, you wouldn't go back to that old life? Say you wouldn't go back."

The almost anguish in her voice penetrated for the first time to Wyndham's ear. He gave her a startled glance, then said with warmth:

"Esther, you and your father have been good Samaritans to me; as long as it is safe I will stay with you."

"It shall and must be safe. Who would look for you here, of all places, when they think you are buried under the waves of the sea?"

"That is true. I expect it is perfectly safe for me to stay."

He lay back in his chair, and gazed into the fire; he had almost forgotten Esther's presence.

"And you like it—you feel happier since you came?" she asked, presently, in a timid voice.

"What did you say?"

"Mr. Wyndham," the forbidden name came out with a burst, "do tell poor Esther Helps that you are happier since she found you."

She had fallen on her knees, the tears were streaming from her eyes; she held out her hands to him.

"Oh," she said, "I would give my life for yours."

In a moment Wyndham's dreamy attitude left him; he sprang to his feet, all alive and keen and watchful. He was the old Wyndham; his eyes were full of pity, which made his whole face radiant.

"Hush," he said. "Get up. Don't say any more. Not another word—not a syllable. You forget yourself. Esther. I saved you once—I must save you again. Sit there, yes, there; I am quite strong. I must tell you the truth. Esther, I said just now that you were the noblest woman I know. You must go on being noble. I will stay here on that condition."

"Oh, sir, will you?" Poor Esther would have liked to shrink through the very boards. "Will you forgive me, sir?"

"Hush; don't talk about forgiveness. There is nothing to forgive. Esther, I will show you how much I trust you. I will talk to you about my wife. I will tell you a little of my story; I mean the part I can tell without implicating others."

CHAPTER XLII

Esther was now seated in the easy-chair; Wyndham stood by the mantel-piece. He had got a shock, and that shock had given him strength, and a good deal of his old manner.

"Esther," he said, "I cannot tell you all the story, but some of it I should like you to hear. You are a friend to me, Esther, and the part that relates to myself I will confide to you."

"Sir, I know the other part; you have been the victim of a wicked man."

"Hush; I don't wish to speak about anyone but myself. I don't blame anyone but myself. I loved a woman, Esther Helps, so much better than myself that for her sake I resolved to die to the world. I need not give you the reason of this. It seemed to me necessary for her happiness that I should do this; and I did not think it too much to do. I married my wife knowing that the great love I had for her was not returned. This seemed all for the best, as when I died, as die to all appearance I should, her heart would not be broken. She could continue to live happy and honored. Do you follow me?"

"Yes, sir, yes. Are you tired? Will you sit, Mr. Wyndham?"

"I was never less tired. When I speak of my wife I feel as if a fresh vigor were coming into me. We were married, and I soon found that I had overtaxed my own resolve. In one particular I could not complete the sacrifice I had undertaken. I tried to make her love me, and for a time—a short time—I thought I had succeeded."

The speaker paused, and the eagerness of his tone changed.

"I failed. The heart that I most craved for was not to be mine. I tested it, but it did not respond. This was best, no doubt, but the fact preyed on me dreadfully. I went on board the Esperance, and, then, God forgive me, the thought took possession of me, the idea overmastered me, that I would make my fictitious death real. Everything had been carefully arranged with regard to my apparent death. That part implicates others, so I will not touch upon it. I resolved to make certainty doubly certain by dying in earnest. Thus my wife's future would be assured. My death would be real, the thing that might come upon her would be averted for ever. I was in a condition when I could not balance right and wrong; but my intellect was sufficiently keen and sensible to make me prepare for the deed I contemplated. I took steps which would prevent anyone on board thinking that I had fallen overboard by design. My death would be attributed to the merest accident. Thus all was made absolutely safe. What is the matter, Esther?"

"Oh, Mr. Wyndham! Oh; you frighten me. Did you—did you think of your soul, sir?"

"I did, Esther. But I loved my wife better than my hope of heaven. I resolved to risk even that for her. As I tell you, I had no sense of personal right or wrong at that time. You see that I am a very wicked man, Estherno heroa man who yielded to a dire temptation. I won't talk about this. The night came, and I dropped into the water. There was a storm that night. It was dark, but now and then the stars could be seen through the rifts of the clouds. As I leapt overboard I looked up, and saw the brightness of the Southern Cross. Then I went under. The great waves closed over my head. The next instant I came to the surface only possessed with one fierce frantic desire, to save the life I meant to throw away. Better be a living dog than a dead lion, I said to myself. Yes, I would liveif only like the miserable dogs of Eastern towns, w ould live as the outcast, as the scum of the earthI would live. I had done a horrible thing in seeking to throw away my life. I cried aloud in an anguish of terror:'God spare me! God leave my breath in my body! Don't take my spirit before the judgment seat!' Through the rifts in the clouds I saw a boat at a little distance manned by some of the sailors who were looking for me. I shouted, but no living voice could be heard in the gale. Then I resolved to husband my strength. I was an excellent swimmer, and I could always float like a cork. I could not swim in that sea, but I could lie quite passive on the waves. I turned on my back, and waited for the issue of events. I closed my eyes and felt myself being moved up and down. The motion in itself was not unpleasant. The waves were wonderfully buoyant. Instead of losing my strength I was rested. My heart beat steadily. I knew that my chance of life depended on my keeping very cool. Presently something struck me. I put out my hand and grasped a floating oar. By means of the oar I knew that unless I froze with the cold I could keep above the water for hours. I placed it under my arms and kept above the water with very little effort.

"The cold, however, was intense, and I doubt that I could have lived till morning had not another chance of deliverance just then appeared. The clouds had almost cleared from the sky, and by the brightness of the southern constellations I saw something gleaming white a little further off. It was not the ship, which must have been a league or two away by now, but something I could see in my present horizontal position. I ventured to raise my head a very little, and saw a boata boat painted whitewhich, strange to say, had not been overturned by the roughness of the waves. It was gently floating onwards in my direction. The name Esperance was painted in gold letters on the outside of the boat, near the bow. I guessed at once what had happened. One of the ships' boats had got loose from its moorings in the gale, and was now sent to me as an ark of deliverance. It was evidently on one of the ship's oars, too, that I was supporting my head.

"Then I saw that God did not mean me to die, and a great glow of gratitude and even happiness ran through me. You will wonder at this, but you don't know how horrible death looked in the jaws of that angry sea.

"The boat came nearer, and nearer and my happiness and sense of relief grew to almost rapture. I cried aloud:'God. I thank Thee! Take the life you have thought worth preserving almost through a miracle, as your own absolutely. Take my body, take my spirit, to spend, to worship, to lose myself in Thee!' Then the boat came up, and I had to duck under to avoid being stunned by her.

"It is no easy matter to get into an empty boat in a rough sea. My hands were almost numb, too, for I had been a couple of hours in the water. I felt, however, quite cool, self-possessed and quiet. I could think clearly, and bring my little knowledge of boats to my aid. I knew my only chance of not upsetting the boat was to climb over by the stern. This, after tremendous difficulties, I accomplished. I lay in the bottom of the boat for some time quite unconscious. When at last I was able to rouse myself, daylight had come and the storm had gone down. My clothes were drenched through with salt water. I could not keep from shivering, and every bone ached. I was not the least hungry, but I was consumed with thirst. There were two or three oars lashed to the side of the boat. I could row, therefore, and the exercise warmed me. Presently the sun came up in the heavens. I was glad of this, but its rays beating on my uncovered head soon produced headache, which in its turn brought on a queer giddiness and a feeling of sickness. I saw now that I was going to be very ill, and I wondered how long I should retain my senses. I knew that it behoved me to be very careful. I was alive, but for my wife's sake I must appear to be dead. I saw that I had taken the very best possible step to insure this end, and if I could only carry on my purpose to its conclusion I should have adopted a far better plan for securing the establishment of my own apparent death than the one originally devised for me.

"Aching as I did from head to foot I found it difficult to keep my thoughts collected. I managed, however, to do so, and also to scratch out the name of the Esperance from the bows of the boat. This I accomplished with my pocket knife. I also cut away my own name from my linen, and from two handkerchiefs which I found in my pockets. These handkerchiefs had been marked by my wife. After this I knew there was no more I could do. I must drift along and take my chance of being picked up. I cannot recall how I passed the day. I believe I rowed a little when I felt cold; but the greater part of the time I simply allowed the boat to drift.

"That evening I was picked up by a trading vessel bound for the Cape. Its crew were mostly Dutch, and several of the sailors were black. I faintly remember going on board the vessel. Then all memory leaves me. I had a long illness─a fever which changed me, turning my hair very grey. I grew a beard in my illness, and would not allow it to be removed when I got better, as I knew that in the future I must live under the shadow of death, I must completely sink the identity which made life of value.

"I was put into hospital when we arrived at Cape Town, and when I got better was given a small purse of money, which had been collected by some people who professed to take an interest in me. On the day I left the hospital I really commenced my new life.

"It is unnecessary to tell you all that followed. I had not forgotten my vow—the vow I made to God verily out of the deeps. I determined, as far as it was in me, absolutely to renounce myself and to live for God as He reveals himself in suffering man. I did not resolve to do this with any ulterior motive of saving my own soul, and atoning for the sin of the past. I felt that God deserved all that I could possibly give Him, and to give it absolutely and without reservation kept me, I believe, from losing my senses. For a time all went well. Then the hunger which had been my curse came back. You will ask what that was. It was a sense of utter starvation which no physical food could satisfy, which no mental food could appease. I must get near my wife. I had sinned for her, and now I could not keep away from her. I must at least live in the same country. I prayed against this hunger; I fought with it. I struggled with it, but I could not beat it down. A year ago I came back to England. I came to London, to the safest place for a man who must hide. Willing hands are always needed to help to lighten some of the load of misery in this great city. I called myself Brother Jerome, and presently I found my niche. I worked, and I could have been happy. Yes, starving in body, with nowhere to lay my head, I could have been happy following The Blessed example, but for the hunger which always drove me mad, which was gnawing at my heart, which gnaws there still—which—Esther—Esther Helps—is—killing me!"

Wyndham dropped his head on his hands. He uttered one groan. When he raised his head again his eyes were wet.

"I am close to my wife," he said; "but I have never heard of her once—not once since I returned."

Then he sat down in the chair which Esther rose from. He began to cough again, and Esther saw the drops of sweat standing large on his forehead.

It was now her turn to speak. She stood upright—a tall, slim woman—a woman who had gone through a change so great as almost to amount to a new birth—while Wyndham had been telling his story.

"Now," she said, "I am happy. I praise God for His mercies, for it is given to me to comfort you."

Wyndham raised his head; he was too exhausted to ask her what she meant, except with his eyes.

"Your wife is well, and from this day forth you shall hear news of her, fresh news, once a week. Every Sunday you shall hear."

"Esther, don't torture me. Are you telling me truth?"

"I am telling you the solemn truth. Would I lie to a man like you? Mr. Wyndham, do you know, has anyone ever told you that you have a child?"

"Nobody. Is this the case? My God, a child!"

"Yes, sir, a little boy; he is called after you. He is three years old. You'd like to see him, maybe?"

"Good heavens, Esther, this is like new wine to me. I have a son of my own—Valentine's son!"

He began to pace the floor.

"And you would like to see him, wouldn't you, sir?"

"Yes—no—the joy might kill me. People have died of joy."

"You wouldn't die of joy, sir. It has always been the other way with you. Joy would make you live, would cure that cough, and that sinking feeling you have told me of."

"And the hunger, Esther—the hunger which gnaws and gnaws. Esther, you are a wonderful woman."

"Sit down, Mr. Wyndham. Keep quiet. Don't get excited. I'll do this for you. I made up the plan this morning. It was about that I came to speak to you. The baby wants a new nurse. To-morrow I am going to offer for the place. I shall get it, too, no fear of that. I shall live in the same house as your wife, every night your son will sleep in my arms. Each Sunday I come here with my news—my weekful of news. Some day I bring your son. What more natural than that I should come to my father once a week. Who will suspect? Mr. Wyndham, that hunger of yours shall have one weekly meal. No fear, no fear. And now, sir, go to bed, and may God Almighty bless you!"

CHAPTER XLIII

Valentine Wyndham had often said that no greater treasure of a nurse could be found than the one who came to her when little Gerald was a month old. When she saw Esther, however, she changed her mind. Esther was superior to Annette in personal appearance, in intellect, and in a curious unspoken intangible sympathy which brought a strange sense of comfort to Valentine's strained and worn heart. Esther was full of tact. She was not demonstrative, but her every look and word expressed loving interest. Baby very soon ceased to fret for Annette. With a child's fickleness he boldly declared that he liked "noo nurse better than old nurse." His most loving word for Esther was "noo nurse," and he was always contented and happy when he lay in noo nurse's arms and listened to her stories. She had wonderful stories for him, stories which she never dreamt of telling in his mother's presence, stories which always led to one termination—a termination which had a wonderful fascination for baby. They were about little fatherless boys, who in the most unlooked for ways found their fathers. Baby revelled in these tales.

"I'se not got a farwer, noo nursie," he would generally end sorrowfully.

Then Esther would kiss him, and tell him to wait, and to watch for the good fairies who were so kind to little boys.

His whooping cough soon got better, and he was able to go out. One day Esther took him early into the Park. He was dressed all in white fur. Esther told him he looked like Baby Bunting.

"But I haven't got a farwer to buy me a wabbit-skin,"
quoth baby.

That day, however, the father he did not know pressed two or three burning kisses on his round cheek. Esther sat down on a chair near a very worn and shabby-looking man. His back was partly to her. She said a word and he turned round. He looked at the child. Suddenly a light filled his sunken eyes—a beautiful light. He stretched out his arms, and straight as an arrow from a bow, Baby Bunting found a shelter in their close embrace.

"Kiss me," said the man.

The little lips pressed his cheek.

"I 'ove oo," said baby, in his contented voice. "Has 'oo little boys of 'oo own?"

"One little boy."

"Oo 'ove him, I pose?"

"Ay."

Three kisses were pressed on baby's face and he was returned to Esther.

"Nice man," he said patronizingly, by-and-bye. "But he gived raver hard kisses when he crunched me up."

That evening baby told his mother that a man met him in the Park, who kissed him and looked sad, and said he had a little boy of his own.

"And he crunched me up with kisses, mover," concluded baby.

"Was this man a friend of yours, Esther?" queried Mrs. Wyndham.

"Yes, madam, a friend of mine, and of my father's. A gentleman with a very sorrowful story. I think it comforted him to kiss master baby."

Esther was a woman of acute observation. It seemed to her that if there was an individual on earth to be envied it was Valentine Wyndham. What matter though she thought herself a widow? Still she had won a love of a quality and depth which surely must satisfy the most exacting heart. Esther often said to herself that if she were Valentine she must surely rest content. As to her forgetting Wyndham that could surely, surely never be.

These were Esther's thoughts, always supposing the case to be her own; but she had not been many weeks in the house in Park-Lane before she began to open her eyes and to suspect that matters were otherwise with her young mistress. Valentine, although still a wife, supposed herself a widow. All the world thought her such. What more natural than that she should turn her thoughts once more to love. At the time of her supposed widowhood she was under twenty years of age. Why should she mourn for her young husband all her days? Surely there was somebody who considered that she ought not to mournsomebody who came almost daily to the house, whom Mrs. Wyndham liked to talk to. For Esther noticed that her eyes were bright after Adrian Carr went away. She did not guess that their brightness was generally caused by the shedding of tears.

Esther began to feel very uncomfortable. Should she or should she not tell Wyndham of the danger which was threatening Valentine?

There came a Sunday when Mrs. Wyndham entered her nursery with a request.

"Nurse, my head aches dreadfully. I know you stipulated to have every Sunday afternoon to yourself, but if you could stay at home to-day I should be grateful."

No one could make requests more sweetly than Valentine, and Esther felt herself coloring up with the pain of refusing.

"I am very sorry, madam," she said in a low constrained voice; "but—but—my father will expect me. You know it was an understood thing, madam, that I was to see him once a week. You remember my telling you I am his only child."

"Yes, yes," said Valentine, "and I have thought of that. If you will take care of Gerry this one afternoon I will send the page in a cab to your home to fetch your father here." Esther changed color, from red to white.

"I am more sorry than I can express, my dear madam, but it would make all the difference to my father seeing me in my own little home and here. My father is very humble in his ways, dear madam. I think, perhaps, if you have a headache, Jane, the under housemaid, might be trusted for once with master baby."

"Jane has already gone out," replied Valentine coldly. Then with an effort she swallowed down her resentment. "I will be frank with you, Esther," she said. "If it was simply a headache I could certainly take care of my little boy, even at some inconvenience. But there is more behind. I promised Miss Wyndham, who is now in town, to meet her this afternoon at Mr. Carr's new church. She is most anxious to hear him preach, and I should be sorry to disappoint her."

"You mean you are anxious to hear him preach," quoth Esther, under her breath. "And is it on that account I will leave a hungry heart to starve?" Aloud she said: "Do you object to my taking master baby with me, madam?"

"I do object. The child must not be out so late. Then you distinctly refuse to accommodate me, Esther?"

"I am obliged to adhere to our arrangement, Mrs. Wyndham. I am truly sorry."

Valentine held out her hand to her little boy.

"Come, then, Baby Bunting," she said. "Mother will play with her boy; and poor Aunt Lilias must go to church alone."

She did not look at Esther, but went quietly away, holding the child's hand.

"What a brute I am," soliloquized the nurse. "And yet, she, poor young lady, how can she—how can she forget?"

Esther's home was in all its Sunday quiet when she reached it. Helps was having his afternoon siesta in the kitchen. Cherry was spending the day with the cousins who admired her recitations. Helps started out of his slumbers when his daughter came in.

"Essie," he said, "I'm glad you've come. That young man upstairs is very ill."

Esther felt her heart sinking down. She pressed her hand to her side.

"Is he worse, father?" she gasped.

"Oh, I don't know that he's worse; he's bad enough as it is, without going in for being worse. He coughs constant, and Cherry says he don't eat enough to keep a robin going. Esther, I wish to goodness we could get him out of this."

"Why so, father? He doesn't hurt you. Even Cherry can't name any fault in him."

"No, but suppose he was to die here. There'd be an inquest, maybe, and all kinds of questions. Well, I'm not hard-hearted, but I do wish he'd go."

Esther sank down into the nearest chair.

"You speak cruel words now and then, father," she said. "Who talks of dying? He won't die. If it comes to that, or any chance of it, I'll come back and nurse him to life again."

"Essie, you think a sight of that young man."

"Well, I do. I'm not going to deny it. I'm going upstairs to see him now."

CHAPTER XLIV

AT THE SOUND OF THE CLOCK

She left the room, tripping lightly upstairs in her neat nurse's dress. When she got to Wyndham's door and knocked gently for admission her heart, however, was beating so wildly that she feared he might notice it.

"Come in," said his voice; she entered.

He was lying back in his easy-chair. When he saw Esther he took off the soft hat which he always wore in Cherry's presence, and greeted her with that brightness in his eyes which was the greatest reward he could possibly offer her.

"You are a little late," he said; "but I thought you would not fail me."

"I won't ever fail you, Mr. Wyndham; you know that."

"Esther, it is safer to call me Brother Jerome."

"Not at the present moment. The house is empty but for my father. Still, if you wish it, sir."

"I think I do wish it. A habit is a habit. The name may slip out at a wrong moment, and then—my God, think what would happen then!"

"Don't excite yourself, sir. Esther Helps is never likely to forget herself. Still I see the sense of your wishes. You are Brother Jerome to me always from this out. And now, before I go any further, I want to state a fact. Brother Jerome, you are ill."

"I am ill, Esther. Ill, nigh unto death."

"My God, you shan't die!"

"Hush; the question of dying does not rest with you or me. I want to die, so probably I shall live."

"You look like dying. Does Cherry feed you well?"

"Better than well. I want for nothing."

"Is your fire kept up all night?"

"Esther, I have not come to requiring a night nurse yet. My fire goes out in the early hours before the dawn."

"The coldest part of the twenty-four hours. Brother Jerome, you must give up visiting in East London at present."

"No, not while I can crawl. You forget that on a certain night I surrendered my body as well as my spirit to the service of comfort. While I can comfort others I will. There is nothing else left to me."

"Then, sir, you will die—you will deliberately kill yourself."

"No, I tried that once. I won't again. Esther, what is the matter? You are a good girl. It is a mistake for you to waste your pity on me."

"You must forgive me, sir. Pity comes to one unbidden. Pity—and—and sympathy. If you get worse, I shall leave my situation and come home and nurse you."

"Then you will indeed kill me. You will take away my last hope. My one goblet of new wine will be denied me. Then I shall truly die. Esther, what is your budget of news? How is my wife? Begin—go on—tell me everything."

"Mrs. Wyndham is well, sir."

"Well? Do you mean by that that she is happy? Does she laugh much? Does she sing?"

"Sometimes she laughs. Once I heard her sing."

"Only once, Esther? She had a very sweet voice. I used sometimes to tell her that it was never silent."

"Once, sir, I heard her sing."

"Oh, once? Was it a cheerful song?"

"It was on a Sunday evening. She was singing to your little boy. I think she sang the 'Happy Land.' I don't quite remember. I came to fetch the boy to bed, and she was singing to him. She took her hands off the piano suddenly when I came in, and there were tears in her eyes."

"Tears? She was always sensitive to music. And yet you say she does not look sad."

"I should not call her sad, Brother Jerome. Her face is calm and quiet. I think she is a very good young lady."

"You need not tell me that, Esther; you managed very well about the boy."

"Thank you, sir. I think I did. What did you feel when you saw him, sir?"

"Rapture. All my blood flowed swiftly. I lived and breathed. I had an exquisite five minutes."

"The boy is not like his mother, sir."

"No, nor like me. He resembles my sister Lilias. Esther, I must see him again."

"You shall, by-and-bye, but not too soon. We must not run any risks."

"Certainly not. I will have much patience. Hold out the hope only, and I will cling to it indefinitely."

"You shall see the child again, Brother Jerome."

"God abundantly bless you. Now go on. Tell me more. How does my wife spend her time? Has she many visitors?"

"Sometimes her father."

"Only sometimes? They used to be inseparable."

"Not now, sir. There is something wrong between them. When they meet they are constrained with one another, and they don't meet very often. I have orders, though, to take the child every morning to see Mr. Paget."

"Have you? I am sorry for that. He kisses my son, does he?"

"Yes, sir. He seems wrapped up in him; he"

"Don't talk of him. That subject turns my blood into vinegar. Go on. Tell me more. What other visitor has my wife?"

"Sometimes your sister, Miss Lilias Wyndham."

"My sister? Esther, you don't know what that name recalls. All the old innocent days; the little hymns before we went to bed, and the little prayers at our mother's knee. I don't think I can bear to hear much about Lilias; but I am glad she loves my wife."

"She does, sir. She is devoted to Mrs. Wyndham. I don't think any other visitors come except Mr. Carr."

"Adrian Carr, a clergyman?"

Wyndham's tone had suddenly become alert and wakeful.

"I believe the gentleman's name is the Rev. Adrian Carr. Brother Jerome."

"Why do you speak in that guarded voice, Esther? Have you anything to conceal?"

"No, sir, no. Don't excite yourself. I conceal nothing; he comes, that is all."

"But surely, not often? He is my father's curate; he cannot often come to London."

"He is not Mr. Wyndham's curate now, sir; he has a church of his own, St. Jude's they call it, at the corner of Butler-street."

"And he comes constantly to my house? To to see my wife?"

"Your—your widow, sir."

"God help me, Esther! God help me! How am I to endure this! My poor—my beloved—my sweet—and are you exposed to this? Esther, Esther, this care turns me into a madman."

"You must stay quiet, Brother Jerome. Mr. Carr comes, and your—your widow sees him."

"Do you think she likes him?"

"Oh, sir, I would rather die than have to tell it to you."

"I cannot listen to your sentimentalisms. Does my wife seem happy when Adrian Carr calls upon her?"

"I think she is interested in him, Brother Jerome."

"Does she see him alone?"

"Often alone."

"And you say she seems pleased?"

"I think so. It is incomprehensible to me."

"Never mind whether you understand it or not. Do you know that by this news you are turning me into a devil? I'll risk everything—everything. I'll expose the whole vile conspiracy if my wife is entrapped into engaging herself to Adrian Carr."

Brother Jerome was no longer a weak-looking invalid; he began to pace his attic floor; a fire burnt in his sunken eyes, and he clenched his thin hands. For the time he was strong.

"Listen to me, Esther Helps. My wife shall run no risk of that kind. It was in the contract that that should be prevented. I sinned for her—yes, I willingly sinned for her—but she shall never sin for me. Rather than that we'll all go to penal servitude. I, and your father, and her father."

"Do quiet yourself, Mr. Wyndham. There may be nothing in what I told you."

Esther felt really frightened.

"Perhaps the gentleman comes to see your sister, Miss Wyndham. He certainly comes, but—but—"

"Esther, the whole thing must be put a stop to—the faintest shadow of risk must not be run. My wife thinks herself a widow, but she must retain the feelings of a wife. It must be impossible for her, while I live, to think of another man."

"Can you not bring yourself back to her memory, sir? Is there no way?"

"That is a good thought. Don't speak for a little. Let me think."

Wyndham continued to pace the floor. Esther softly built up the fire with trembling fingers. In this mood she was afraid of Wyndham. That fire in his eyes was new to her. She was cowed—she shivered. With her mental vision she already saw her grey-headed father in the prisoner's dock.

"Esther," said Wyndham, coming up to her suddenly. "I have thought of a plan. It won't implicate anyone, and if a chord in Valentine's heart still beats true to me this must touch it. At what hour does Carr generally call to see my wife?"

"He is a busy man; he comes mostly at night, about nine o'clock. He has a cup of tea, and goes away at ten. When Miss Wyndham is there he sometimes stays on till nearly eleven."

"He comes every night?"

"Almost every night."

"And he leaves at ten?"

"A few minutes after ten. When the clock strikes ten it seems to be a sort of a signal to him, and he gets up and goes away."

"Thank you. Ten, then, will be the hour. Esther, something else may happen at ten of the clock. You need not look so white. I said no risk would be run. It is possible, however, that my wife may be agitated. No, you don't suppose I am going to reveal myself to her—nothing of the sort. Still, something will happen which may break down her nerve and her calm. In that case she may even appeal to you, Esther, you will be very guarded. You must remember that on the success of this scheme of mine depends your father's safety, for if she engages herself to Carr I swear by the God above me that we three, Paget, your father, and I, go to prison."

"Sir, I must own that I feel dreadfully frightened."

"Poor Esther! And you don't deserve it, for you are the best of girls and quite innocent. But that is ever the way. The innocent bear the sins of the guilty. In this matter, however, Esther, you must trust me, and keep your own counsel. Now, I want to know if you have any money you can lend me?"

"I have two sovereigns in my purse, sir. Will that do?"

"Plentifully. I will tell you what I want the money for. I want to hire a violin—a good one. Once, Esther. I used to express my feelings through the violin. It talked for me. It revealed some of the tortures of my soul. The violin shall speak again and to my wife. Now you are prepared at all points. Good-bye. Be as brave as you are good, and the worst may be averted."

CHAPTER XLV

On the following night, as Esther was preparing to go to bed, the nursery door was suddenly opened and Mrs. Wyndham entered.

"Esther," she said, "I want baby."

"He is sound asleep, madam. You would not wake him?"

"He can be moved without disturbing him. I want him to sleep in my bed. I want his company. My little child?"

She was trembling. She caught hold of the rails of the baby's cot.

"Little children are sacred innocent things, aren't they, nurse? I want my little child to-night."

"Strange," thought Esther. "I listened with all my might, and I could not hear anything except the usual barrel organs and German bands in the street. But she has heard something, there isn't a doubt. How queer and shaken she looks. Poor young thing, I do pity her; she can't help thinking she is a widow when she is a wife."

Aloud Esther complied with Mrs. Wyndham's request cheerfully.

"Certainly, madam. The child will never know that we are moving him. If you will go on to your room, ma'am, I'll follow with master baby."

Mrs. Wyndham turned away at once.

When the nurse entered her mistress' room with the child, there was a soft nest made in the big bed to receive him, and the fire in the grate cast a cheerful glow over everything.

"Let me kiss him," said the mother. "My darling, my beloved. I'll take him into my arms presently, nurse, and then all fears will fly away."

"Fears, Mrs. Wyndham? No one ought to fear in this cheerful room."

"Perhaps not, nurse; but sometimes I am superstitiouspainfully so. Yes, put baby there. Is he not a handsome boy? Although I could wish he were more like his father."

"He seems to feature your sister-in-law, Miss Lilias Wyndham, madam."

"How queer that you should find that out! He is not like what Lilias is now, but they all say she was just such another little child. Nurse, I hate high winds—there is going to be a storm to-night."

"Would you like me to sleep on the sofa in your room, madam?"

"Yes, no—yes, oh, yes."

"I will bring a shawl, and wrap it round me and lie down."

"No, don't, nurse, don't. I must not yield to this nameless thing. I must—I will be brave. And the child, my own little child, will comfort me."

"What is the nameless thing, dear madam?"

"I cannot—I won't speak of it. Esther, are you—are you going?"

"Certainly not, Mrs. Wyndham. I mean, not yet."

"That is right. Take this chair; warm yourself. Esther. I don't look on you as an ordinary nurse. Long ago I used to be so much interested in you."

"It was very kind of you, madam; young ladies, as a rule, have no time to interest themselves in poor girls."

"But I had plenty of time, and did interest myself. My father was always so much attached to yours. I was an only child and you were an only child. I used to wonder if you and your father cared for each other as passionately, as loyally, as I and my father cared."

"I don't know that, madam; we did love each other. Our love remains unchanged. True love ought never to change, ought it?"

"It ought never to change," repeated Mrs. Wyndham. Her face grew white, her lips trembled. "Sometimes true love is killed by a blow," she said suddenly. Then her expression changed again, she tried to look cheerful. "I won't talk any more. I am sleepy, and that nest near baby looks inviting. Good-night, dear nurse."

"Let me undress you, ma'am. Let me see you in your nest beside the child."

"No. Go now. Or rather—rather—stay a moment or two longer. Esther, had you ever the heartache?"

"There are a few women, madam, who don't know what the heartache means."

"I suppose that is true. Once I knew nothing about it. Esther, you are lucky never to have married."

Esther Helps made no response.

"To marry—to love—and then to lose," dreamily murmured Mrs. Wyndham. "To love, and then to lose. Esther, it is a dreadful thing to be a widow, when you are young."

"But the widow can become a wife again," suddenly replied Esther.

The words seemed forced from her lips; she was sorry the moment she had uttered them.

Mrs. Wyndham opened her big eyes wide.

"I suppose the widows who can become wives again have not lost much," she responded in a cold voice.

Then she moved over to the bedside and began to undress.

A few moments later Esther left her. She felt puzzled, perplexed, unhappy. She had no key to the thoughts which were passing in her mistress' mind. Her impression was that Valentine loved Carr, but felt a certain shame at the fact.

The next evening the vicar of St. Jude's called again. He came hurriedly to the door, ran up the stairs without being shown the way, and entered Valentine's presence with a brisk step. Esther leant over the banisters to watch him as he entered the drawing-room. It was half-past nine when he arrived; he had been conducting a prayer meeting and was later than usual.

The drawing-room door was shut on the two, and Esther, who had been sitting with the child, now crept softly downstairs and entered a small bedroom at the back of the drawing-room. This bedroom also looked on the street. It was the room occupied by Lilias when she visited her sister-in-law. Esther closed the door softly behind her. The room was dark. She went up to the window and looked eagerly up and down the gaily-lighted street.

She could distinguish no words, but the soft murmur of voices came to her through the drawing-room wall.

"You are better to-night?" said Carr, in a cheery, confident tone; "although you took it upon yourself to disobey me."

"I could not go to the prayer-meeting. I could not."

"Well, well, you must act as you think best; only I don't think staying at home is the best thing for you."

"Oh, I shan't get over-nervous; and Lilias is coming to me next week."

Carr's eyes brightened.

"That is good," he said. "Well, I must not stay. I just looked in for a moment. I knew you would not let these superstitious fears get the better of you. Good-night."

He held out his hand. Valentine put hers behind her.

"No," she said; "you always stay until past ten. It was at ten o'clock last night" She trembled more words would not come.

"And I will stay until past ten to-night," responded Carr resuming his seat. "Now, don't look at the clock. Turn your thoughts to me and my affairs. So Miss Wyndham comes here next week?"

"She does."

"Shall I put everything to the test, then?"

Valentine's face grew bright.

"Oh how earnestly I wish you would," she cried, clasping her hands.

"Do you, indeed? Then you must think there is some chance for me. The fact is, Mrs. Wyndham, I am the veriest coward that ever breathed. If I win, I win for ever. I mean that I am made, body, soul, and spirit. If I lose, I think morally I shall go under. A main spring will be broken which has kept me right, kept my eyes looking upwards ever since I knew your sister Lilias."

"But even if she refuses you, you will live on," said Valentine, in a dreamy voice. "We often have to live on when the main spring is broken. We creep instead of running, that is all."

"Now you are getting gloomy again. As your spiritual adviser I cannot permit it. You have put a daring thought into my head, and you are bound to think of me, not yourself, at present. Will you sing something to me before I go? You know Lilias' song of triumph; you taught it to her. Sing it to me to-night, it will be a good omen."

Valentine hesitated for a moment. Then she went over to the piano and opened it. Her fingers touched one or two chords tremblingly. Suddenly she stopped, her face worked. She looked at Carr with a piteous expression.

"I cannot sing the triumph song," she said, "it is not in me. I should do it no justice. This must take its place. But it is not for you, remember. Oh, no, I pray God never for you. Listen, don't scold me afterwards. Listen."

Her fingers ran over the keys, her voice swelled and filled the room:

"The murmur of the mourning ghost
That keeps the shadowy kine.Oh, Keith of Ravelston.
The sorrows of thy line!
Ravelston, Ravelston.
The merry path that leadsDown the golden morning hill.
And through the silver meads.
Ravelston, Ravelston.
The stile beneath the tree.The maid that kept her mother's kine.
The song that sang she.
She sang her song, she kept her kine.
She sat beneath the thorn.When Andrew Keith of Ravelston
Rode through the Monday morn.
His henchmen sing, his hawk bells ring.
His belted jewels shineO, Keith of Ravelston.
The sorrows of thy line!"

"Now, good-night," said Valentine, springing to her feet. "Don't question me about the song. I sang it, but I cannot speak of it. The clock is about to strike. It is your hour for farewell. Oh, yes, I wish you all luckall luck. The clock is striking! Oh, what a noise there is in the street!"

"What a silence you mean," said Carr, as he took her hand.

It was true. The thunderous rattle of a heavy waggon, the discordant notes of a brass band, the din of a hurdy-gurdy frightfully out of tune, suddenly stopped. It was as if a wave of sound had been arrested, and in the quiet floated up the passionate wail of a soul. There are no other words to describe what the sound meant. It had a voice and an interpretation. It was beautiful, but its beauty was torture. Trembling in every limb, Valentine sprang away from Carr, flew to one of the French windows, wrested it open, and stepped on to the balcony. She was in white, and the people in the street could see her. She pressed to the front of the balcony and looked eagerly up and down.

The wailing of the lost soul grew more feeblemore faint. It stopped. There was a pause of half a minute, and then the waggon lumbered on, and the hurdy-gurdy crashed out its discordant notes.

"I saw nothing," said Carr, who had followed Mrs. Wyndham on to the balcony and now led her back to the drawing-room. "I saw nothing," he repeated. "I mean. I did not see the man who played."

"But you heard?"

"Oh, yes, I heard."

"You could not see. That was spirit music. My husband played. Don't speak to me; don't touch me; you tried to argue me out of my belief last night, but even you heard to-night. My husband has come back in the spirit, and he has played for me. Only he knows that aironly he in all the world. That was 'Waves.' Once I told you the story of 'Music waves.'"

She did not faint, she crouched down by the fire; but no face to be alive could be whiter than hers.

"What is the matter, Mr. Carr?" she said suddenly. "Why cannot my husband's spirit rest? They say that those spirits that are hurried out of life before their time cannot rest. O, tell me what you think. O, tell me what it means. You heard the music yourself to-night."

"I did. I certainly heard it."

"And at the same hour. When the clock struck."

"That is a mere coincidence, not worth considering."

"I don't believe in its being a coincidence."

She beat her hands passionately together.

"The thing was planned—he planned it. He will come again to-morrow night when the clock strikes ten."

Again she beat her hands together; then she covered her face with them.

Carr looked at her anxiously. The weird soft wailing music had affected even his nerves. Of course he did not believe in the supernatural element, but he was touched by the distress of the woman who was crouching at his feet. This mental unrest, this superstitious terror, might have a disastrous effect. He must do his utmost to check it. If necessary he must even be cruel to be kind.

"Mrs. Wyndham," he said, "you must go away to-morrow; you must go into the country for a few days."

"I will not. I won't stir a step."

"You ought, your nerves are shaken. There is nothing for shaken nerves like change of air. Go to Jewsbury-on-the-Wold, and talk to Lilias. She, too, loved your husband; she will sympathize, but she will not lose sight of common-sense."

"I will not stir from here."

"I think for your child's sake you ought. The child belongs to your husband as well as you, to your dead husband. The child is fatherless as far as this world is concerned. You have no right—it is very, very wicked of you to do anything to make him motherless."

"What do you mean? Why do you speak to me in that tone? I don't deserve it."

"You do."

"I think you are cruel."

Valentine's eyes filled with sudden tears.

"What do you mean by saying that I will leave baby motherless?"

"I mean that if you encourage the fancy which has now taken possession of you you are extremely likely to lose your senses—to become, in short, insane. How can you train your child if you are insane?"

Valentine shuddered.

"But I did hear the music," she said. "The old story music that he only played. How can I doubt the evidence of my senses? Last night at ten o'clock I heard 'Waves' played on the violin, my husband's favorite instrument—the melody which he made, the harmony and melody with all the passion and its story, which he made about himself and me. No one else could produce those sounds. I heard them last night at ten o'clock, you were here, but you heard nothing. To-night there was silence in the street, and we both heard—we both heard."

"I certainly heard some very melancholy music."

"Played on the violin?"

"Yes, played on the violin."

"In short, you heard 'Waves.'"

"I heard something which I never heard before. I cannot tell the name."

"No. What you heard was 'Waves,' in other words the cry of a soul."

"Mrs. Wyndham, get up. Give me your hand. Look me in the face. Now, that is better. I am going to talk common-sense to you. You have been from the first impressed with the idea that foul play was done to your husband. For a time I own I shared your apprehension. I discovered one or two things in connection with his death which far more than your words inclined me to this belief. Since I came to London I have thought a great deal over the matter. Last week a lucky chance brought me in communication with Captain Jellyby of the Esperance. Ah, you start. I saw him. I think you would like me to bring him here some night. He entered into minute particulars of Wyndham's last days. He would like to tell you the story himself. I can only say that a fairer story could not be recorded of any man. He was beloved by every one on board the ship. 'We all loved him,' said Captain Jellyby. 'Emigrants, passengers, sailors, all alike. Sir,' he said, 'when Mr. Wyndham was washed over, there wasn't a dry eye on board. But if ever a man humbly and cheerfully went forth to meet his Creator, he was the man, sir. He met his death trying to help the man at the wheel. Bless his heart, he spent all his life trying to help other people.'"

Valentine was silently crying.

"You comfort me," she said; "you comfort me much. Go on."

"That is all, my dear friend, that is all. It set my mind at rest with regard to your husband. It ought to set yours at rest also. He is a glorious, and happy spirit in heaven now. Is it likely that he would come back from there to frighten you for no object or purpose? No, you must dismiss the idea from your mind."

"But the music—the unearthly music."

"Played by a strolling musician with a talent for the thing. That was all."

"His air and mine—'Waves.' The air that no one else knew, that was never written down."

"You imagined the likeness to the air you mention. Our imaginations play strange tricks with us. The air played to-night was of a very minor character, and had notes in common with the one your husband composed. Hence a fleeting resemblance. It is more natural and in accordance with sense to believe this than to suppose that your husband came back from heaven to torture you. Now, good-night. You are good. You will try and be brave. I ask you to be brave for the sake of your noble husband's child."

CHAPTER XLVI

As Carr was leaving the house he came across Esther, who, very white, but with a resolute look on her face, met him on the stairs.

"How is my mistress, sir?"

Carr felt nettled at her tone.

"Why do you ask?" he said shortly; "when last you saw her I presume she was well."

"No, sir."

"No?"

Carr paused. He gave Esther a quick piercing look, and his manner changed. Her face was strong, it could be relied on.

"You are the little boy's nurse, are you not?"

"I am, Mr. Carr."

"And you are attached to your mistress?"

Esther hesitated.

"II am," she said, but her voice trembled.

"Mrs. Wyndham wants some one who can be kind and sympathetic near her. Some one who can be tactful, and full of common-sense. Her nerves are greatly shaken. For instance she was much agitated at some music she heard in the street to-night."

"I heard it, sir. I was surprised. It wasn't like ordinary music."

"Oh, you thought so, did you? For heaven's sake don't repeat your thoughts to Mrs. Wyndham. You look a sensible young woman."

Esther dropped a curtsey.

"I hope I am," she said in a demure voice.

"Has your mistress a maida maid she likes?"

"No. I render her what little services are necessary."

"Can you stay in her room to-night? She ought not to be alone."

"I will sleep on the sofa in my mistress' room."

"That is right. Don't allude to the music in the street if you can help it."

Carr ran downstairs and went away, and Esther, slowly and hesitatingly, entered the drawing-room.

Mrs. Wyndham was standing with her two arms clasped round her husband's violin. The tears were raining from her eyes. Before she could disengage herself Esther saw the action, and a queer pang, half of pleasure, half of pain, shot through her. She saw at a glance that Gerald Wyndham's wife cared for no one but her husband. She stepped across the room quickly, and without any thought of the familiarity of the action put her hand through her mistress' arm, and led her towards the door.

"Come," she said, "you are tired and weak. Master baby is in his nest, and he wants you. Come, I am going to put you to bed."

Valentine raised no objection. She was trembling and cold. The tears were undried on her cheeks; the look of infinite pathetic patience in her eyes almost crushed Esther Helps.

"What a fool I was to suppose she didn't love her husband," she murmured. "As if any woman could be much with him and not love him. Ah, lucky Mrs. Wyndhamnotwithstanding all your sorrow you are the woman I envy most on earth."

Valentine did not object to her maid's attentions. She felt shaken and worn out, and was glad passively to submit. When she was in bed she spoke for the first time.

"Esther, get a shawl, and lie here, outside the clothes. It comforts me to have you near."

Esther obeyed without any comment. She wrapped a thick shawl around her, and lay down near the edge of the big bed. Valentine took her little rosy boy into her arms.

"Now you must go to sleep, Mrs. Wyndham," said the maid, and she resolutely shut her own dark eyes.

For an hour she lay motionless, every nerve keenly awake, and on tension. For an hour she never lifted her eyelids. At the end of that time she opened them, and glanced at her mistress. Valentine was lying as still as if she were carved in marble. Her eyes were wide open. They were looking straight before her out into the big room. She scarcely seemed to breathe, and never saw Esther when she glanced at her.

"This won't do," thought the maid. "Poor little soul, she has got an awful shock. She will be very ill if I don't do something to rouse and interest her. I know she loves her husband—I will speak of him."

Esther moved on purpose somewhat aggressively. Valentine's wide-open eyes never flinched or changed their expression. The maid touched her mistress on the shoulder.

"This isn't good of you," she said; "you ought to be asleep."

Valentine started and shivered violently.

"I thought I was asleep," she said. "At any rate I was far away."

"When people sleep they shut their eyes," quoth Esther.

"Were mine open? I did not know it. I was looking at a picture—a picture in real life. It was lovely."

"I like beautiful pictures," said Esther. "Tell me what you saw."

By this time these two women had forgotten the relative positions they bore to each other. Valentine observed no familiarity in Esther's tone. Esther spoke and thought as though she were Valentine's social equal. She knew she was above her mentally just then; it was necessary for her to take the lead.

"Tell me what you saw, madam," she said. "Describe your beautiful picture."

Valentine obeyed with the docility of a child.

"It was a seaside picture," she began. "The sun was setting, and there was a path of light across the waters. The path seemed to go right up into the sky, and melt, and end there. And I—I thought of Jacob's ladder, from earth to heaven, and the angels walking up and down. On the shore a man and a girl sat. He had his arm round her waist; and she was filling her hands with the warm soft sand and letting it dribble away through her fingers. She was happy. She felt warm and contented, and protected against the whole world. Although she did not know that she loved it so much, it was the arm that encircled her that gave her that feeling."

Valentine stopped suddenly.

"That was a pretty picture, madam," said Esther. "A pretty picture, and you described it well. I suppose the gentleman was the girl's lover or husband."

"Her lover and husband in one. They were married. They sat like that once during their honeymoon. Presently he, the husband, took up his violin, which he had beside him, and began to play."

"Don't go into the music part, please, Mrs. Wyndham. I want just to keep to the picture alone. I want to guess something. I am good at guessing. You were the happy young girl."

"I was; oh, I was."

"And the gentleman was your husband; yes, your husband, whom you dearly loved."

"Don't talk of him, he is lost, gone. Esther, I'm a miserable, miserable woman."

Her icy quiet was broken up. Long-drawn sobs escaped her; she shivered as she wept.

"It is an awful thing to love too lateto love loo late," she moaned.

"Madam, I'm going to give you some sal-volatile and water: when you have taken it you shall tell me the whole story from first to last. Yes, you had better; you have said too much or too little. I may be able to comfort you if I know all."

Esther administered the restorative. When the distressful sobs were quieted, and Mrs. Wyndham lay back exhausted on her pillow, she took her hand, and said with infinite tact and tenderness:

"You love him you have lost very deeply. Is that not so?"

"Beyond words to describe."

"You were young when you were married, Mrs. Wyndham; you are a very young woman still. Perhaps, as a young girl, as almost a child-girl, you did not know what great love meant."

"I always knew what great love meant. As a little girl I used to idolize my father. I remember when I was very young, not much older than baby here, lying down on the floor and kissing the carpet over which his steps had walked. I used to steal into his study and sit like a mouse; perfectly happy while I was watching him. When I saw his face that was bliss; when he took me in his arms I thought Heaven could give me no more. You are an only child. Esther Helps. Did you feel like that for your father?"

"No, madam, I always loved my father after a quiet fashion; I love him after a quiet fashion still. That kind of intense love I did not know. And you feel it still for Mr. Paget? I suppose it is natural. He is a handsome gentleman; he has a way about him that attracts people. For instance, my father would do anything for him. It is still bliss to you, Mrs. Wyndham, to watch your father's face."

"Come near to me, Esther; let me whisper to you. That love which I thought unquenchable isdead!"

"Madam, you astonish me! Dead?"

"It died, Esther Helps, on the morning my husband sailed away."

"Then you only love your husband now?"

"I love many people. For instance, this little child; for instance, my sister Lilias. What I feel for my husband is high above all these things. I cannot describe it. It lies herein my heartand my heart aches, and aches."

"It would make Mr. Wyndham very happy to hear you," said Esther.

Her words were unguarded. Valentine began to sob feebly.

"He can never hear me," she said. "That is the dreadful part. I loved him when we were married, but I did not know it. Then the knowledge came to me, and I was so happy. One evening I told him so. I said, 'I love you!' I shall never forget his face. Often he was sad, but his face seemed to shine when I said those words, and he took me in his arms, and I saw a little way into the depth of his great heart. Soon after that something happened—I am not going to tell it, it doesn't matter—please don't hold my hand, Esther. It is very queer that you should be with me to-night."

"Why, dear madam? Don't you like to have me with you?"

"I think I do. I really quite think I do. Still it is strange that you should be here."

"Your story interests me wonderfully, Mrs. Wyndham. Will you tell me more?"

"There is not a great deal to tell. For a time I misunderstood my husband, and the love which really filled my heart seemed to go back and back and back like the waves when the tide is going out. Then the time came for him to go to Sydney. He could not say good-bye; he wrote good-bye. He said a strange thing in the middle of the letter; he asked me if I really loved him to join him the next morning on board the Esperance. Loved him! Of course I loved him! I was so relieved. Everything was made clear to me. He was first—all others everywhere were second. My father came in, and I told him what I meant to do. He was angry, and tried to dissuade me. When he saw that I would not yield he appeared to consent, and promised to go with me the next morning to Southampton. The Esperance was not to sail until noon. There seemed lots of time. Still, for the first time, I began to doubt my father. I determined not to wait for the train he had arranged to travel by with me, but to go down by a much earlier one. I went to Southampton with a German maid I had at the time. We arrived there at eight in the morning, we reached the docks soon after nine, the Esperance was away—she had sailed at eight. Don't question me about that day, Esther Helps. It was on that day my love for my father died."

CHAPTER XLVII

It was nearly morning before Mrs. Wyndham fell asleep. Before then, Esther had said a good deal.

"I am not surprised at your loving your husband," she began. "Men like your husband are worth loving. They are loyal, true, and noble. They make the world a better place. Once your husband helped me. I am going to tell you the story.

"Three years ago, Mrs. Wyndham, I was a very different girl from the one who now is by your side. I was handsome, and vain, and empty-headed. I thought most of dress and of flirting. I had the silliest form of ambition. I wanted to be a gentleman's wife. My mother had been a lady by birth, and I thought it was only due to me to be the same. My only chance of becoming a lady was by marrying a gentleman, and I thought surely someone would be found who would make me his wife for the sake of my handsome face. I had nothing else to recommend me. Mrs. Wyndham, for I was empty-headed and untrained, and I had a shallow, vulgar soul.

"One day I was skating in Regent's Park with some friends. I fell on the ice and hurt my foot. A gentleman picked me up. I looked into his face in the bold way I had, and then all of a sudden I felt ashamed of myself, and I looked down, and a modest, humble womanly feeling crept over me. The gentleman was your husband, Mr. Wyndham; the expression on his face impressed me, and I could not forget it. He came to our house that evening and brought a book to my father, and a present of flowers from you to me. I felt quite silent and queer when he was in the room; I did not talk, but I listened to every word he said. He was so uncommon. I thought what a clergyman he'd make, and how, if he were as eloquent in his words as in his looks, he might make us all good in spite of ourselves. He made a great impression on me, and I did not like to think my low silly thoughts after he had gone.

"Soon afterwards I made the acquaintance of a Captain Herriot, in the th Hussars; he was a very fine gentleman, and had very fine words, and although I did not love him a bit nor a scrap, he turned my head with his flattery. He did go on about my faceI don't know how I ever was goose enough to believe him. He managed to get my secrets out of me though, and when I told him that I meant to be a gentleman's wife some day, he said that he was the gentleman, and that I should marry him, and him alone. I thought that would be fine, and I believed him. He made all arrangementsoh, how I hate to think of what I afterwards saw was his real meaning.

"I was not to let out a thing to my father, and on a certain night we were to go together to the Gaiety, and he was to take me home afterwards, and the next morning we were to go to church and be married. He showed me the license and the ring, and I believed everything, and thought it would be fine to be the wife of Captain Herriot.

"I kept my secret from my father, but Cherry, a cousin who lives with us, got some of it out of me, for I was mad with vain triumph, and it was indirectly through her that I came to be delivered. The night arrived, and I went away from my home thinking how proudly I'd come back to show myself in a day or two; and how Cherry would open her eyes when I told her I was the wife of Captain Herriot, of theth Hussars. I reached the theatre, and Captain Herriot gave me his arm, and led me into the house, and we took our places in the stalls. People turned and looked at me, and Captain Herriot said it was no wonder, for I was the most beautiful woman in the Gaiety that night.

"Then the curtain rose, the house was darkened, and some one took the empty stall at my other side. I turned my head, Mr. Wyndham was sitting near me. He said a courteous word or two. I bowed my head; I could not speak. Madam, I did not see that play; I was there, looking on, but I saw nothing. Captain Herriot whispered in my ear; I pushed away from him. Suddenly he was horrible to me. I felt like a girl who was placed between an angel and a devil. Instantly the mask fell from my eyes. Captain Herriot meant to ruin me, never to marry me. Mr. Wyndham scarcely said a word to me till the play was over, then he spoke.

"'Your father wants you,' he said. 'Here is a cab, get into it. I will take you to your father.'

"He spoke out, quite loud and clear. I thought Captain Herriot would have fought him. Not a bit of it. His face turned an ugly color. He took off his hat to me, and slunk away through the crowd. That was the last straw. He had not even spirit to fight for the girl who thought she was about to become his wife.

"Mr. Wyndham got on the box of the cab, and took me to Mr. Paget's offices. My old father came out, and helped me out of the cab, and put his arms round me. He wrung Mr. Wyndham's hand, and said 'God bless you, sir;' and then he led me inside, and told me how Cherry had betrayed me, and how he (my father) had taken that stall ticket intending to sit beside me that night, and give Captain Herriot a blow in his face afterwards, as he was known to be one of the greatest scoundrels going. Pressing business kept my father at the office that night, and Mr. Wyndham promised to go in his place.

"'There isn't another young gentleman who would do it,' said my father. 'No not another.'

"After that, madam, I was changed; yes, a good bit. I thought I'd live more worthy. Mr. Wyndham's face used to come between me and frivolous ways and vain sins. It seemed as if his were the hand to lead me up. You don't mind, do you, madam, that he should have rescued one poor girl from the pit of destruction, and that she should love him—yes, love him for what he has done?"

"Oh, Esther, do I mind? Come here, Esther, come here. Let me put my arms round you. Kiss me. You have lifted something from my heart—how much you can never know. Esther, I was at the Gaiety that night, and I saw my husband with you, and I—I doubted him."

"Madam—you?" Esther sprang away—her whole face became crimson.

"I did, Esther; and that was when my love went away like the tide going out; but now—now—Esther, lie down. Let me hold your hand. I am sleepy. I can sleep sweetly now."

CHAPTER XLVIII

When the wandering minstrel, with his violin under his arm, left the neighborhood of Park-lane, he walked with a somewhat feeble and faltering step through Grosvenor-square and into Bond-street. A few people looked at him as he passed, and a hungry-looking girl who was leaning against a wall suddenly asked him to play for her. He stopped at the sound of her voice and said a word or two.

"I am sorry my violin only knows one air, and I have played it."

"Can you not play it again?"

"It is not meant for you, poor girl. Good-night."

"Good-night, kind sir. I'll say a prayer for you if you like; you look miserable enough."

The minstrel removed his soft hat, made a gesture of thanks, and hurried on. He was going to Queen's Gate. The walk was long, and he was very feeble. He had a few coins in his pocket from the change of Esther's sovereigns; he determined to ride, and mounted on the roof of a Hammersmith omnibus in Piccadilly.

By-and-bye he reached his destination, and found himself in familiar ground. He walked slowly now, hesitatingsometimes inclined to turn back. Presently he reached a house; he went up the steps, and took shelter for a moment from the biting east winds under the portico. It was late, but the lights were still shining in the great mansion.

He was glad of this; he could not have done what he meant to do except under strong excitement, and sheltered by the friendly gas light. He turned and gave the visitor's bell a full peal. The door was opened almost instantly by a liveried footman.

"Is Mr. Paget within?"

The man stared. The voice was not only refined, but to a certain extent familiar. The voice, oh, yes; but then the figure, the thin, long reed-like figure, slouching forward with weakness, buttoned up tight in the seedy frock coat whose better days must have been a matter of the very distant past.

"Is Mr. Paget within?"

The tone was so assured and even peremptory that the servant, in spite of himself, was overawed.

"I believe so, sir," he said.

"Ask if I can see him."

"Mr. Paget is not very well, sir, and it is late."

"Ask if I can see him."

The footman turned a little surly.

"I'll inquire," he said; "he's sure to say no, but I'll inquire. Your name, if you please. My master will require to know your name."

"I am known as Brother Jerome. Tell your master that my business is urgent. Go; I am in a hurry."

"Rum party, that," murmured the servant. "Don't understand him; don't like him. All the same, I can't shut the door in his face. He's the sort of party as has seen better days; 'ope as the umbrellas is safe."

Then he walked across the hall and entered his master's study.

The room, with its old oak and painted glass, and electric light, looked the perfection of comfort. The tall, white-headed man who sat crushed up in the big armchair was the envied of many.

"If you please, sir," said the servant.

"Yes; don't leave the door open. Who were you chatting to in the hall?"

"A man who has called, and wants to see you very particular, sir."

"I can't see him."

"He says his name is Brother Jerome."

"I can't see him. Go away, and shut the door."

"I knew it would be no use," muttered the footman. "Only he seems a sort of a gentleman, sir, and in trouble like."

"I can't see him. Shut the door and go away!"

"Yes, you can see me," said a voice.

The minstrel walked into the room.

"Good heavens!"

CHAPTER XLIX

At the sound of his voice the footman fell back as white as a sheet. Mr. Paget rose, walked over to him, took him by the shoulders, and pushed him out of the room. He locked the door behind him. Then he turned, and backing step by step almost as far as the window, raised his hands, and looked at his forbidden visitor with a frozen expression of horror.

Wyndham took his hat off and laid it on the table. Mr. Paget raised his hands, covered his face with them, and groaned.

"Spirit!" he said. "Spirit, why have you come to torment me before the time?"

"I am no spirit," replied Wyndham, "I am a living man—a defrauded and injured man—but as much alive as you are."

"It is false—don't touch me—don't come a step nearer—you are dead—you have been dead for the last three years. On the th April, , you committed suicide by jumping into the sea; you did it on purpose to revenge yourself, and since then you have haunted me, and made my life as hell. I always said, Wyndham, you would make an awful ghost—you do, you do."

"I am not a ghost," said Wyndham. "Touch me, and you will see. This wrist and hand are thin enough, but they are alive. I fell into the sea, but I was rescued. I came to you to-night—I troubled you to-night because you have broken our contract, because—What is the matter? Touch me, you will see I am no ghost."

Wyndham came nearer; Mr. Paget uttered a piercing shriek.

"Don't—don't!" he implored. "You are a lying spirit; you have often lied—often—to me. You want to take me with you; you know if you touch me I shall have to go. Don't—oh, I beseech of you, leave me the little time longer that I've got to live. Don't torment me before the time."

He dropped on his knees; his streaming white hair fell behind him, his hands were raised in supplication.

"Don't," said Wyndham, terribly distressed. "You have wronged me bitterly, but I, too, am a sinner; I would not willingly hurt mortal on this earth. Get up, don't degrade yourself. I am a living man like yourself. I have come to speak to you of my wife—of Valentine."

"Don't breathe her name. I lost her through you. No, you are dead—I have murdered you—your blood is on my soul—but I won't go with you yet, not yet. Ha! ha! I'll outwit you. Don't touch me!"

He gave another scream, an awful scream, half of triumph, half of despair, sprang to the door, unlocked it and vanished.

Wyndham took up his violin and left the house.

"Mad, poor fellow!" he muttered to himself. "Who'd have thought it? Even from a worldly point of view what fools people are to sin! What luck does it ever bring them? He made me his accomplice, his victim, in order to keep his daughter's love, in order to escape dishonor and penal servitude. He told me the whole story of that trust money—to be his if there was no child—to be kept for a child if there was. He was a good fellow before he got the trust money I have no doubt. The friend died, and soon afterwards Paget learned that he had left a son behind him. Mr. Paget told me—how well I remember his face when he told me how he felt about the son, who was then only an infant, but to whom he must deliver the trust money when he came of age. 'I wanted that money badly,' he said, 'and I resolved to suppress the trust papers and use the money. I thought the chances were that the child would never know.'"

The chances, however, were against Mr. Paget. The friend who had left him the money in trust had not so absolutely believed in him as he supposed. He had left duplicate papers, and these papers were in the boy's possession. One day Mr. Paget learned this fact. When he knew this he knew also that when his friend's son came of age he should have to repay the trust with interest; in short, he would have to give the young man the enormous sum of eighty thousand pounds or be branded as a thief and a criminal.

"I remember the night he told me this story," concluded Wyndham with a sigh.

He was walking slowly now in the direction of the Embankment.

"So the plot was made up," he continued. "The insurance on my life was to pay back the trust. Valentine would never know her father's dishonor. She would continue to love him best of all men, and he would escape shame, ruin—penal servitude. How have matters turned out? For the love of a woman I performed my part: for the love of a woman and self combined, he performed his. How has he fared? The woman ceases to love him, and he is mad. I—how have matters fared with me? How? The wages of sin are hard. I saw a sight to-night which might well turn a stronger brain than mine. I saw my wife, and the man who may soon be her husband. I must not dwell on that, I dare not."

Wyndham walked on, a burning fever gave him false strength. He reached the Embankment and presently sat down near a girl who looked even poorer and more miserable than himself. There were several men and girls occupying the same bench. It was a bitter cold, frosty night; all the seats along the Embankment were full, some poor creatures even lay about on the pavement. Wyndham turned to look at the slight young creature by his side. She was very young, rather fair in appearance, and very poorly clad.

"You are shivering," said Wyndham, in the voice which still could be one of the kindest in the world.

The poor worn young face turned to look at him in surprise and even confidence.

"Yes," said the girl. "I'm bitter cold, and numb, and starved. It's a cruel world, and I hate God Almighty for having made me."

"Hush, don't say that. It does no good to speak against the one who loves you. Lean against me. Let me put my arm round you. Think of me as a brother for the next hour or two. I would not harm a hair of your head."

"I believe you," said the girl, beginning to sob.

With a touching movement of absolute confidence she laid her faded face against his shoulder.

"That is better, is it not?" said Wyndham.

"Yes, thank you, sir. I'm desperate sleepy, and I shan't slip off the bench now. I was afraid to go to sleep before, for if I slipped off somebody else would get my seat, and I know I'd be dead if I lay on the pavement till morning."

"Well, go to sleep, now. I shan't let you slip off."

"Sir, how badly you are coughing."

"I am sorry if my cough disturbs you. I cannot help giving way to it now and then."

"Oh, sir, it is not that; you seem like a good angel to me. I even love the sound of your cough, for it is kind. But have you not a home, sir?"

"I certainly have a shelter for the night. Not a home in the true sense of the word."

"Ought you not to go to your shelter, sir?"

"No, I shall stay here with you until you have had a good sleep. Now shut your eyes."

The girl tried to obey. For about ten minutes she sat quiet, and Wyndham held her close, trying to impart some of the warmth from his own body to her frozen frame. Suddenly the girl raised her eyes, looked him in the face, and smiled.

"Sir, you are an angel."

"You make a great mistake. On the contrary I have sinned more deeply than most."

"Sir?"

"It is true."

"I don't want you to preach to me, sir; but I know from your face however you have sinned you have been forgiven."

"You make another mistake; my sin is unabsolved."

"Sir?"

The girl's astonishment showed itself in her tone.

"Don't talk about me," continued Wyndham. "It is a curious fact that I love God, although it is impossible for Him to forgive me until I do something which I find impossible to do. I go unforgiven through life, still I love God. I delight in His justice, I glory in the love He has even for me, and still more for those who like you can repent and come to Him, and be really forgiven."

He paused, he saw that he was talking over the girl's head. Presently he resumed in a very gentle pleading voice:

"I don't want to hear your story, but"

The girl interrupted him with a sort of cry.

"It is the usual story, sir. There is nothing to conceal. Once I was innocent, now I am what men and women call lost. Lost and fallen. That's what they say of girls like me."

"God can say something quite different to you. He can say found and restored. Listen. No one loves you like God. Loving He forgives. All things are possible to love."

"Yes, sir; when you speak like that you make me weep."

"Crying will do you good. Poor little girl, we are never likely to meet again in this world. I want you to promise me that you won't turn against God Almighty. He is your best friend."

"Sir! And He leaves me to starve. To starve, and sin."

"He wants you not to sin. The starving, even if it must come, is only a small matter, for there is the whole of eternity to make up for it. Now I won't say another word, except to assure you from the lips of a dying man, for I know I am dying, that God is your best friend, and that He loves you. Go to sleep."

The girl smiled again, and presently dropped off into an uneasy slumber with her head on Wyndham's shoulder.

By-and-bye a stout woman, with a basket on her arm, came up. She looked curiously at Wyndham. He saw at a glance that she must have walked from a long distance, and would like his seat. He beckoned her over.

"You are tired. Shall I give you my seat?"

"Eh, sir, you are kind. I have come a long way and am fair spent."

"You shall sit here, if you will let this tired girl lay her head on your breast."

"Eh, but she don't look as good as she might be!"

"Never mind. Jesus Christ would have let her put her head on His breast. Thank you, I knew you were a kind hearted woman. She will be much better near you than near me. Here is a shilling. Give it her when she wakes. Good-night."

CHAPTER L

Esther longed to go to Acacia Villas during the week. She often felt on the point of asking Mrs. Wyndham to give her leave, but then again she felt afraid to raise suspicions; and besides her mistress was ill, and clung to her. Although Esther listened with a kind of terror on the following evening, the sound of the violin was not again heard.

Sunday came at last, and she could claim her privilege of going home. She arrived at Acacia Villas with her heart in a tumult. How much she would have to tell Wyndham! It was in her power to make him happy, to relieve his heart of its worst load.

Cherry alone was in the kitchen when she arrived, and Cherry was in a very snappish humor.

"No, Esther, I don't know where uncle is. He's not often at home now. I hear say that Mr. Paget is very badgone in the head you know. They'll have to put him into an asylum, and that'll be a good thing for poor uncle. Take off your bonnet and cloak, Esther, and have a cup of tea cosy-like. I'm learning one of Macaulay's Lays now for a recitation. Maybe you'd hear me a few of the stanzas when you're drinking your tea."

"Yes, Cherry, dear, but I want to go up to Brother Jerome first. I can see him while you're getting the kettle to boil. I've a little parcel here which I want him to take down to Sister Josephine to the Mission House to-morrow."

Cherry laughed in a half-startled way.

"Don't you know?" she said.

"Don't I know what?"

"Why Brother Jerome ain't here; he went out on Tuesday evening and never came home. I thought, for sure, uncle would have gone and told you."

"Never came home since Tuesday? No, I didn't hear."

Esther sat down and put her hand to her heart. Her face was ghastly.

"I knew it," murmured Cherry under her breath. "She have gone and fallen in love with a chap from one of them slums."

Aloud she said in a brisk tone:

"Yes, he's gone. I don't suppose there's much in it. He were tired of the attic, that's all. I sleep easy of nights now. No more pacing the boards overhead, nor hack, hack, hack coughing fit to wake the seven sleepers. What's the matter, Esther?"

"You are the most heartless girl I ever met," said Esther. "No, I don't want your tea."

She tied her bonnet strings and left the house without glancing at her crestfallen cousin.

That very same afternoon, as Mrs. Wyndham was sitting in her bedroom, trying to amuse baby, who was in a slightly refractory humor, there came a sudden message for her. One of the maids came into the room with the information that Helps was downstairs and wanted to speak to her directly.

Mrs. Wyndham had not left her room since Tuesday evening. There was nothing apparently the matter with her, and yet all through the week her pulse had beat too quickly, and a hectic color came and went on her cheeks. She ate very little, she slept badly, and the watchful expression in her eyes took from their beauty and gave them a strained appearance. She did not know herself why she was watchful, or what she was waiting for, but she was consciously nervous and ill at ease.

When the maid brought the information that Helps was downstairs, her mistress instantly started to her feet, almost pushing the astonished and indignant baby aside.

"Take care of Master Gerry," she said to the girl. "I will go and speak to Mr. Helps; where is he?"

"I showed him into the study, ma'am."

Valentine ran downstairs; her eagerness and impatience and growing presentiment that something was at hand increased with each step she took. She entered the study, and said in a brusque voice, and with a bright color in her cheeks:

"Well?"

"Mr. Paget has sent me to you, Mrs. Wyndham," said Helps, in his uniformly weak tones. "Mr. Paget is ill, and he wants to see you at once."

Valentine stepped back a pace.

"My father!" she said. "But he knows I do not care to go to the house."

"He knows that fact very well, Mrs. Wyndham."

"Still he sent for me?"

"He did, madam."

"Is my father worse than usual?"

"In some ways he is worse—in some better," replied Helps in a dubious sort of voice. "If I were you I'd come. Miss Valentine—Mrs. Wyndham, I mean."

"Yes, Helps, I'll come; I'll come instantly. Will you fetch a cab for me?"

"There's one waiting at the door, ma'am."

"Very well. I won't even go upstairs. Fetch me my cloak from the stand in the hall, will you? Now I am ready."

The two got into the cab and drove away. No one in the house even knew that they had gone.

When they arrived at Queen's Gate, Helps still took the lead.

"Is my father in the library?" asked the daughter.

"No, Mrs. Wyndham. Mr. Paget has been in his room for the last day or two. I'll take you to him, if you please, at once."

"Thank you, Helps."

Valentine left her cloak in the hall, and followed the old servant upstairs.

"Here's Mrs. Wyndham," said Helps, opening the door of the sick man's room, and then shutting it and going away himself.

"Here's Valentine," said Mrs. Wyndham, coming forward. "I did not know you were so ill, father."

He was dressed, and sitting in a chair. She went up to him and laid her hand gravely on his arm.

"You have come, Valentine, you have come. Kneel down by me. Let me look at you. Valentine, you have come."

"I have come."

Never did hungrier eyes look into hers.

"Kiss me."

She bent forward at once, and pressed a light kiss on his cheek.

"Don't do it again," he said.

He put up his hand and rubbed the place that her lips had touched.

"There's no love in a kiss like that. Don't give me such another."

"You are ill, father; I did not know you were so very ill," replied his daughter in the quiet voice in which she would soothe a little child.

"I am ill in mind, Valentine, and sometimes my mind affects my body. It did for the last few days. This afternoon I'm better—I mean I am better in mind, and I sent for you that I might get the thing over."

"What thing, father?"

"Never mind for a moment or two. You used to be so fond of me, little Val."

"I used—truly I used!"

The tears filled her eyes.

"I thought you'd give me one of the old kisses."

"I can't. Don't ask it."

"Is your love dead, child, quite dead?"

"Don't ask."

"My God," said the sick man; "her love is dead before she knows—even before she knows. What a punishment is here?"

A queer light filled his eyes; Valentine remembered that whispers had reached her with regard to her father's sanity. She tried again to soothe him.

"Let us talk common-places; it does not do every moment to gauge one's feelings. Shall I tell you about baby?"

"No, no; don't drag the child's name into the conversation of this hour. Valentine, one of two things is about to happen to me. I am either going to die or to become quite hopelessly mad. Before either thing happens I have a confession to make."

"Confession? Father!"

Her face grew very white.

"Yes. I want to confess to you. It won't pain me so much as it would have done had any of your love for me survived. It is right you should know. I have not the least doubt when you do know you will see justice done. Of late you have not troubled yourself much about my affairs. Perhaps you do not know that I have practically retired from my business, and that I have taken steps to vest the whole concern absolutely in your hands. When you know all you will probably sell it; but that is your affair. I shall either be in my grave or a madhouse, so it won't concern me. If any fragment of money survives afterwards—I mean after you have done what you absolutely consider just—you must hold it in trust for your son. Now I am ready to begin. What is the matter, Valentine?"

"Only that you frighten me very much. I have not been quite—quite well lately. Do you mind my fetching a chair?"

"I did not know you were ill, child. Yes, take that chair. Oh, Valentine, for you my love was true."

"Father, don't let us go back to that subject. Now I am ready. I will listen. What have you got to say?"

"In the first place, I am perfectly sane at this moment."

"I am sure of that."

"Now listen. Look away from me, Valentine, while I speak. That is all I ask."

Valentine slightly turned her chair; her trembling and excitement had grown and grown.

"I am ready. Don't make the story longer than you can help," she said in a choked voice.

"Years and years ago, child, before you were born, I was a happy man. I was honorable then and good; I was the sort of man I pretended to be afterwards. I married your mother, who died at your birth. I had loved your mother very dearly. After her death you filled her place. Soon you did more than fill it; you were everything to me; you gave early promise of being a more spirited and brilliant woman than your mother. I lived for you; you were my whole and entire world.

"Before your birth, Valentine, a friend, a great friend of mine, left me a large sum of money. He was dying at the time he made his will; his wife was in New Zealand; he thought it possible that she might soon give birth to a child. If the child lived, the money was to be kept in trust for it until its majority. If it died it was to be mine absolutely. I may as well tell you that my friend's wife was a very worthless woman, and he was determined she should have nothing to say to the money. He died—I took possession—a son was born. I knew this fact, but I was hard pressed at the time, and I stole the money.

"My belief was that neither the child nor the mother could ever trace the money. Soon I was disappointed. I received a letter from the boy's mother which showed me that she knew all, and although not a farthing could be claimed until the lad came of age, then I must deliver to him the entire sum with interest.

"From that moment my punishment began. The trust fund, with interest, would amount to eighty thousand pounds. Even if I made myself a beggar I could not restore the whole of this great sum. If I did not restore it at the coming of age of this young man, I should be doomed to a felon's cell, and penal servitude. I looked into your face; you loved me then; you worshipped me. I idolized you. I resolved that disgrace and ruin should not touch you.

"Helps and I between us concocted a diabolical plot. Helps was like wax in my hands; he had helped me to appropriate the money; he knew my secrets right through. We made the plot, and waited for results. I took you into society, I wanted you to marry. My object was that you should marry a man whom you did not love. Wyndham came on the scene; he seemed a weak sort of fellow—weak, pliable—passionately in love with you—cursedly poor. Did you speak, Valentine?"

"No; you must make this story brief, if you please."

"It can be told in a few more words. I thought I could make Wyndham my tool. I saw that his passion for you blinded him to almost everything. Otherwise, he was the most selfless person I ever met. I saw that his unselfishness would make him strong to endure. His overpowering love for you would induce him to sacrifice everything for present bliss. Such a combination of strength and weakness was what I had been looking for. I told Helps that I had found my man. Helps did not like it; he had taken an insane fancy for the fellow. What is the matter, Valentine? How you fidget."

"You had better be brief. My patience is nearly exhausted."

"I am very brief. I spoke to Wyndham. I made my bargain; he was to marry you. Before marriage, with the plausible excuse that the insurance was to be effected by way of settlement, I paid premiums for insurances on the young man's life for eighty thousand pounds. I insured his life in four offices. You were married. He knew what he had undertaken, and everything went well, except for one cursed fact—you learned to love the fellow. I nearly went mad when I saw the love for him growing into your eyes. He was to sail on board the Esperance. He knew, and I knew that he was never coming back. He was to feign death. Our plans were made carefully. I was to receive a proper certificate, and with that in my hand I could claim the insurance money. Thus he was to save you and me from dishonor, which is worse than death.

"All our plans were laid. I waited for news. Valentine, you make me strangely nervous. What is the matter with you, child? Are you going to faint?"

"No—no—no! Go on—go on! Don't speak to me—don't address me again by my name. Just go on, or I—Oh. God, I am a desperate woman! Go on, I must hear the end."

As Valentine grew excited her father became cool and quiet: he waited until she had done speaking, then dropping his head he continued his narrative in a dreary monotone.

"I waited for news—it was long in coming. At last it arrived on the day my grandson was born. Wyndham had outwitted me. He could not bear the load of a living death. Shame on him. He could take his bliss, but not his punishment. He leaped overboard the Esperance—he committed suicide."

"What? No, never. Don't dare to say such words."

"I must say them, although they are cruel. He committed suicide, and then he came to haunt me; he knew that his blood would rest on my soul; he knew how best to torture me for what I had done to him."

"One question. Was the insurance money paid?"

"Was it? Yes. I believe so. That part seemed all of minor importance afterwards. But I believe it was paid. I think Helps saw to it."

"You believe that my husband committed suicide, and yet you allowed the insurance offices to pay."

"What of that? No one else knew my thoughts."

"As you say, what of that? Is your story finished?"

"Nearly. I lost your love, and for the last three years I have been haunted by Wyndham. I see his shadow everywhere. Once I met him in the street. A few nights ago he came into the library and confronted me; he spoke to me and tried to touch me; he pretended he was not dead."

"What night was that?"

Valentine's voice had changed; there was a new ring in it. Her father roused himself from his lethargic attitude to look into her face. "What night did my husband come to you?"

"I forget—no, I remember. It was Tuesday night."

"Did he carry a violin? Speak—did he?"

"He carried something. It may have been a violin. Do they use such instruments in the other world? He was a spirit, you know, child. How queer, how very queer you look!"

"I feel queer."

"He wanted me to touch him, child, but I wouldn't. I was too knowing for that. If you touch a spirit you must go with him. No, no, I knew a thing worth two of that. He went on telling me he was alive. But I knew better, he couldn't take me in. Valentine, everything seems so far away. Valentine, I am faint, faint. Ah, there he is again by the door. Look! No, he must not touch me—he must not!"

Valentine glanced round. There was no one present. Then she rang the bell. It was answered by the old housekeeper.

"Mrs. Marsh, my father is ill. Will you give him some restorative at once? And send for the doctor, if necessary. I must go, but I'll come back if possible to-night."

She left the room without glancing at the sick man, who followed her to the door with his dim eyes. She went downstairs, put on her cloak and left the house.

She had to walk a little distance before she met a hansom, and one or two people stared at the tall, slim figure, which was still young and girlish, but which bore on its proud face such a hard expression, such a burning defiant light in the eyes. Valentine soon reached home. Everything was in a whirl in her brain. Esther Helps was standing on the steps. She flew to Esther, clasped her hands in a grasp of iron, and said in a husky choked voice:

"Esther, my husband is alive!"

"He is, dear madam, he is, and I have come to take you to him!"

"Oh, Esther, thank God!"

"Come indoors, madam, you have not a moment to lose. We will keep that cab, if you please. I have only just come back. I was going to seek you. Stay one moment. Mrs. Wyndham. You are in black; will you put on your white dress—the one you wore on Tuesday night."

"Oh, what does it matter? Let me go to him."

"Little things sometimes matter a great deal; he saw you last in your white dress."

"He was really there on Tuesday night?"

"He was there. Come, I will fly for the dress and put it on you."

She did so. Valentine put her cloak over it, and the two drove away in the hansom. Valentine had no ears for the direction given to the cabman.

"I am in heaven," she said once, under her breath. "He lives. Now I can forgive my father!"

"Madam, your husband is very ill."

Valentine turned her great shining eyes towards Esther.

"All the better. I can nurse him," she said, with a smile, and then she pulled the hood of her cloak over her head and did not speak another word.

The cab drew up at one of the entrances to St. Thomas' Hospital.

CHAPTER LI

"What place is this?" asked the wife.

She was unacquainted with hospitals and sickness.

"This is a place where they cure the sick, and succour the dying, dear Mrs. Wyndham," gently remarked Esther Helps.

"They cure the sick here, do they? But I will cure my husband myself. I know the way." She smiled. "Take me to him, Esther. How slow you are. Beloved EstherI don't thank youI have no words to say thank youbut my heart is so happy I think it will burst."

The porter came forward, then a nurse. Several ceremonies had to be gone through, several remarks made, several questions asked. Valentine heard and saw nothing. Esther helped Valentine to take off her cloak; and she stood in her simple long plain white dress, with her bright hair like a glory round her happy face.

The nurse who finally conducted them to the ward where Wyndham lay looked at her in a sort of bewilderment. Esther and the nurse went first, and Valentine slowly followed between the long rows of beds; some of the men said afterwards that an angel had gone through the ward on the night that the strolling minstrel, poor fellow, died. The sister who had charge of the ward turned and whispered a word to Esther, then she pushed aside a screen which surrounded one of the beds.

"Your husband is very ill," she said, looking with a world of pity into Valentine's bright eyes. "You ought to be prepared; he is very ill."

"Thank you, I am quite prepared. I have come to cure him."

Then she went inside the screen, and Esther and the nurse remained without.

Wyndham was lying with his eyes closed; his sunken cheeks, his deathly pallor, his quick and hurried breath might have prepared the young wife for the worst. They did not. She stood for a moment at the foot of the bed, her hands clasped in ecstasy, her eyes shining, a wonderful smile bringing back the beauty to her lips. Then she came forward and lay gently down by the side of the dying man. She slipped her hand under his head and laid her cheek to his.

"At last, Gerald," she said, "at last you have come back! You didn't die. You are changed, greatly changed; but you didn't die, Gerald."

He opened his eyes and looked her full in the face.

"Valentine!"

"Hush, you are too weak to talk. Stay quiet, I am with you. I will nurse you back to strength. Oh, my darling, you didn't die."

"Your darling, Valentine? Did you call me your darling?"

"I said it. I say it. You are all the world to me; without you the world is empty. Oh, how I love you—how I have loved you for years."

"Then it was good I didn't die," said Wyndham, he raised his eyes, looked up and smiled. His smile was one of ecstasy.

"Of course it was good that you didn't die, and now you are going to get well. Lie still. Do you like my hand under your head?"

"Like it?"

"Yes; you need not tell me. Let me talk to you; don't answer me. Gerald, my father told me. He told me what he had done; he told me what you had done. He wants me to forgive him, but I'm not going to forgive him. I'll never forgive him, Gerald. I have ceased to love him, and I'll never forgive him; all my love is for you."

"Not all, wife—not quite all. Give him back a little, and—forgive."

"How weak you are, Gerald, and your voice sounds miles away."

"Forgive him, Valentine."

"Yes, if you wish it. Lie still, darling."

"Valentine—that money."

"I know about it—that blood-money. The price of your precious life. It shall be paid back at once."

"Then God will forgive me. I thank Him, unspeakably."

"Gerald, you are very weak. I can scarcely hear your words. Does it tire you dreadfully to talk? See, I will hold your hand; when you are too tired to speak your fingers can press mine. Gerald, you were outside our house on Tuesday night. Yes, I feel the pressure of your hand; you were there. Gerald, you were very unhappy that night."

"But not now, darling," replied Wyndham. He had found his voice; his words came out with sudden strength and joy. "I made a mistake that night, wife. I won't tell it to you. I made a mistake."

"And you are really quite, quite happy now."

"Happy! Sorrow is put behind methe former things are done away."

"You will be happier still when you come home to baby and me."

"You'll come to me, Val; you and the boy."

"What do you say? I can't hear you."

"You'll come to me."

"I am with you."

"You'll comeupto me."

Then she began to understand.

Half-an-hour later the nurse and Esther drew the screen aside and came in. Valentine's face was nearly as white as Wyndham's. She did not see the two as they came in. Her eyes were fixed on her husband's, her hand still held his.

"He wants a stimulant," said the nurse.

She poured something out of a bottle and put it between the dying man's lips. He opened his eyes when she did this, and looked at Valentine.

"Are you still there? Hold my hand."

"Do you think I would let it go? I have been wanting this hand to clasp mine for so long, oh, for so long."

The nurse again put some stimulant between Gerald's lips.

"You must not tire his strength, madam," she said. "Even emotion, even joyful emotion is more than he can bear just now."

"Is it, nurse? Then I will sit quiet, and not speak. I don't mind how long I stay, nor how quiet I keep, if only I can save him. Nurse, I know he is very ill, but, but"

Her lips quivered, and her eyes, dry and bright and hungry, were fixed on the nurse. Wyndham, too, was looking at the nurse with a question written on his face. She bent down low, and caught his faint whisper.

"Your husband bids you hope," she said then, turning to Valentine. "He bids you take courage; he bids you to have the best hope of allthe hope eternal. Madam, when you clasp hands up there you need not part."

"Did you tell her to say that to me, Gerald?" asked the wife. "Oh, no, you couldn't have told her to say those words. Oh, no, you love me too well to go away."

"God loves you, Valentine," suddenly said Gerald. "God loves you, and He loves me, and His eternal love will surround us. I up there, you here. In that love we shall be one."

Only the nurse knew with what difficulty Wyndham uttered these words, but Valentine saw the light in his eyes. She bowed her head on his thin hand, her lips kissed itshe did not speak.

To the surprise of the sister who had charge of the ward. Wyndham lingered on for hoursduring the greater part of the night. Valentine and Esther never left him. Esther sat a little in the shadow where her pale face could scarcely be seen. If she felt personal grief she kept it under. The chief actors in the tragedy, the cruelly-wronged husband and wife, absorbed all her thoughts. No, she had no time, no room, to think of herself.

Wyndham was goingBrother Jerome would no longer be known in the streets of East London; the poor, the sorrowful, would grieve at not seeing his face again. The touch of his hand could no longer comfortthe light in his eyes could no longer bless. The Mission would have to do without Brother Jeromethis missioner was about to render up his account to the Judge of all.

The little attic in Acacia Villas would also be empty; the tired man would not need the few comforts that Esther had collected round him—the tiresome cough, the weary restless step would cease to disturb Cherry's rest, and Esther's chief object in life would be withdrawn.

He who for so long was supposed to be dead would be dead in earnest. Valentine would be a real widow, little Gerald truly an orphan.

All these thoughts thronged through Esther's mind as she sat in the shadow behind the screen and listened to the chimes outside as they proclaimed the passing time, and the passing away also of a life.

Every moment lives of men go away—souls enter the unknown country. Some go with regret, some with rejoicing. In some cases there are many left behind to sorrow—in other cases no one mourns.

Wyndham had sinned, he had yielded to temptation; he had been weak—a victim it is true—still a victim who with his eyes open had done a great wrong. Yet Esther felt that for some at least it was a good thing that Wyndham was born.

"I, for one, thank God that I knew him," she murmured. "He has caused me suffering, but he has raised me. I thank God that I was permitted to know such a man. The world would, I suppose, speak of him as a sinner, but to my way of thinking, if ever there was a saint he is one."

So the night passed on, and Valentine remained motionless by the dying man's bed. What her thoughts were, none might read.

At last, towards the break of day, the time when so many souls go away, Wyndham stirred faintly and opened his eyes. Valentine moved forward with an eager gesture. He looked at her, but there was no comprehension in his glance.

"What is the matter?" said Valentine to the nurse. "I scarcely know him—his face has altered."

"It looks young, madam. Dying faces often do so. Hark, he is saying something."

"Lilias," said Wyndham. "Lilly—mother calls us—we are to sing our evening hymn.

'Bright in the happy land!'
Lilias, do you hear mother; she is calling? Kneel down—our evening prayers—by mother—we always say our prayers by mother's knee. Kneel, Lilias, see, my hands are folded—'Our Father'"

There was a long pause after the last words, a pause followed by one more breath of infinite content, and then the nurse closed the dead man's eyes.

CHAPTER LII

TWO YEARS AFTER

Augusta Wyndham was pacing up and down the broad gravel walk which ran down the centre of the rectory garden in a state of great excitement. She was walking quickly, her hands clasped loosely before her, her tall and rather angular figure drawn up to its full height, her bright black eyes alert and watchful in their expression.

"Now, if only they are not interrupted," she said, "if only I can keep people from going near the rose-walk, he'll do it—I know he'll do it—I saw it in his eyes when he came up and asked me where Lilias was. He hasn't been here for six months, and I had given up all hope; but hope has revived to-day—hope springs eternal in the human breast. Tra la, lala, la. Now, Gerry, boy, what do you want?"

A sturdy little fellow in a sailor suit stood for a moment in the porch of the old rectory, then ran with a gleeful shout down the gravel walk towards Augusta. She held out her arms to detain him.

"Well caught, Gerry," she said.

"It isn't well caught," he replied with an angry flush. "I don't want to stay with you, Auntie Gussie; I want to go to my—my own auntie. Let me pass, please."

"You saucy boy, auntie's busy; you shall stay with me."

"I won't. I'll beat you—I won't stay."

"If I whisper something to you, Gerry—something about Auntie Lil. Now be quiet, mannikin, and let me say my say. You love Auntie Lil, don't you?"

"You know that; you do talk nonsense sometimes. I love father in heaven, and mother, and Auntie Lil."

"And me, you little wretch."

"Sometimes. Let me go to Auntie Lil now."

"I want to whisper something to you, Gerry. Auntie Lil is talking to someone she loves much better than you or me or anyone else in the world, and it would be very unkind to interrupt her."

Gerry was sitting on Augusta's shoulder. From this elevated position he could catch a glimpse of a certain grey dress, and a quick flash of chestnut hair, as the sun shone on itthat dress and that hair belonged to Auntie Lil. It was no matter at all to Gerry that someone else walked by her side, that someone was bending his dark head somewhat close to hers, and that as she listened her steps faltered and grew slow.

Gerry's whole soul was wounded by Augusta's words. His Aunt Lilias did not love anyone better than him. It was his bounden duty, his first duty in life, to have such an erroneous statement put right at once.

He put forth all his strength, struggled down from Augusta's shoulders, and before she was aware of it was speeding like an arrow from a bow to his target, Lilias.

"There, now, I give it up," said Augusta. "Awful child, what mischief may he not make? Don't I hear his shrill voice even here! Oh, I give it up now; I shall go into the house. The full heat of the sun in July does not suit me, and if in addition to all other troubles Lilias is to have a broken heart, I may as well keep in sufficient health to nurse her."

Meanwhile Gerry was having a very comfortable time on Carr's shoulder; his dark eyes were looking at his Aunt Lilias, and his little fat, hot hand was clasped in hers.

"Well," he said suddenly, "which is it?"

"Which is what, Gerry? I don't understand."

"I think you are stoopid, Auntie Lil. Is it him or me?"

Then he laid his other fat hand on Carr's forehead.

"Is it him or me?" said Gerry, "that you love the most of all the peoples in the world?"

"It's me, Gerry, it's me," suddenly said Adrian Carr; "but you come next, dear little man. Kiss him, Lilias, and tell him that he comes next."

"Gerald's dear little boy," said Lilias. She took him in her arms and pressed her head against his chubby neck.

"Dear, dear little boy," she said. "I think you'll always come second."

She looked so solemn when she spoke, and so beautiful was the light in her eyes when she raised her face to look at Gerry, that even he, most despotic of little mortals, could not but feel satisfied.

He ran away presently to announce to all and everyone within reach that Mr. Carr had kissed Auntie Lil like anything, and the newly-betrothed pair were left alone.

"At last, Lilias," said Carr.

She looked shyly into his face.

"I thought I should never win you," he continued. "I have loved you for years, and I never had courage to tell you so until to-day."

"And I have loved you for years," replied Lilias Wyndham.

"But not best, Lilly. Oh, I have read you like a book. I never came before Gerald in your heart."

"No," she said letting go his hand, and moving a step or two away, so that she should face him. "I love you well, beyond all living men, but Gerald stands alone. His place can never be filled."

The tears sprang into her eyes and rolled down her cheeks.

"And I love you better for loving him so, my darling," answered her lover. He put his arms round her, and she laid her head on his breast.

For a long time they paced up and down the Rose-walk. They had much to say, much to feel, much to be silent over. The air was balmy overhead, and the rose-leaves were tossed by the light summer breeze against Lilias' grey dress.

Presently she began to talk of the past. Carr asked tenderly for Valentine.

"Valentine is so noble," replied her sister-in-law. "You don't know what she has been to me since that day when she and I looked together at Gerald's dead face. Oh, that day, that dreadful day!"

"It is past, Lilias. Think of the future, the bright future, and he is in that brightness now."

"I know."

She wiped the tears again from her eyes. Then she continued in a changed voice:

"I will try and forget that day, which, as you say, is behind Gerald and me. At the time I could scarcely think of myself. I was so overcome with the wonderful brave way in which Valentine acted. You know her father died a month afterwards, and she was so sweet to him. She nursed him day and night, and did all that woman could do to comfort and forgive him. His brain was dreadfully clouded, however, and he died at last in a state of unconsciousness. Then Valentine came out in a new light. She went to the insurance offices and told the whole story of the fraud that had been practised on them, and of her husband's part in it. She told the story in such a way that hard business men, as most of these men were, wept. Then she sold her father's great shipping business, which had all been left absolutely to her, and paid back every penny of the money.

"Since then, as you know, she and Gerry live here. She is really the idol of my old father's life; he and she are scarcely ever parted. Yes, she is a noble woman. When I look at her I say to myself, Gerald, at least, did not love unworthily."

"Then she is poor now?"

"As the world speaks of poverty she is poor. Do you think Valentine minds that? Oh, how little her father understood her when he thought that riches were essential to her happiness. No one has simpler tastes than Valentine. Do you know that she housekeeps now at the rectory, and we are really much better off than we used to be. Alack and alas! Adrian, you ought to know in time, I am such a bad housekeeper."

Lilias laughed quite merrily as she spoke, and Carr's dark face glowed.

"It is a bargain," he said, "that I take you with your faults and don't reproach you with them. And what has become of that fine creature, Esther Helps?" he asked presently.

"She works in East London, and comes here for her holidays. Sometimes I think Valentine loves Esther Helps better than anyone in the world after Gerry."

"That is scarcely to be wondered at, is it?"

Just then their conversation was interrupted by some gleeful shouts, and the four little girls, no longer so very small, came flying round the corner in hot pursuit of Gerry.

"Here they is!" exclaimed the small tyrant, gazing round at his devoted subjects, and pointing with a lofty and condescending air to Adrian and Lilias. "Here they is!" he said, "and I 'spose they'll do it again if we ask them."

"Do what again?" asked Lilias innocently.

"Why, kiss one another," replied Gerry. "I saw you do it, so don't tell stories. Joan and Betty they wouldn't believe me. Please do it again, please do. Mr. Carr, please kiss Auntie Lil again."

"Oh, fie, Gerry," replied Lilias. She tried to turn away, but Carr went up to her gravely, and he kissed her brow.

"There's nothing in it," he continued, looking round at the astonished little girls. "We are going to be husband and wife in a week or two, and husbands and wives always kiss one another."

"Then I was right," said Betty. "Joan and Rosie wouldn't believe me, but I was right after all. I am glad of that."

"I believed you, Betty. I always believed you," said Violet.

"Well, perhaps you did. The others didn't. I'm glad I was right."

"How were you right, Betty?" asked Carr.

"Oh, don't ask her, Adrian. Let us come into the house," interrupted Lilias.

"Yes, we'll come into the house, of course. But I should like to know how Betty was right."

"Why you wanted to kiss her years ago. I knew it, and I said it. Didn't you, now?"

"Speak the trufe," suddenly commanded Gerry.

"Yes, I did," replied Carr.

When Adrian Carr left the rectory that evening he had to walk down the dusty road which led straight past the church and the little village school-house to the railway station. This road was full of associations to him, and he walked slowly, thinking of past scenes, thanking God for his present blessings.

"It was here, by the turnstile, I first saw Lilias," he said to himself. "She and Marjory were standing together, and she came forward and looked at me, and asked me in that sweet voice of hers if I were not Mr. Carr. She reminded me of her brother, whom I just barely knew. It was a fleeting likeness, seen more at first than afterwards.

"Here, by this little old school-house the villagers stood and rejoiced the last day Gerald came home. Poor Wyndham—most blessed and most miserable of men. Well, he is at rest now, and even here I see the cross which throws a shadow over his grave!"

Carr looked at his watch. There was time. He entered the little church-yard. A green mound, a white cross, several wreaths of flowers, marked the spot where one who had been much loved in life lay until the resurrection. The cross was so placed as to bend slightly over the grave as though to protect it. It bore a very brief inscription:

In Peace

www.ingramcontent.com/pod-product-compliance
Lightning Source LLC
Chambersburg PA
CBHW081718100526
44591CB00016B/2422